Inescapable Data
Harnessing the Power of Convergence

Inescapable Data
Harnessing the Power of Convergence

Chris Stakutis, CTO VitalFile/FilePath
& SANergy, IBM

John Webster, Senior Analyst and Founder,
Data Mobility Group

IBM Press
Pearson plc
Upper Saddle River, NJ • Boston • San Francisco • New York
Toronto • Montreal • London • Munich • Paris • Madrid
Capetown • Sydney • Tokyo • Singapore • Mexico City

www.phptr.com/ibmpress

IBM Press Program Manager: Tara Woodman, Ellice Uffer
Cover Design: IBM Corporation
Published by Pearson plc
Publishing as IBM Press

Library of Congress Catalog Number 2004117648

IBM Press offers excellent discounts on this book when ordered in quantity for bulk purchases or special sales, which may include electronic versions and/or custom covers and content particular to your business, training goals, marketing focus, and branding interests. For more information, please contact:

U. S. Corporate and Government Sales
1-800-382-3419

For sales outside the U. S., please contact:

International Sales
international@pearsoned.com

Pearson Education, Inc.
Rights and Contracts Department
One Lake Street
Upper Saddle River, NJ 07458

ISBN 0-13-185215-9
Text printed in the United States at R. R. Donnelley in Crawfordsville Indiana.

First printing, April 2005

This book is dedicated to the one passion of my life that expects nothing other than reciprocal devotion, my wife, Cheryl.

Chris Stakutis

To my wife, Penny, and my business partners, Dianne McAdam and Joe Martins, who gave me the latitude to work on this. This is also dedicated to Robert Tasker, who launched me as an industry analyst.

John Webster

Contents

Foreword

To get anywhere, or even to live a long time, a man has to guess, and guess right, over and over again, without enough data for a logical answer.

—*Robert Heinlein*

Guess what. Lack of data will no longer be the problem. To the contrary, the challenge will be to use and manage enormous quantities of data effectively. Covering many examples in personal and business life, *Inescapable Data* details the coming data explosion and how it will be exploited in new and exciting ways. It is about the far-reaching impact on a personal, work, and cultural level when diverse technologies evolve and are brought together in life-altering ways. Most importantly, it is about how it will impact you and those around you.

People generally fall into three camps when it comes to technology. Some people love it and are fascinated with it. I am in this category. In my personal life, I tend to be an early adopter of gadgetry, from computers and handheld communication devices, to home electronics such as TiVo, to high-tech kitchen gizmos such as remote-control cooking thermometers. In my professional life, I deal with data protection and storage management and helping organizations more effectively manage their ever-growing volumes of information.

Others hate technology or at least are highly suspicious of it. My brother-in-law, for example, avoids new technology and is often frustrated when he is forced to use it. He prefers tellers to ATM machines, full-service over self-service, and vinyl to CDs. He is particularly concerned about privacy rights and the potential for intrusion that the "online" world represents.

The majority of people fall into a third category. They take technology for granted and do not really think a whole lot about it. My wife belongs to this group. Like my brother-in-law, she does not seek out technology and often has a quizzical or skeptical look on her face when I try to get her interested in one of my new gadgets. Until she is fully convinced that this is going to make her life better or easier, she really is not interested. So, for example, she never warmed up to PDAs or programmable remote controls, but she loves cell phones and TiVo.

With *Inescapable Data*, Chris Stakutis and John Webster have produced a fascinating and thought-provoking book that has something for everyone, regardless of their disposition toward technology. The technophile will appreciate the authors' identification and analysis of how disparate technologies come together to create a whole that is far greater than the sum of its parts. Among the things I learned was the surprising connection between analyzing the genome sequence and fighting e-mail spam as well as about the many technological advances that will help us to manage the enormous growth of data.

The technophobe will be both disturbed and challenged by much of what he reads in this book. Inescapable Data is just that: *inescapable*. My brother-in-law will find it harder and harder to avoid its impact, such as the ability of stores to observe his patterns of movements and buying habits. His very real concerns about privacy and the opportunities for misuse of information are significant and must be addressed on a societal level. He will have to balance these concerns against the equally real opportunities for saving lives that Inescapable Data brings to the fields of medicine and national security.

The techno-agnostic will become enlightened. After scanning the first two chapters, my wife, who views technology strictly as a matter of convenience, immediately leapt upon the notion of how helpful it would be if she could check the contents of our pantry while she was at the supermarket. The authors have done an impressive job of providing examples of the impact Inescapable Data will have on medicine, manufacturing, sports, retail, and everyday life. You will come away from this book with a fresh perspective on the issues—both the positive and the negative.

Inescapable Data is all around us today; this book will help people spot its growing effect on their lives and prepare them to deal with it more effectively at home, at work, and at play. What will be the impact on your family, your job, your industry? Read on to find out.

Jim Damoulakis
GlassHouse Technologies, Inc.
February 2005

Preface

Overview

Greetings. Technology and technological advances are always interesting. The intention of this book is not just to showcase new technologies and their specific values, but rather to examine the special values that emerge when some key technologies are intermixed, and primarily intermixed with many different (usually *real-time*) sources of data.

Data is all around us and it is growing at a furious pace—from cellular-controlled ovens to video-controlled manufacturing to embedded chips in our bodies—and we cannot help but wonder whether the new pervasive wireless technologies will allow for unforeseen power to come from all this gathered data. The Inescapable Data environment specifically looks for new streams of data to be combined and analyzed against other streams or historical data in an effort to drive higher personal or business value. For example, although it might be interesting to have your child's school record available electronically, it is perhaps more interesting to be able to correlate various achievements and progress against a wide population—and even further interesting to correlate that data against a detailed analysis of his or her medical history.

In a more business-oriented example, technology might enable us to track inventory levels better and in real time. However, inventory-level information might be the wrong question to ask? New levels of efficiency appear in the Inescapable Data world because business systems are tied so closely together, across company boundaries, that inventory level no longer becomes the question and is replaced by "are any manufacturing dependencies suggesting date-skew anywhere in our outside supply chain for product X?" In the Inescapable Data world, we allow our business systems to join together throughout a product's value chain—and even perhaps to competitors—for the sake of efficiency and flexibility.

Similarly, our personal lives demand continuous connectivity to all the activities that comprise our days. Whether it is communication with customers in different time zones or e-sending to the team a better map to the soccer field, we discover time efficiencies that in turn give us more flexibility. The tools of our business lives have become the exact same tools used in our personal lives, allowing for a convenient blending of activities.

Most of this, we believe, is for the good. Some of it brings new worries and exposures. But as notable Harvard sociologist Nicholas Christakis says, "There is a way in which technology is inexorable, so I doubt there is a way to stop any of this."

Intended Audience

This book is designed to inform the modern business manager (as well as the techno-curious) about important developments and usage of data-everywhere devices and networks. Our mission is to help a wide range of decision makers learn to spot the emergence of Inescapable Data and capitalize on it appropriately. A wider audience for this book includes individuals from engineering through marketing in high-technology companies who want to be informed of trends outside of their more narrow industry segments. That said, the book is broad enough in scope and written with only a modest assumption of technical understanding so that most adults can understand, appreciate, and possibly value the information.

The Interviews as a Foundation

Although we consider ourselves knowledgeable regarding computing, networking, and data storage, we wanted to get out on the street and talk firsthand with key people from many different disciplines. We reached out to nearly 50 different executives and experts for one-on-one interviews (the vast majority conducted in person). We wanted to learn what these people are seeing, and then showcase their knowledge in a broader light, supplemented by heavy direct research.

The inside front cover of this book identifies the various people whom we interviewed at length to gain a richer understanding of the technology and trends occurring in a variety of industries, thus supplementing our general research. Their thoughts and views assisted in formulating the notions presented throughout this book.

Acknowledgments

We want to acknowledge the time and education provided by Mark Palmer of Progress Software regarding the state and future of RFID and similar rapid data and complex event systems.

About the Authors

Chris Stakutis is a renowned data storage industry inventor, technologist, and visionary with more than 20 years of industry experience. He holds more than 6 U.S. patents (eight more filed) along various data and networking inventions. Currently working for IBM managing cutting-edge data storage research and development, he was the founder and CTO of SANergy (high-speed data sharing), which was sold to IBM in 2000. Mr. Stakutis is often published in industry journals and seen speaking at industry events. Mr. Stakutis graduated from Worcester Polytechnic Institute in an accelerated 3-year program and then went on to obtain an MBA from Babson College at a leisurely 10-year pace. He has held key engineering and product management roles in various high-technology companies, including Mercury Computer Systems, Precision Robots, MIT Lincoln Laboratories, and many start-ups.

John Webster is senior analyst and founder of Data Mobility Group. Mr. Webster is responsible for directing Data Mobility Group's ongoing research into storage management and the management of data from the standpoint of the storage domain. Prior to founding DMG, Mr. Webster was senior analyst and

IT advisor for Illuminata, Inc., where he founded and developed Illuminata's storage-related market research and analysis practice. Mr. Webster has held the positions of director of computing research with Yankee Group's Management Strategies Planning Service, and senior analyst with Clipper Group and International Data Corporation. He is a member of the SNIA's Storage Management Forum and serves as liaison to the SNIA's End User Council. He is also past chairman of the Greater Boston Regional Computer Measurement Group. He is a graduate of Boston University.

CHAPTER ONE

The Inescapable Data Vision

There is a way in which technology is inexorable, so I doubt there is a way to stop any of this.
—*Harvard University Sociologist Nicholas Christakis*

If you look closely, you will see data collection and emission devices all around, often discreetly located and sometimes barely detectable—things such as mobile phones that double as Internet gateways, chemical sniffers in major cities, discrete radio tags on commercial products, and video cameras (seemingly everywhere, and sometimes in some curious places).

These devices are already ubiquitous, and their numbers are growing at a furious pace—from home electronics and appliances to video-surveillance cameras on school buses to sensory microchips embedded in our bodies. We cannot help but wonder whether these new and increasingly pervasive wired and wireless data collection technologies will usher in as yet unforeseen benefits or become the electronic sentinels of Big Brother's kingdom. Those who choose to master this Inescapable Data environment will specifically look for new streams of data that can be combined and analyzed (often in real time) against streams of historical data in an effort to derive both business and personal power.

In Inescapable Data, we see the beginnings of a fusing of technologies—data collection on a massive scale with wired and wireless communications coupled with a steady advance of information processing—that could, for example, enable a manufacturer to track inventory levels better and in real or near-real time. But that could be just the first link in a massively strengthened value chain that also pulls together raw materials suppliers, distributors, and retailers; that crosses corporate boundary lines and, for the sake of efficiency and flexibility, even includes companies that normally compete with each other. The same fusing of technologies will also make your child's medical record available to you electronically and enable you to correlate that record with those of thousands of other children (and even generate a detailed analysis of his or her personal genome).

Demand continues to grow for continuous connectivity with the important people in our lives (our spouses, our bosses, our customers), sharing data that has become a part of our everyday lives (our shopping lists, sales orders, and inventory levels). Whether it is in instant message communication with customers in different time zones, or e-mailing better directions to a soccer field where a game is being played, we have discovered the value of being and staying connected. In fact, many of the tools we use in our business lives have become the exact same tools we use in our personal lives, allowing for a blending of both—wonderfully liberating for some, stressful for others.

Here's our vision: We are about to see an onslaught of massive data collection and delivery capabilities that will usher in both opportunities and some worries. It is not about Internet II; that is only part of the story. It is more about what can happen when billions of wired and wireless data collection and delivery devices are attached to networks, possibly empowering our businesses, reaching into our homes, and even improving our bodies. It is also about huge data stores and computer processing capable of making sense of this new world, and entry points that enable each of us as individuals or businesses (even individuals *as* businesses) to tap in.

We happened on this vision over lunch. Professionally, we are both in computing technology—one a data-networking industry inventor, the other a data storage industry analyst—and we have come together over low-carb salads and a mutual interest in all things data related. We identify that the fundamentals of computing (data and networking) are being energized by both the solid pace of data growth as well as dramatic changes in communication style and information exchange. So we started with a pen and paper napkin and made a list of computing's new fundamentals and the impact of the coming fusion:

- *Data.* Data-everywhere devices—full-function cell phones, biosensors, miniature digital video cameras, GPS transceivers— all generate massive amounts of new data that can be captured and mined for new value in real time.
- *Communications.* Demand for more "asynchronous-yet-immediate" conversation technologies such as wireless e-mail and instant messaging will drive further conveniences and efficiencies in both our personal and business lives.
- *Networking.* Radical new strategies for the networking of anything electrified. Things as common as refrigerators and automobiles can and will be given wired or wireless networking interfaces.
- *Information processing.* Information will become more easily accessible to increasingly greater numbers of people—people with only a modicum of computing smarts. Information traditionally locked up within machines, available to only those with degrees in computer science, will rapidly become more open, aided by self-describing data representation styles.

Staring down at the list we created, we began to think that we were looking at the cusp of a new world, where data will not only be everywhere but it will be fully interconnected, delivering us values that were never before anticipated. Historically, businesses were driven exclusively by higher profit and individuals by greater personal freedom. In the new world we envision, the synergy of both personal and business goals can drive unprecedented values for both, made possible by pervasive devices that generate massive new volumes of data, their processing counterparts collecting and transforming that data into information, and by the invisible wired and wireless networks that will blanket our lives.

We decided to call this phenomenon *Inescapable Data.* Our Inescapable Data vision suggests that it is not just advances in each of these technologies, it is the *combination* of these fundamental elements that will break barriers and magnify gains to levels not yet anticipated. We think these new combinations will lead to an explosion of benefits driving both higher personal and economic satisfaction. That is the upside. The downside could be loss of personal privacy, identity theft on a monumental scale, and trust in information sources whose authenticity cannot be verified.

Great vision we thought. So we decided to see whether we could find it—or at least its beginnings—among the tangle of technologies here today, those promised to arrive soon, and the purported creative future visions. Our path through this exploration took us to prominent computer industry people, testing our visions while exploring theirs. Our interviews also extended to a variety of industry segments, from mundane footwear to medicine to sports to business to warfare. We conferenced with notable sociologists, leaders of computers and networks, military thinkers, and, of course, those money-gambler "venture capitalists" who fuel revolutions.

Inescapable Data is at once empowering and worrisome. It is up to us as members of an increasingly techno-savvy society to determine how it will best be used. One thing we can say with certainty: It is coming.

CHAPTER TWO

The Connectivity Divide

Let's start with a simple test. Draw a line under the last question to which you can answer yes.

Toddler

I sometimes receive postal mail.
I have a home phone.
I have cable TV at home (or satellite).
My home phone is cordless.
I use the Internet from home.
I have at least one cell phone.
I use e-mail for either work or family matters from home.
I have high-speed Internet (cable or DSL) at home.

Crossing

I use instant messaging either at home or work.
I sometimes work from home instead of going into the office.
I carry my cell phone wherever I carry my wallet.
I use text messaging (via cell or PDA).
I usually pay (if necessary) at hotels for high-speed Internet access.

Connected

I could make use of an XML document if I wanted.

I use a hybrid PDA (cell, e-mail, text services).

I use "virtual office" groupware tools (document sharing, messaging).

I sometimes work at 3:30 in the morning.

I expect airports, campgrounds, rest stops, trains, buses, and planes to have WiFi service. Actually, I expect it absolutely everywhere.

I sometimes make free voice calls over the Internet.

I usually work from home and have given up my true office.

There is a dividing line between the truly connected members of our society and those who are not. The value of Inescapable Data technologies can only be realized by crossing the line. In 2005, most career-oriented adults fall somewhere between being connected newborns to having advanced to the toddler stage. Teens and twenty-somethings, the future workforce, are another story. They are showing their parents the way.

Introduction

"There is a way in which technology is inexorable, so I doubt there is a way to stop any of this," explains Dr. Nicholas Christakis, notable Harvard University sociologist. "Is there a socioeconomic class getting left behind? Sometimes, technology improves standards of living, and sometimes, it increases the difference between the top and the bottom. Regarding data and connectivity, like the washing machine and dishwasher benefits, we're all better off. Sure, there is still a difference between the top and the bottom, but the fundamental benefits are realized by all. We all drive cars; some drive Mercedes and some drive Hyundais, but we all get places."

Inescapable Data and the value of connectivity will be available to everyone, eventually. We may cross into the competence zone at different times and with varying degrees of sophistication with regard to the use of our new "toys." As we approach the middle years of the first decade of the twenty-first century, the main issue will be building the wireless "information" infrastructure, much as the main issue of the early 1990s was building the Internet infrastructure. Here, we examine the status and future of the great wireless build-out, because only when that is fully in place can society as a whole cross the connectivity divide.

Wireless and WiFi: From Confusion and Competition to Possible Synergy

Steve Nicolle, CEO of Tatara Systems, a company focused on the convergence of cellular services and wireless Ethernet (WiFi) once overheard a CTO of an unnamed wireless carrier say of WiFi, "If I could squash it, I would." Things are moving quickly in the wireless communications industry, and confused consumers are having trouble keeping up with the torrid pace. A clear understanding of the major communication denominations is definitely needed. What the average consumer thinks of as "cell service" is more broadly termed "wireless" (not to be confused with "cordless," as in cordless phones, and definitely not to be confused with WiFi or 802.11)—three commonly used "wire-free" communications methods based on three different technologies—confusion right off the bat.

Many wireless carriers, such as AT&T and Verizon (once known as New England Telephone), have been around since the days of the Bell network, huge long-distance phone bills, and POTS (plain old telephone service). Others such as Sprint are relative newcomers. Carriers actually "carry" voice and data over long distances and comprise the Internet backbones (appropriate given their wireline history and the Internet's continuing dependence on wired communications). Carriers owned what was once known as the "Iron Triangle"—the phones, the network, and the support services—a comfortable situation that is now limiting broader user adoption. The Iron Triangle carriers hold the keys to introducing new cell-based applications that we believe would attract even more users. However, they have tended to lock out the smaller more aggressive players offering more advanced and creative applications. Fortunately, times are changing.

"Wireless Ethernet (WiFi, or often called 802.11) put a wedge in that triangle," explains Nicolle. "Wireless Ethernet devices are made by typical computer communication companies such as Cisco. All was well when WiFi was an in-office–only technology because the cellular wireless carriers never serviced that computer end user. This is now all changing as a result of cell phones that have data services making them more computer-like and computers having cell capabilities making them far more portable." The confusion and competition begins.

The cellular wireless carriers have had to upgrade their communications technologies to better deal with data. (For example, voice traffic places less demand on a network for communications bandwidth than data.) Early cell-data services offered approximately 64 kbps (kilobits per second) connections to the network, not too unlike the old 56 kbps dialup modems of the early Internet days. However, you got 64 kbps if no one else was using the wireless service at the same time. Bandwidth is shared among all active users in a particular cell zone, so actual data communication rates could be closer to 1 kbps—nearly impractical for any serious data use.

The cellular services carriers are not sitting idly by, however. New technology is being rolled out now that greatly increases data communications rates. Not one, but two entirely different and competing high-bandwidth wireless communications technologies are now in use: Code Division Multiple Access (CDMA) and Global System for Mobile Communications (GSM). CDMA is more prevalent in the United States and is carried by Verizon and Sprint. Although GSM's penetration of the U.S. market is reasonably large (by virtue of the fact that it is carried by AT&T and Cingular), it is virtually the only technology outside of the United States.

Unfortunately, the technologies are incompatible. Proponents of either standard push roadmaps along that reflect parallel visions, yet never is convergence of the two competing standards foreseen. This echoes the early days of local-area network (LAN) data communications, which began with three LAN technologies (Token Ring, Ethernet, and AppleTalk). However, the marketplace eventually settled on Ethernet. So now, all computers that use wireless Ethernet are derived from one family, 802.11, where one finds a more or less smooth path of technological advancement waiting ahead.

The cellular wireless carriers are heading toward a new generation of technology known as 3G (third generation), which will boost wireless data speeds into the multimegabit per second range and higher—still shared among many other members of a cell site that could be physically large compared to a section of an office building or home. Although the cellular carriers might fantasize about 3G's potential as being *the* communication technology to the end point, that is likely too impractical of a scenario.

Too often, wireless-enabled laptop computers (and other endpoint devices) will be useable within distance of WiFi access points that will offer data rates that are far in excess of what can be experienced by sharing a 3G connection with potentially hundreds of other users. Because users will always clamor for the higher speed and will only tolerate lower speeds as a last resort (such as at the beach, on a mountain, or on the highway), we will probably see a combination of wireless communications standards going forward. "The cellular wireless carriers are finally embracing the notion of working with the WiFi camps because it is now the same end-point customer," explains Nicolle. One of net effects of the Inescapable Data world is that the business user and the citizen share the same technology needs. "Furthermore, the carriers have a critical piece—the backbone infrastructure. Wireless Ethernet still has to ultimately hit the Internet and that 'backhaul' interface is expensive."

Travel Notes from a Connected Cognoscenti

Although I always prefer WiFi when possible, I am truly grateful to have the slower cellular "data" services to keep me connected in between. Recently, I vacationed in St. John, U.S. Virgin Islands, with my family. One beautiful day we rented a rubber "dingy" and motored halfway to St. Thomas. We dropped anchor to eat lunch while bobbing in the waves. (The anchor, of course, did no good because the water was too deep, but the effect was comforting.) While sitting on the edge of the dingy (which is how one sits when in a dingy), I was happily e-mailing two customers that had a technical problem and updating our family relatives regarding our current boating adventure. After a soggy sandwich, I surfed various Web reviews to settle on a restaurant for the evening (all from my PDA). We then motored back and jumped the boat across many turbulent but exhilarating waves. Having *any* sort of data access in uncommon places is fantastic—speed merely improves the experience.

In the end, we as consumers will win. In the meantime, there is confusion over what standards we should adopt and some spotty service. The Blackberry, for example, uses cellular, and although it is somewhat slow for Internet surfing, connectivity is ubiquitously available no matter where one is, and the data rates are perfectly practical for e-mail and text messaging. Laptop computers with nearly gigabit WiFi work fine in key locations such as at home or in the office (or even better, in the home office); in fringe locations such as campgrounds or airports, however, one can be forced to pay separately for access via some other service provider or have no access at all. Although wireless communication may seem more or less pervasive, connectivity is not yet everpresent—a temporary barrier to an absolute Inescapable Data world and wide-scale connectivity for us all.

Nokia and DoCoMo Versus the Old Guard

Mike Hill, general manager of IBM's Global Communications business, described for us the changing climate in the wireless carrier space. "Voice revenues (as an application) are declining as far as the price point, but the volumes are going up. Cell companies have to continue to provide voice services, but the costs for providing them are increasing. How will they recover that revenue and grow? By offering new applications, most telcos are gearing themselves up for this new opportunity landscape." A market that has more than 170 million subscribers in the United States alone—nearly every American adult—is an attractive market opportunity for additional services.

But it's not so straightforward. First, there are two competing approaches. Some device manufacturers, such as Nokia, want to build more intelligent devices that run a number of applications locally (i.e., with much of the application processing done by the cellular device or PDA itself). The other camp favors a "thin-client" model with minimal processing at the consumer end of the connection and more processing at the service provider end, resulting in lighterweight (and cheaper) handheld devices. "We've seen such pendulum swings many times in the regular computer industry. Typically, as speed and ubiquity of communication infrastructure increases, services migrate back to the center and allow for thinner clients. We're seeing wireless speeds and coverage soar, so we're likely heading for service provider services," extols Hill.

Electronic Jack Knives

Our cell phones are rapidly turning into "everything" devices. Candide Media Works (www.candidemedia.com) offers a service called Talking Street (www.talkingstreet.com). For a few dollars, Candide takes you on a pay-per-use walking tour of city sites that would be of interest to you as a tourist, hosted via your cell phone. Dial in to an interactive walking tour; then, as you roam around to various landmarks, pressing different keys activates recordings of scenic details and history. Listen to the tour at your own pace (asynchronously) over the course of a week if you want. Candide Media currently uses celebrities such as Sigourney Weaver or Steven Tyler as the narrators and is appearing in various cities around the United States (Boston, New York City, and Washington, D.C. so far, with more to come).

One could imagine that PDA-cellular devices could augment such a tour with pictures and short video clips. A GPS-enabled device could perhaps guide you along a path during the tour as well. Perhaps even an RFID reader in the phone could detect specific objects in the area and activate recordings for additional details.

Cell phones can also be used as a payment device for services and products; NTT's DoCoMo phones can now be used for retail purchases simply by waving the phone at the checkout in some locations. Such a phone can also be used as a "wireless key" to allow entry into your house or office or admission to a movie. Going forward, it appears that our cell phones (or PDAs) will become our electronic jack knives.

Hill goes on to explain that the adoption rate of any new cellular service is highly dependent on availability of a wide range of extremely easy-to-use applications available for it. We saw that the success of the PC in the 1980s was driven largely by the broad availability of applications made possible by Microsoft's development model, which encouraged a multitude of small software companies to write application software specifically for MS-DOS first and Windows later on (far unlike Microsoft's rivals of the period). However, playing out a similar scenario would be more problematic for the U.S. cell industry. As Hill puts it, "The only model our telcos know is a world where they own everything." In contrast, DoCoMo in Japan is fabulously successful because it has recruited 80,000 software vendors (ISVs) to write applications for its infrastructure. "The DoCoMo model succeeds in Japan partly because they have crafted a win-win model between themselves and the application and content providers, which allows many firms to develop services on a profitable basis. That is a lesson that all service providers should learn from," continues Hill.

Why is this interesting to us as hunters of Inescapable Data incarnations? The apparent rigidity of old-line telcos is currently a barrier to a wider adoption and wider penetration of wireless data connectivity for those interested in crossing the connectivity divide. In the interim, the only people crossing the divide are those who are sufficiently attracted by the limited number of applications available. Thus, the "have nots" presently outnumber the "haves." In time, the logjam of have nots will loosen and break free as more compelling applications bring ubiquitous wireless communication services to all who will embrace them.

Cell Phones That Rock

The music-download industry has been growing rapidly as evidenced by the phenomenal success of Apple's iPod and download services offered by a growing list of e-tailers and retailers (Apple, Microsoft, Sony, and even Wal-Mart and eBay). Apple sells nearly a million iPod-type devices per quarter, resulting in yearly revenue of $320 million.[1]

Think of it, though. For the connected cognoscenti, carrying both an iPod (or other portable MP3 player) and a cell phone is cumbersome and unnecessary (and maybe not even cool anymore). Enter mobile phones that can also store and play music. Additionally, some forward-looking wireless carriers offer both music-download and streaming services. (Remember, it is all about the application.) Strategic Analytics expects that 54 percent of cell phones by 2009 will be capable of storing and playing digital music.[2]

Chaoticom Inc, a start-up based in Andover, Massachusetts, makes software that allows carriers to offer music-download services for properly equipped phones. Europe appears to be ahead of the United States in this new trend, with more than 20 million subscribers signed on through Telenor (a Norwegian carrier).[3] Some analysts predict that within a few years, as much as 20 percent of all music downloads will be to cell phones. The lure for wireless companies is (what else?) increased revenue. In Europe, cell bills are 14 percent higher on average for those with the music-download service versus those without, and in a marketplace characterized by keen price competition, music could be an attractive way to add a higher-margin, value-add service to a base service offering.

It is unclear, however, whether the current approach that puts cell carriers in the position of being download "gatekeepers" will have staying power. As hybrid PDAs start adding in MP3 capabilities in addition to wireless Internet access (and thus access to the traditional Internet-based pay-per-download sites), will there be any need for special software and services from the wireless companies? Currently, the wireless data speeds are still

---

[1] http://www.macworld.com/news/2004/07/14/numbers/.
[2] http://www.strategyanalytics.com/press/pr00134.htm.
[3] http://boston.bizjounrnals.com/boston/stories/ 2004/08/16/story8html.

relatively slow and the extra compression afforded by specialty software is needed, but 3G services will soon start to roll out higher-speed wireless data communications. In any case, there is a huge demand for digital music provided by electronic distribution avenues, and the invisible cell network is not only an additional pathway but one that drives more convergence of devices such as PDAs, cell phones, and laptops.

Connecting You

Additional applications will increase wireless data penetration. These applications will have two key attributes:

- They will enable you to wirelessly collaborate with others using the same or other applications.
- They will get your data to you (because you're never in one place anymore or using only one type of device).

"It is no longer about computers being networked together," begins Kenneth Kuenzel, CEO of Covergence, a start-up in the area of network convergence, "it is now about people being networked together without actually being together." People and processes need to rendezvous in real time in the Inescapable Data world. Some of us (those who have crossed the communication divide) often carry three devices, all of which could receive a communication (laptop with e-mail, cell with SMS, PDA with instant messenger and e-mail, and so forth). Sometimes, we are closer to one of those devices. Sometimes, we want a message as e-mail and sometimes as an instant message and hardly ever do we want to process the same message more than once (in case two different devices received it). This is a significant problem for the connected cognoscenti among us because there is not a single infrastructure nor a single provider of all these services.

Furthermore, as we become more connected, we risk erosion of some important social conventions. "IM is invasive," continues Kuenzel, "we don't want the mailroom guy IM'ing the CEO on a whim. We need to be able to maintain some degree of established social hierarchy. Yet, the real value in data today is in its timeliness. Devices and software therefore need to provide a more casual indication of how willing you are to collaborate using a particular format to a particular party at any given instant."

Connectedness will require some readjustments. On one hand, as connected members of society, we are saying we want information absolutely instantaneously, and to be sure that we receive it, we carry every communication device possible at all times. On the other hand, we are saying that we worry about being too reachable by both people we do not believe should have access to us as well as by rightful people at inopportune times. We wind up giving some people our cell numbers, different people our e-mail addresses, and different people our instant messaging handles. We need to learn how to manage our new connected lives or all of this will lead to confusion and an unwillingness on the part of neophytes to go deeper.

Some improvements will be made to current connectivity tools such as instant messaging and text messaging, but most likely, new applications will be developed that correctly merge the various communication technologies and add in a renaissance of social hierarchy—connected style—and more end-user awareness. It would not be surprising to see such tools come out of the open-source community given the current disparity between competing tools (which often drives the development of open-source solutions). For sure, there's a waiting market out there for stuff that helps us better manage our connected lives.

As users of Inescapable Data devices, some of us will find that what is good for business is also good for personal use. Instant messaging (or text messaging) can have as much utility in our home and family lives as it does in business. Some of the connected cognoscenti among us would not expect a child to call just to ask to be picked up from the mall. (We are likely on a conference call anyway.) Instead, a text message can be processed in full multitasking glory. When driving to a soccer game away from the home field, a text message with the field location (rather than a phone call) obviates the need to write down an address while driving, or the need to "thumb" it into a PDA. If one's favorite Little Leaguer had a great first at-bat, one could clandestinely text message Mom and effect a remote smile. In perhaps the most bizarre communication twist, the acceptance and use of text and instant messaging has changed how we talk when actually using the phone now. Our conversations are choppy, extremely short, and end abruptly (gtg [got to go]); often, we just hang up now without any "goodbye." Guilty?

Connected and Truckin'

Think that this connected vision is still a vision of the future? Think again. There are already pockets of advanced connectivity hidden away within our society that are doing incredible things with what is available to them now.

Truckstop.net and Sprint have rolled out WiFi service to more than 3,000 truck stops across the United States.[4] There are more than 4.5 million truckers in the United States, and approximately half of them are avid laptop users. Surprised? Don't be. Laptops deliver many benefits to both truckers and the companies they work for, some of which are not immediately obvious.

"A trucker's cab is his mobile office," explains Alan Meiusi, COO of Truckstop.net, "and as such, they should be able to access the services that they would regularly enjoy as if they were back at headquarters or at home. Enabling them to do more out on the road allows them more time with their families when at home instead of paperwork and business arrangements. It is more than having truckers surf Web sites and send e-mail. It is an integral part of running their business."

Meiusi goes on to explain that truckers use e-mail for order and delivery confirmation, and they use the Web to post available truck capacity or inventory. They also search the Web for freight opportunities and use wireless/GPS for remote check-in and tracking. A typical tractor trailer is an asset worth more than $100,000, excluding cargo. Add insurance and the driver's salary and the value of that asset triples. There is great interest on the part of the trucking companies to track the asset, maximize usage, and ensure the safety and health of both the tractor and the driver.

WiFi access at rest stops is today being used to upload engine and equipment information automatically back to the operations center. In the future, trucking operations centers will be able to track an individual truck's braking performance, engine efficiency, mileage, and other details. This will greatly increase the safety and reduce the cost of maintaining the vehicle. As importantly, with wireless access, new trip itineraries can be easily downloaded that take into consideration weather, roadwork, and any shift in customer requirements and delivery information.

---

[4] http://www3.sprint.com/PR/CDA/PR CDA Press Kits Detail/1,3685,146,00.html.

Some trucking companies distribute training videos and material directly over the Internet to wireless trucker hotspots. Drivers who are required to complete some number of safety-training hours each year can now take those courses from the comfort of their cabs—off road, we hope. By law, drivers are required to be off the road for a set number of hours per day to allow for rest. Tracking the truck in a WiFi hotspot enables the company to prove compliance while at the same time allowing the trucker to be more efficient and catch up on electronic paperwork, training, maintenance instructions, and so forth.

Truckers benefit from and enjoy being connected as well. Being a segment of society that lives largely away from home, WiFi spots give them a sense of community with fellow truckers and open another communication channel with family members. Truckers now rely on e-mail to keep in close touch with their families and can do so at rest stops during normal off hours. Many truckers carry digital cameras and upload pictures of their travels to family members as well as pictures of cargo and receipts back to the operations center. For independent truckers, WiFi connectivity enables them to schedule trips, better optimize loads, and be more accessible to customers during trips. Truckers have also discovered that, by using Voice over IP (VoIP; the technology that allows telephone communication over the Internet) they can place a call to anywhere for free and avoid costly cell phone roaming charges.

So, here is an industry segment that on the surface seems mundane and low tech, but that has not only adopted data connectivity, it now requires it for reasons ranging from increased efficiency to regulated tracking of loads across interstate and international borders. The WiFi technology that allows a large trucking firm's operations center to run its business better is the same technology that allows its employees more comfort and happiness away from home. Large and small firms alike can leverage its values; it is easily within the economic reach of all involved. In the future, we will see tie-ins with more data sources that, for example, could allow a trucker's onboard system to check live road-condition data as reported by nearby truckers and public roadwork databases, access a customer's loading dock status in real time, and so on (from among the many yet-to-be-thought-of data sources).

City-Wide WiFi

A number of cities are either in the process of rolling out city-wide WiFi access to the Internet or evaluating such a venture. Philadelphia is considering creating a $10 million city-wide WiFi hotspot.[5] If implemented, this would be the world's largest hotspot. They would locate transmitters on streetlights and other public utility areas around the city to form a large, seamless hotspot. Philadelphia officials are leaning toward making access to the service free in an effort to help make the Internet more available to those city residents who cannot afford to pay monthly service fees, allowing more people to cross the divide.

Other cities already have areas with municipal WiFi networks. Among others, these include Corpus Christi, Texas; Cleveland, Ohio; Long Beach, California; and Spokane, Washington. A prominent Boston city councilor named John M. Tobin wants to establish a pervasive city-wide WiFi network, believing that it will not only promote community awareness, but get both residents and tourists out of their apartments and hotel rooms and into the parks and restaurants. Although Tobin states that his initiative is all about "fairness and accessibility," we note that it could draw more visitors to the city who will spend money and thereby increase tax revenues. (Similarly, a for-profit company is attempting to WiFi-enable a sizeable chunk of Nantucket Island, including the waterways). However, we surmise that, over time, a price will be paid for accessing city-wide WiFi services, either in the form of a direct payment for WiFi access time (the Starbucks/T-Mobile model) or in obtrusive advertisements as a city tax you pay electronically. Are we as connected cognoscenti at the beginning phases of having pervasive (and perhaps free or low-cost) WiFi access (i.e., WiFi wherever we go)? Keep your PDA-tapping fingers crossed.

---

[5] http://arstechnica.com/news/posts/20040901-4149.html.

Staying Connected Down on the Farm

Modern farming has become a large operation physically and complex from a management standpoint. Many farming processes have become highly scientific in nature and need constant monitoring of things such as soil conditions and irrigation. Other processes are reminiscent of manufacturing plants, with supply chains that extend into and out of the farm.

With the new complexity and level of investment in technology required to succeed, it is no wonder that large commercial farms now account for more than 50 percent of the U.S. total agricultural output and are the most willing to deploy computer and now networking technologies. Farming is increasingly a global market, and to compete with lower land and labor costs abroad, technology is squeezing unprecedented efficiencies and economies.

For example, wireless and GPS technologies are now being used to guide and drive tractors in real time. John Deere has a set of technologies marketed as GreenStar Guidance that use GPS and can accurately locate tractors down to a few *inches* in the field. Tilling and other similar operations are traditionally a manual operation that can result in nonparallel tracking, which means that either sections are missed or overtilled (leading to measurable wasted time). Some tractors even have the actual "turning" automated so that the lane tracking can be 100 percent controlled remotely, perhaps even operated at night for even more efficiency.

Certainly, GPS/WiFi-equipped farm equipment also aids in inventory tracking of these expensive assets, but the values go far beyond asset tracking. *Precision agriculture* is a fairly recent term used to describe some new methods of farming that exploit remote-sensing information to drive a number of values. Crop quality and yield can vary greatly based on specific characteristics of a small region of the land, yet historically fertilizing and irrigating are uniformly applied to large areas of a farm. Information can now be gathered in-field and in real time for every square inch of land. For example, the new harvester machines can measure the amount of grain and its moisture content on-the-fly[6] of each swath (and coordinates) and transmit that data in real time (wirelessly) back to the operations center. This data can then be correlated and saved for use in seeding, fertilizing, and irrigation, controlled again by automated machinery

---

[6] http://www.geotimes.org/nov03/feature agric.html.

that knows precisely where it is in the field. Essentially, every square inch of land can be treated uniquely and automatically controlled by computers through wireless networks, and those computers know *exactly* where the equipment is.

Many data streams come together to help the modern farmer. One is real-time remote sensing, such as the harvester previously mentioned, and similar devices that taste the soil as machinery moves across it. Another is weather forecasts and real-time weather-related data, such as wind direction and speed and cloud cover. Satellite imagery, topographical data, and thermal data can all be combined to understand how to best deal with a given set of conditions. (It turns out that plants grow better in the cooler sections of a farm because of a complicated energy-balancing operation constantly navigated by the plant). This in turn leads to more accurate fertilizing and pesticide usage, higher yields, and less pollution.

On the more business side, real-time yield information coupled with real-time market prices nets more accuracy in managing the supply-demand balance. WiFi-connected farms now have data streams and databases that match real-time inventory and projected inventory against market feeds and price fluctuations. Like other businesses we will examine, the connected farmer has real-time links to his suppliers and can better negotiate prices and far more accurately estimate quantities.

The farmer in the Inescapable Data world is a business man now using connectivity as one of his primary tools—completely unrealistic just a handful of years ago due to the lack of wireless technology and nonexistent data sources. A 1 percent efficiency increase nets more than $2B in the U.S. $200B farming business. Wireless, GPS, satellite images, soil tasters, yield-measuring equipment, climate databases, weather forecasts, spot and future prices, and so on combine to bring a new level of efficiency. If it is part of business, any business, it is going to be connected and exploited and in real time. Even farming. Crossing the divide.

Connected Camping

In 2004, a surprising number of campgrounds across the United States began to offer WiFi services at no additional charge. (In fact, this chapter itself was written while at a campground in Massachusetts and was shared between the authors and editorial staff while 2.7 children were roasting marshmallows and hoping for cooler weather.) While staying at one such campsite during the summer of 2004 in the Northeast, an observational survey of campers was made to determine the extent and nature of connected camping. Here are the results of this highly informal survey:

+ The campground community was almost evenly divided between retired couples over 60 and families whose adults were under 40 and had several kids in tow.
+ Casual observance at this particular campground showed that the main users of WiFi were those in the over-60 group, who were primarily keeping in touch with distant family members and participating in various virtual community groups. (They were *not* managing their supply chains.)
+ The members of the under-40 group were typically on shorter stays at the campground and could *suffer through* with mere cell phone connectivity for a couple of days.
+ One member of the under-40 group was able to barter his way to Internet access for a beer.

Campground owners and operators provide WiFi connectivity as a value-add service because they have somehow gotten the message that it is not only good for business, but that keeping campers happily clicking away in their tents, RVs, campers, and Winnebagos contributes to crowd control. Whether addicted to instant messaging or just keeping up with the Joneses in the neighboring Winnebago, those of us who have crossed the divide have done so for personal reasons that often outweigh the business drivers. Once over the divide, they prefer to carry their connected lives with them.

The connected cognoscenti among us now expect wireless Internet access no matter where they are. They find it critical for continued business operations (no matter what business they are in) or essential to their personal lives. The list of venues where the connected cognoscenti now expect to find WiFi would be astounding to the unconverted observer. (You want to use that thing *here*?) But make no mistake, challenges faced by carriers and conflicting technologies aside, the list of the connected among us grows by the thousands daily, and ubiquitous connectivity is now their expectation with regard to the future. In the words of Dr. Christakis, "Many people, myself included, find it absolutely absurd that they cannot keep current with their e-mail while in a taxi riding through farmland outside of London." Connectivity expectations abound.

Untethered Displayable Data

Might there be too much data heading our way? How will we deal with the on-slaught of even the digested data (information)? Will our thumbs be sore from constant PDA and cell phone surfing? People considering crossing the divide will need more comfortable ways to deal with the onslaught of data.

Some forward-thinking people are convinced that the solution for data over-load is to have at least some of the data (or information) presented to us using non-computer–related methods or tools. Data that is presented via small de-vices that could appear in and around our lives and deliver data in mechanical or color form could relieve our brains from the unwanted overload. "There is the notion that cognitive psychologists call 'pre-attentive processing'—things that your brain can process without any apparent cognitive load," explains David Rose, president of Ambient Devices, an MIT spin-off. "Things you don't per-ceive as distracting—color, angle, shape, pattern, motion, for example—will allow your brain to focus on more pressing issues. This then frees up your brain for either more difficult cognitive problems or life's daily challenges."

"Hmmm," we think. How so?

It turns out that the concept of displayable data, in spite of all the cognitive load stuff, is straightforward and easily explained through example. One such displayable device available today is called an Orb (from Ambient Devices); it is a small globe-like object that is capable of glowing in different colors while con-nected wirelessly to a data source. Let's say the Orb is monitoring the price of your favorite stock (Microsoft, maybe?) in near-real time while perched atop a bookcase in your office. As Microsoft's share price goes up during the trading day, the Orb glows green. And, of course, it glows red when the price declines. Perhaps it could be trained to flash red if the decline is precipitous. Deceptively simple, eh? Well, that is the idea. No complex spreadsheet manipulations, no sneaking over to the Yahoo! financial Web site to check the share price during work hours, no thumbing through the financial pages on your way to work. You look, you know. In fact, you may not even have to look directly at the Orb. A mere glance in its direction would tell all. Far less cognitive processing is re-quired on your part and it does not interrupt your train of thought.

Here is another use (albeit less practical) for an Orb-like device: periodically monitor in real time the distance between you and a loved one. Suppose that your significant other travels frequently on business. Give your significant other a cell phone with GPS capability, and you could program the Orb to radiate warm roseate hues when he or she gets closer, or icy blue tones when moving farther away. How about a pictorial rendering of a nearby city, or an appropriate song, like "I Left My Heart in San Francisco"? As the kids leave for school in the morning, they can "observe" that Mom is still far away but heading home. Later, the Orb glows a loving amber hue as Mom is just about to be dropped off outside.

Along far more practical lines, the cities of San Francisco, Denver, and Chicago are experimenting with displayable data devices that tell bus riders waiting at a bus stop how close the next bus is. The device glows a particular color to indicate the distance or time-wait for the next bus arrival. NextBus manufactures small GPS "pucks" that are placed on the tops of public transportation buses. A NextBus monitoring system aggregates the location information of all buses into a Web-available database. "The public transportation budget in San Francisco is a half of a billion dollars and they loose $400M a year. They have to run buses every 15 minutes, otherwise people won't take the bus," describes Rose (presumably due to too long of a wait period). "If you can increase the awareness of the time of the 'next bus,' you can decrease the frequency that buses run and save money." Those cities are currently using NextBus' service and giving away Orb-like devices to riders for free. They have experienced a 15 percent increase in ridership simply by giving people a convenient and nontechnical visual tool that helps them know when to get on the bus.

Such bus-monitoring technology will likely be rolled out to school children as well. A major morning stress factor in nearly every U.S. household with school-age children is the mad dash that often occurs when preparing for the arrival of the school bus. Typically, parents send their children out to the bus stop 10 or so minutes early just to be sure that they do not miss it, even in the rain and in freezing weather. Real-time bus-distance information conveyed by a simple observable object near the front door could alleviate much of this stress.

How about some other creative uses for display information technology:

+ IBM is experimenting with using a displayable technology to indicate a project's status (Are we behind? How far?) that hangs on a wall much like a clock.
+ Orbs could be used to suggest vacation-area sailing conditions for those avid sailors among us (cue up the sound of waves crashing against the hull).

+ Or skiing conditions atop your favorite mountain (an Orb with miniature swirling snowflakes inside).
+ Or the three-day weather forecast (images of sunglasses or galoshes are projected on the wall).
+ Or your wife's fertility (bells and whistles).

Some of the information is for fun; some of it is for practical purposes. A somewhat surprising benefit of displayable data lies in the presumed ability to actually change behavior patterns. If your electric company placed an energy-efficiency Orb next to your thermostat, you might become a more efficient energy user. If you see that the project at work is slipping, you might work a bit harder. If you could see that your own personal body metrics (heart rate or temperature, for example) were meandering away from normal, you might behave differently or eat differently, or maybe even exercise more regularly. Displayable data could enable a wider set of people to cross the connectivity divide.

Those of us already living deep into full connectivity can survive with the rudimentary PDA-based Web surfing (and other similar technologies) available today to access data. But this is not sufficient for a large section of the population, such as urbanites waiting for the bus to get to work. In many ways, we are already trained and willing for more passive display sources. We populate our homes with clocks, with thermostats, with outside temperature gauges, humidity sensors, and a battery of gauges. More pervasive wireless coverage and decreasing costs of computer and cell equipment will help the new forms of data presentation, but we will not become a fully connected society until all of us have mass means to exploit information. Displayable data can politely push information to large audiences. When the average lower-income city dweller can waste as little time waiting for the bus as the adjacent luxury condo owner, we have achieved a new value in the saturation of data in our lives. As with the washing machine, all classes benefit.

Religion and the Connected

Many of the world's religions are adapting to connected technologies at different speeds. Religion, at its core, is all about communicating, and thus connected technologies should naturally find a home. Although there seems to be a spottiness in the patterns of technology adoption at the local level, there are some notable happenings in the broader world view.

Muslims pray five times per day—at sunrise, at noon, afternoon, sunset, and midnight—and they have to face in the direction of Mecca. In the dessert and in other areas, it can be difficult to find the right direction. They can now use their cell phones to respectfully find the correct direction of Mecca for their daily prayers.[7] LG Electronics (and others) are making cell phones with an embedded compass and an ability to point to a particular direction.[8] LG's G5300 phone is able to indicate to the user the correct direction of Mecca after being fed some location information. There are more than 1.1 billion Muslims in the world, and a relatively ordinary cell phone can now allow them to tend to their daily prescribed ritual more easily. LG is specifically targeting this audience.

In another example, the Vatican issues text messages (SMS) to subscribers' phones containing daily prayers. A service from www.popemessage.com will send a daily message taken from the pontiff's teachings to subscribers' cell phones. To subscribe, users just send an initial SMS message 'POPE ON' to the number 24444, and the process starts automatically. There is a small fee of between 10 and 30 cents per message received. This service has been received sincerely by subscribers who welcome a short daily papal message as a welcome interruption to an otherwise harried day. (Note here the value of immediate yet asynchronous nonvoice messaging—a theme we explore in the following chapter). This service is overwhelmingly successful and follow-on services with more rich features are in the works. Many priests, reverends, and rabbis have similarly started text messaging their parishioners' cell phones, for those who could use a little prayer boost in a time of need, or simply as a reminder that a spiritual leader is thinking of them.

Some effort is even being made to produce live masses (or other services) from locations around the world broadcast to your cell phone. Perhaps during an afternoon lunch walk to get away from the stresses of the office cube (or cubeless) society, you'll take in a live evening Irish mass. Perhaps you'll "message" a clergyman in some far-off country encouraging him in his missionary work. In much the same way that technology allows businesses to be more continuously

---

[7] http://www.wired.com/news/culture/0,1284,64624,00.html.

[8] http://www.lge.com/ir/html/ABboards.do?action=read&groupcode=
AB&list code=RND MENU&seq=3179&page=1&target=rndnews read.jsp.

connected, so too it seems that our religious lives could be enriched with closer (albeit less physical) contact.

PDA devices have been a boon for biblical scholars and general civilians. Selected portions of the Bible or the entire Bible (or other religious doctrine) can be downloaded and rapidly cross-referenced to easily find a needed passage wherever you are. Online services offer to download specialty material daily that users can read at their leisure. PDAs and cell devices are now an additional tool for religion that provides convenience and saves time.

Tech News World (www.technewsworld.com) recently interviewed Tom Ferguson, associate deputy of interfaith relations for the Episcopal Church.[9] "Religion is not embracing the information revolution; it's reaping what it sowed hundreds of years ago. Religion created the information revolution that has been ongoing," explains Ferguson in the interview. "People crave religion and spirituality without having it crammed down their throats in church. Anonymity and having the user be the one in charge have driven the [...] spirituality engines. Technology has allowed thousands—if not millions—of people to begin to develop spirituality outside of the traditional power structures."

Ferguson acknowledges that elements of religion are going through a telecommuting style change much like businesses are seeing. "I live in Los Angeles and work for the New York office. While this is common most everyplace and is a no-brainer to most people reading this, it's taken the church a long time to fully embrace telecommuting. There's so much in religion that needs a home, a center—a Vatican, Jerusalem, a Mecca, a Ganges River. This is going to be broken down in coming years. The definition of place and center will have to be re-imagined."

Indeed, finding "place and center" will have to be re-imagined in the connected world as technology allows a stretching of physical boundaries. Religion can thrive in the newer, more connected world, given the vastness of Web connections allowing people to self-organize and more easily share common views and find the information that most interests them. It will be different, no doubt, from the religious experience of our youth.

In pockets, members of religious communities are crossing the divide, to their benefit.

---

[9] http://www.technewsworld.com/story/33078.html.

Summary

Years ago, the concept of a digital divide drew a line between the computer literate and illiterate. Both companies and people took varying lengths of time to embrace the power of computing technology and cross the digital divide. We observe that our culture remained essentially unchanged when the majority of the general population was in the precrossing phase. However, as momentum built behind PCs first and then the Internet, cultural foundations such as education, government, entertainment, and health care began to change and adapt to the newly computer literate majority. Over time, those who remain on the other side of the divide become more disconnected from the cultural mainstream that is increasingly driven by the computer-literate majority.

We see a similar phenomenon emerging with data and information connectivity. Here, the new divide to be crossed is the connectivity divide. We see our children crossing this divide in droves, as evidenced by their seeming addiction to wireless text messaging and IM. In time, the two will represent the connected majority, and a similar cultural shift will follow.

For now, most of us have crossed the digital divide (perhaps more so than we would care to admit at times). Pervasive connectivity (wired and wireless) will allow information to ebb and flow through our digital networks more freely and to more places, increasing business and personal productivity, and enhancing entertainment, enticing us over the connectivity divide. In a more perfect Inescapable Data world, cellular carriers will be driven to adopt standard communication methods on a worldwide basis such that we can experience seamless connectivity from home, to work, to the beach. Network intelligence will be cognizant of and embrace the fact that we could have many modes of communication at our disposal and will streamline the appropriate messages to the appropriate devices. We will continue to use synchronous and wired communication modes for both voice and data, but we will increasingly seek wireless modes for the freedom they allow. We will also learn to appreciate the many new ways in which we will be able to acquire information, ways that could be non-numeric, nontextual, and unobtrusive, yet every bit as effective as a red stop light or a blinking elevator button.

CHAPTER THREE

Inescapable Data Fundamentals

Lounging in the sun on one side of the club pool, thumbing through the Internet via my PDA, my kids on the other side of the pool text message me about it being time "definitely" to leave. There are many comments to be made here, but the most significant is that their chosen mode to reach me was immediate, personal, and did not require voice. Yet, the method they chose was cool to them. For me, it was perfectly asynchronous, meaning that at the time the message is sent, the receiver of the message (myself, in this case) can either answer it immediately or answer it at a more convenient time.

Introduction

As a foundation for the remaining chapters, we explore the four fundamental ingredients of the new information world we introduced in the introductory chapter:

- *Communications.* Modern, high-value, multifunctional communications methods, such as instant messaging and others
- *Data.* Fundamental data-everywhere devices such as radio frequency identification devices (RFID) and video, among many others

+ *Networking.* Pervasive everywhere networking, primarily the wireless family
+ *Infochange.* Metadata and XML to bring it all together by virtue of data now being able to describe itself as it travels

In later chapters that delve deeper into specific technical and business details, we refer to these fundamentals because they create the foundation of the Inescapable Data vision.

What Is Important in Communication?

Communication has always been essential in our business and personal lives. Over the years, changes in communication techniques and devices have brought varying levels of new efficiencies. We examine some historical and current communication methods—from postal mail to voice mail and beyond—against five key attributes: immediacy, time efficiency, utility, awareness, and happenstance; because communication is the heart of a connected world. It is important to start with a clear understanding of these attributes because they help define the overall value of new communications methods for the Inescapable Data world:

+ *Immediacy.* This measures how quickly a message is received by the target. Postal mail is hardly immediate. E-mail is faster, text or instant messaging is faster still, and a meeting or phone conversation is probably the fastest. We have been somewhat fooled to think that the higher the immediacy, the more valuable a communication method is. We value immediacy up to the point where it turns "synchronous" (as in an interactive meeting or phone call); once synchronous, we become less time efficient.
+ *Time efficiency.* The more asynchronous a communication method is, the higher the time efficiency. Postal mail, for example, is very asynchronous, and while waiting for the delivery, other work is being performed. Once received, whatever task lies within is triaged and will be dealt with at the most efficient time (which is not necessarily when the message is received). E-mail carries the same value (but is notably more immediate). Instant messaging and text messaging are still asynchronous (but less so), and they too are time efficient. A phone call or meeting is not asynchronous—we will see less of those in the Inescapable Data world.

+ *Utility.* Utility (in the Inescapable Data world) is defined as the ability to package an object along with the message. An example is a postal package that contains both a letter about the family and a Christmas present. In the more electronic world, an example might be an e-mail containing a message and an actual purchase order (digitized document or similar).

+ *Awareness.* In office settings, we are aware of others around us. Both casual and formal meetings can take place with little or no notice. In our new more mobile work society, we do not always have the luxury of bumping into people or looking over a cube wall to see what someone is working on. This could lead to productivity loss, and so some new communication technologies strive to bring back a level of awareness. Groupware, for example, allows a concept of "team rooms" and might show live information about who else is "in" that team room and which documents they are working on.

+ *Happenstance.* Happenstance refers to accidental (but often productive) meetings and exchanges that take because of the physical proximity of the players (hallway chats, water-cooler chitchat, etc.). Similar to awareness, in our new mobile work society, we have lost a great deal of happenstance. Instant messaging, text messaging, and groupware bring back informal and impromptu conversations (for the same good and bad values happenstance has always had).

As you go forward in the Inescapable Data world, examine your current and new communication techniques against this list of attributes. Does the technique enable you to get information to the right party with great speed? Does it enable the target party to multitask and prioritize his or her message handling easily? Can you include the actual business object or directions to the soccer field? Does it provide a level of insight wherein you can learn whether your intended target is available for an exchange? Finally, does it provide a sense of community and encourage impromptu useful exchanges?

From Postal Mail to Voicemail to E-Mail to IM and Beyond

Old-fashioned postal mail dates back to Babylonian times. It introduces the concept of asynchronous communication and, as such, is perhaps the first major productivity enhancement in communications. (We will leave the discussion about smoke signals and drum beating to sociologists.) More modern times witnessed the advent of the telephone. Phone communications provided sharply increased immediacy and synchronicity. Phones meant that businesses could get answers and agreements days faster than any previous method. Phones, however, took communication back to a synchronous mode—both parties had to be simultaneously available, and both had to devote full attention to the meeting. Because of this, synchronous phone communication could not replace asynchronous postal mail; it was still essential to have both written communication (which could be digested at the leisure of the target person and be retained for future reference and legal tracking) as well as the immediacy of phone communications.

Phone communication evolved new fascinating features to address its shortcomings. The most significant feature was the introduction of voicemail in the 1990s. Voicemail made it possible to "reach" someone beyond business hours and either deposit a communication or arrange to have a communication. As the world economy turned more global, this was an important development in allowing businesses to run faster and more efficiently. Voicemail is a purely asynchronous communication method and appropriately boosted efficiency. Today, we just assume that no matter whom we call (person or business), we can leave a message—100 percent universal capability within a mere 15 years.

The early years of voicemail were a relearning experience in asynchronous communication for most of us. Too often, messages would be something like this, "Joe, this is Hank, please get back to me." How useful is that? Could you imagine sending a business postal mail like that? Nevertheless, millions of us left such messages for years. After struggling with phone tag and watching lack of immediacy lead to frustration, today's messages are more like this, "Joe, we have the product in stock, and I can get it out to you tomorrow if I hear back from you with the PO number." Finally, "information" is being productively exchanged and in an asynchronous but timely manner. It was this redeveloped social skill that led to the entrance and success of e-mail. (The asynchronous and detail focus of e-mail correspondence felt comfortable to business people after years of voicemail.) Furthermore, voice phone communication completely lacks the utility attribute (per our definition) because it cannot contain an actual business object.

During the late 1990s, the importance of e-mail soared. Finally as ubiquitous as phones, businesses could count on the availability of the e-mail communication mechanism. E-mail offers three dramatic enhancements to human communication:

+ It is completely asynchronous yet fast, giving it the quality of immediacy when desired.
+ It contains information that would normally be spoken via phone or voicemail and thus is at least as useful as asynchronous voicemail.
+ It can actually contain a business object (digitized) along with other message content.

Whereas in a sales situation, a phone call could not actually contain a proposal, an e-mail can. A phone call cannot contain a document, a manual, a price list, a program, or a schedule; however, an e-mail can. Those items were formerly relegated to postal mail. So, e-mail ranks very high in terms of time efficiency and utility, and hence its widespread use. Similar to postal mail, e-mails can be retained for later digestion and legal tracking.

E-mail, however, is evolving to a state of lesser and lesser immediacy. Businesspeople are becoming inundated with e-mails to such an extent that the piling up of messages meant that most messages would go unprocessed for many days. Ironically, this phenomenon puts e-mail somewhat back into the category of postal mail, although it is still far more immediate. E-mail overload brought stress upon individuals and led to spotty responses (akin to voicemails piling up and seldom being returned). More technological innovation was due.

Enter instant messaging. Instant messaging (IM) allows one party to get a message directly to another party and have that message "pop up" on the other person's computer screen (typically). Perfectly immediate. Perfectly targeted. And yet, asynchronous as well—the targeted party can respond when convenient and can be simultaneously performing other tasks, such as phone calls, processing e-mail, or real work (significant efficiency boost). IM is also the first communications technology to introduce happenstance. We can see who is connected and ready to communicate—whether they are physically present of not—by virtue of the software panel that displays communities of people and shows exactly who is currently "on." This leads to critical ad-hoc exchanges that can take place within a community that spans the globe's time zones. Most IM packages allow attachment of digital objects as well.

But we're not always at work or in front of our computer, so IM is not a universal and pervasive capability. Yet it did pave the way for one that is: text messaging. While IM was building momentum like crazy, coincidentally so was the pervasiveness of cell phones. Cell phone usage went from being a business traveler's device or an in-car–only device to one that is now as commonly found in someone's pocket as is a wallet (and within a short three-year period).

A communication device on its own, cell phones are now the conduit for messaging: text messaging. (Instant messaging and text messaging, by the way, are essentially the same thing; the difference is primarily whether you use a full computer or a personal cell-type device). The significant advance that text messaging brings is universal availability because everyone is tethered to their cell phone at all times in the new Inescapable Data world.

So, we have examined the highlights of communication history from a productivity viewpoint. We have seen that the world operates more efficiently if communication can be asynchronous as well as immediate. Our style of communication has evolved to now better match the technology at hand, and technology has similarly evolved to match our needs. Interestingly, the devices for communication today are exactly the same in business as they are in our personal lives—cell phones, e-mail, instant messaging, and now cellular text messaging—and share the exact same worldwide backbones. This is what the Inescapable Data vision is all about—the reach and blur of business into our civilian lives. Let's now shift and examine the new world of everywhere-emitting data.

Data-Everywhere Devices

Now that we have examined a brief history in communication methodologies, it is time to move to the next fundamental element in the Inescapable Data world: data-everywhere devices. A handful of radically new technologies will be pervasive in our business and personal lives, spewing volumes of data continuously. Like fuel in a rocket, data is the "energy" of the new world. This section explores a few of the base (or dominant) new sources of data to provide some background for later chapters.

RFID

We refer to radio frequency identification (RFID) often throughout this book because it is a foundational Inescapable Data technology. An introductory discussion is warranted up front. An RFID tag is a small electronic device that can be affixed to a box, product, or crate and wirelessly announces itself to a nearby RFID reader. They are somewhat similar to UPC bar codes, with the advantage of using radio signals and thus do not have to be carefully scanned. Some "tags" are large and more costly, holding a great deal of information, whereas others are quite small and can be embedded in clothing, for example.

RFID receivers and tags have been around for well over a decade (they were actually invented after World War II), but they have not gained widespread visibility until recently. Their recent popularity has been driven partly by the technological improvements and costs shrinking and partly in relation to critical mass.

Consider the history of those ubiquitous, black-bar UPC labels you now see on the side of every container of any consumer or business product. UPC coding was in use for over a decade before the introduction of supermarket scanners. Why? Often in technology, widespread adoption cannot occur until there is significant market penetration (the "tipping point"), thus making it worthwhile for businesses to make the often-considerable investment required to implement the new technology. Are we presently moving in the direction of ubiquitous RFID? "Absolutely," says Mark Palmer, a prominent RFID expert, "Wal-Mart alone drove 25 percent of all retail productivity increases in the last decade, and they are now mandating all their suppliers confirm to their 100 percent RFID expectations." What Wal-Mart does, the retail world does. So begins RFID's pervasiveness.

What is in an RFID tag? Well, that depends. Some of them today are as large as a small palm print and perhaps a $1/2$" thick. These tend to be the reprogrammable ones that contain a great deal of information. According to Palmer, "In the Iraq war, RFID tags were on nearly every major shipping container. The tag listed exactly the contents of the container—boots, masks, bricks, etc.—as well as the exact location within the container, avoiding unnecessary searching or dumping. The efficiency gains alone, versus paper tracking slips, which where often lost, are simply staggering." Such tags could cost perhaps $5 to $50, but are easily offset by the high value of the container goods. "Reprogrammable tags can also accurately reflect the contents of a container as parts are being depleted; a level of detail and tracking never before realized," claims Palmer.

Similar but cheaper tags are now being used extensively in warehouses. Currently, we find them on the edge of forklifts, the exteriors of crates and pallets, and on the insides of cartons (e.g., a 24-pack of corn flakes), and soon we will see them on the actual products themselves—all driven by mass retailers such as Wal-Mart. A massive acceleration takes place due to the widespread adoption (albeit perhaps through some industry economic pressure), which drives the pricing for RFID tags even lower. Newer tags are interestingly becoming less capable (and thus cheaper) and merely announce a single number (akin to a UPC value). "The goal," says Palmer "is to ultimately replace the printed UPC label with an ink-based printed RFID tag costing pennies."

The Inescapable Data interest in RFID will be clearer in subsequent chapters. As a quick prelude, the ability to know exactly where everything is at all times is critical to business optimizations and even personal (home-life) efficiencies.

Hybrid PDAs (Personal Communicators)

Hybrid PDAs combine three entirely different business and personal communication mechanisms (cell, e-mail, IM) into a single embraceable device. Their expected ubiquity will enable significant efficiency gains in our business and personal lives. Although many thought that the older PDAs would be a dominant device in our lives, they were unable to achieve penetration beyond a few small business circles. Hybrid PDAs will succeed because of three important conditions:

- Ubiquity of cell phone use. After all, it is no longer "weird" to be on your phone while in a supermarket, and you can be sure that someone next to you on the street is carrying a cell phone (to the same extent that you can be sure that those around you are wearing shoes).

- Seemingly overnight change from one type of cellular technology optimized for voice to a completely different architecture optimized for data, and without anyone even noticing.

- The increased business and social needs for higher immediacy of digital information sharing when *away* from a computer for down-right normal citizen needs (e.g., "Change of field for baseball practice tonight" or "Meeting at the alternate customer site up the road").

We use the term *hybrid PDA*, or simply HPDA, because some confusion exists within the industry as to the proper terminology. Existing PDAs that now have cell capabilities are called one thing by some manufacturers, and cell phones that now have e-mail are called something different. If the device is capable of voice, e-mail, and messaging, we call it an HPDA.

The trend toward holding your electronic life in the palm of your hand started when cell phones were crossed with PDAs. The result was a cell phone that could also keep your calendar and your contact database. Next, text messaging was added, and then Internet access and e-mail. There appears to be no end in sight to the future versatility of these multifunction handheld devices.

For example, NTT DoCoMo has introduced in Japan a cell phone with so many functions, one could get lost trying to find them all. This unit does the following:

- Sends and receives e-mail
- Plays games online
- Accesses iMode compatible Web sites and plays downloaded music
- Takes digital photographs
- Records sound
- Reads bar codes (and someday RFID tags)
- ... Oh, and makes phone calls

The phone also contains a specialized Sony-developed chip called a FeliCa chip or "smart card" that enables users to pay bills and make purchases over a wireless electronic banking system, operate appliances that can be controlled via a connection to the Internet, unlock doors, and the list goes on.

Consider the previous section where we examined various communication methodologies. Sometimes, an e-mail is the best way to deliver a message (perhaps something less time critical, possibly larger, or something that requires some deeper thought). Sometimes, IM is the best method (for quick and important correspondence). Sometimes, even a phone call is appropriate. Imagine the utility of having access to all those modes from a single device that you carry with you (pervasively) anyway.

The relevant point to Inescapable Data is that now we all carry with us an intelligent device that is wirelessly connected to the world's vast data networks continuously. This is monumental and has quietly snuck up on us. The utilities that will be discovered will be mind numbing.

Why Not Just Call Someone?

If we admit that we are heading toward a world where 100 percent of people carry cell phones, why not just call someone when you have a desire to communicate? The answer: because synchronous communication is a poor use of time. You have to interrupt your targeted party, the targeted party has to give you full attention for the duration of the exchange, and the targeted party cannot prioritize and optimize his or her communication exchanges. Furthermore, you cannot give the target the actual business object (e.g., the soccer schedule, the competitive analysis report, the "pictorial" directions to the airport). Even a message such as, "Mom, I'm outside Macy's waiting for you" is best delivered asynchronously yet immediately (given that Mom is finishing a client interview). The significance of cell phones *plus* text messaging is that these devices provide a way to reach nearly everyone nearly every hour of the day now, which is ideal for high-immediacy asynchronous communication without forcibly interrupting the target.

Video Cameras and Webcams

The popularity of consumer digital cameras has driven down the price of their main components and the quality up. The key component of a digital camera of any type is the CCD element (the chip that actually "sees" a scene and turns it into a digital blip); the price of this component has dropped so low that high-resolution color video-capture devices can be built in to nearly anything. In parallel, wireless networking stormed through the computer industry over the same time period and has a natural home with video cameras. It is now trivial to litter an environment with video-capture devices because the costs and wiring complexity have been nearly eliminated.

Certainly, we discuss the values of video in surveillance, for both home security and the larger societal (public) security. But as interesting is the deployment of this new source of data for real-time business optimizations—from observing shoppers' habits to tracking products to inspecting and controlling manufacturing machines. Advances in image-processing algorithms now enable machines to actually *understand* scenes. Video is perhaps the largest data source we have ever had to wrestle with in the computer world. Whereas a single text page may consume a mere 1,000 bytes of information, a single video frame typically contains megabytes of information. Multiply that by 30 frames per second and we are dealing with streams of data that are unprecedented.

In our Inescapable Data world, we will see video capture everywhere, and forevermore video data streams will be an integral part of our information lives.

Wireless Pervasive Monitoring and Sensing Devices

It is now possible to equip just about any electronic sensing device with a wireless network interface such that the entire electronic package, including power source, is no larger than your thumb. These include chemical sensors that can alert people working in manufacturing plants of hazardous chemical spills, for example, or biosensors that can alert communities when a toxic airborne virus is released into the atmosphere by terrorists, or bracelets on your infant used to monitor body temperature. These interfaces can be wirelessly networked together to form an invisible sensory "mesh." The list of potential applications for these highly discreet but powerful sensory networks is nearly endless. Because the sensors themselves transmit their data over wireless networks, they are much easier and quicker to deploy than their wired counterparts and, therefore, will become far more pervasive.

We examine many such devices throughout a wide variety of industries. The point to Inescapable Data is this: We are entering an age where just about everything (and everyone) will be emitting data and forming ad-hoc data networks. Together, we will discover values in intertwining different data sources and trending and analyzing these new streams.

Enabling Pervasive Networking

The next element in the Inescapable Data world is pervasive networking. "If I asked my kids today what is Token Ring, they'd first look at me queerly and then cite some reference to a Hollywood movie about forest battles," says Robert LeBlanc, GM of IBM's Tivoli software division. "In what seems like overnight to me, we've gone from a business world that had very unique machinery and intermachinery connections to one whose foundation networking technologies are the same as we now use everyday in our own homes."

This comment came up in the middle of a conversation about the evolution of computer networking. LeBlanc was referring to the old IBM local area network (LAN) protocol that was prevalent during the late 1980s and 1990s. In fact, many other protocols also existed, such as AppleTalk, thin- and thick-wire Ethernet, and some other specialty types. In the early days of networking, there were many vendor-specific networking devices because, by and large, companies settled on a single vendor for the majority of their computing needs. As the mid and late 1990s rolled around, interoperability became paramount, and the world settled on Ethernet as the standard machine-to-machine network.

In the early years of this new century, communication chip speeds greatly increased, costs fell, and building devices around communication chips simplified; therefore, Ethernet-enabled devices proliferated. At the same time, a couple of other trends were taking place. Broadband connections (cable and DSL) to the home became prevalent. In addition, the appearance of the sub-$1,000 PCs made it possible, even desirable, to have more than one PC in the home. To receive broadband in the home, a special device is needed (to adopt the broadband protocol). It was trivial for manufacturers to add the chip set that allowed that device to also be a "networking hub," which enabled users to attach multiple computers to the same broadband connection. (Note that Microsoft did its part and finally made small area networking possible.) The home network was born (long after predicted), and made possible by the simple fact that the networking technology already in use by businesses was the same technology needed in the home. In fact, the mass market for networking gear created by home use brought the cost of networking gear down dramatically for home and business users alike.

Early on, home-based Ethernet networking (i.e., networking with physical wires) would only capture the interest of the techno-savvy. Thankfully, at the exact same time that broadband was entering more and more homes, wireless Ethernet technology (networking without physical wires) was turning a corner. Wireless Ethernet had been around for more than a decade, but had never taken hold; in fact, many of the companies that had painstakingly pioneered the technology went out of business. Why?

Prior to the early 2000s, the business desktop world was dominated by machines that were fixed to one spot in the office. The need for wireless computing was not acute. Soon enough, however, laptops became the dominant business PC platform. Laptops virtually scream *mobility*—take me with you wherever you go. As business laptop users exploited computing mobility, the need for wireless connectivity soared, which drove the prices down and the performance up. (Before this, wireless speeds were too slow for business users.)

However, as inexpensive as 802.11b (wireless Ethernet) has now become, it is not suitable for mass deployment into devices smaller than computers because of its size, power, and cost. We are increasingly a society that needs to have everything interconnected, and we are learning to hate anything wired. We expect our home phones to be cordless. We want the ear buds for our MP3 players to connect to our hip-side devices without dangles. We have tasted the freedom 802.11b gave, and we cherish the connectivity. Enter Bluetooth.

Bluetooth is a short-range wireless networking communication method that boasts low costs and low power consumption as its main features, enabling just about anything that runs on electricity (even tiny battery electricity) to communicate with something else (as long it is only a few feet away). The magic of Bluetooth is that any and every device that has even a wisp of electricity, from an ear bud to a toaster to a flat-panel display, will now have some type of wireless communication interface. As wireless communication needs and capabilities grow, a networking hierarchy will fall out of the process that will extend the tentacles of the Inescapable Data network to many of the most commonly used electrified devices in our lives. Computers within our living spaces will be connected to the Internet via broadband. In turn, our computers will communicate via Ethernet (wired and/or wireless or Bluetooth types of technology) with our refrigerators, ovens, air-conditioning systems—any electrified device or appliance.

It is both interesting and important that the general tools and technologies used throughout office buildings are now the same as those used in our own homes. This enables an acceleration of technology use. Similar to how we all instinctively know how to drive a car on any road in any city, we now all know how to live and work in any modern location. LeBlanc added, "My kids come into the office here and walk the hallways. They see an occasional Ethernet wire and a smattering of wireless hubs on the ceilings and walls, ultimately leading to the Internet, which is where they work and play, as do we. Do you see? The home and business worlds have blurred."

Question: In a world where everything is a source of data connected to a vast network with global reach, is it realistic to expect any really useful exchange of data between all these very different devices? And will information then rise to the surface of these oceans of data? If history has shown us anything in the computer world, useful information exchange has always been challenging, if not elusive, between disparate machines. XML, discussed next, holds at least part of the solution.

XML...Describing It All

The data communication world has seen so many challenges over the decades that it is difficult to point out any single one as the most troublesome. If we were to choose one, however, it would be a lack of interoperability between devices, characterized by dissimilar computing machinery, incompatible wiring types and protocols, and dissimilar data protocols. Luckily, the computing world has now embraced the notion that nonproprietary standards for physical networking are good and that we all win when devices talk to each other no matter what they do or who made them. Even if new networking technologies come forward, the people designing and building the gear are now more willing to work together to standardize on their interface than ever before. But what about the actual data being exchanged?

The last element in the Inescapable Data world is intelligent and simple information exchange by using self-describing data techniques.

Until fairly recently, storing, processing, and managing large amounts of data was expensive. It was expensive to store on disk, expensive to move through networks, and expensive to process. In the early 2000s, we saw a dramatic drop in the cost of data storage because disk-drive manufacturers could double the capacity of a single drive without substantially increasing the cost to manufacture that drive. (Laptops, a case in point, will soon be sold with 1 terabyte—1,000 gigabyte—disks). We similarly saw networking performance go from 10 megabits per second to 100 to 1,000 and now 10,000 megabits per second with no increase in device cost. Of course, CPU processing power has followed Moore's law all the while (doubling every 18 months) without doubling in cost. We think that these advances, when combined, have enabled something magical to occur: We can now be more "verbose" in our data usage. We have the processing power, the data storage, and the network bandwidth to actually *describe* data as it is used and transferred. This capability would have been unheard of prior to the dawn of the twenty-first century.

So what does it mean to describe data? Typically, data in a computer is stored in binary form and stored in its most compact state. The numeral 5, for example, might be stored in as few as 8 bits (1 byte). With such a tight format, there is little room left to include information to tell what that 5 might actually represent. Does it mean 5 dollars? Five cents? Is it what your balance due is, or the cost of a particular item?

For years, computer systems could easily talk to each other electrically (via Ethernet) but labored to exchange meaningful information. It took teams of well-trained people to write special software that could decompose business databases created for a single use into data that could be used in other contexts and by other software applications. To some extent, this was acceptable because business systems were fairly customized to a particular business or business process. However, the Web dissolved business barriers and created a need for business information exchange. All of a sudden, the need to exchange information between millions of computers materialized, almost overnight.

At the inception of the Web, people first thought that the Web would be so vast that we would need special sites just to collect other sites and help us navigate through the maze. History has often taught us that hierarchical organizations are what we deploy to solve problems of complexity. Look, for example, at your local library—painstakingly, every book is cross-referenced in three directions and stored in a massive index. Hierarchical and index solutions work as an organizational tool for large data sets, but fail for massive ones—such as the Web—which need ad-hoc and quasi relationships.

The Web dictated that to display information, you had to first format it in a simple text-describing nomenclature called Hypertext Markup Language (HTML). A Web page is a collection of text and pictures with various formatting information. Unlike databases, the language of the formatting is human readable and human understandable. For example, a Web page may have such statements as <Title>This is my title</Title><Body>This is the main text area</Body>, where <Title> and <Body> are known as tags.

HTML represents a special kind of magic—a blending of human and machine intelligence. Web "pages" written in HTML are readable by machines and humans alike. As such, it is simple to create search tools that just run around surfing the Web much like we do, but they can read and index the content they find far faster and present it back to us in human-readable form. As an added bonus, they do so continuously without breaks for meals, sleep, or days off from work. Every Web page contains vast amounts of associated information, such as the author, the hosting company site, adjacent pages, pages it references, and pages that reference it. Google and other search engines use all this plus the embedded "tag" information to provide a detailed inventory of this massive resource.

All this leads us to eXtensible Markup Language (XML), which is much like the Web language HTML. Documents are not binary; instead, they are human-readable text, and every element is encapsulated within human-readable tags. We might have a brief XML document such as the following:

```
<CustomerRecord>
 <ItemPurchased>
 <ItemType> Shoes </ItemType>
 <ItemPrice> 5.00 </ItemPrice>
 </ItemPurchased>
 <ItemPurchased>
 <ItemType> Toys </ItemType>
 <ItemPrice> 3.45 </ItemPrice>
 </ItemPurchased>
 </CustomerRecord>
```

XML formatting allows proprietary databases and records to now have a nearly universal method for describing their contents. The binary representation of 5.00 from our example is now clearly a price, and the price of a specific type of shoe. You do not need to be a sophisticated programmer who understands how to read a "schema" document or how to encode SQL statements to make sense of XML statements. Your 13-year-old could happen upon such an XML fragment and derive some value from it. He or she could likely import it into a favorite spreadsheet package and sort or average or trend it with a few keystrokes. We refer to this capability often in later chapters.

Suppose, for example, that airline landing data was available nationwide in XML format (listing the airline, flight number, time of arrival, arrival airport, and so forth). A college student in Ludwig, Texas, with an interest in statistics and the correlation of flights to weather to economic conditions could, without ever writing any specialty software, correlate massive tables of flight data and massive tables of weather data along with published economic data from the Federal Reserve, all without changing out of his or her pajamas. Using some macros in an Excel spreadsheet and some cross-tabulation tricks, the student might tease out a relationship that was somewhat counterintuitive. This "tidbit" then becomes a tool for investment transactions or a tip back to an airline for an efficiency-consulting arrangement.

Note that this brief XML document is perhaps 100 times thicker (data-wise) than a simple 5, and therefore has a comparatively huge impact on the amount of disk space required to store the document and the bandwidth required to send it from one computer to another, not to mention the processing power needed to translate the human-readable statements into machine-readable form, and back again. This is why XML was not practical until available networking bandwidth, CPU horsepower, and storage densities hit their current levels.

Business back ends are now XML crazy. Any information that needs to be expressed to another computer system is now expressed in some XML format. (Data might still be stored in databases in a more native format, but we predict that these formats will eventually disappear.) Most significantly, XML enables far higher business-to-business cooperation squarely aligned with the Web's chief goal: information exchange (as opposed to data exchange). XML has been wholeheartedly embraced by business and is allowing for significant efficiency gains and better customer experiences. We are now finding XML reaching into the consumer world and our homes for many of the same values. To the Inescapable Data world, XML is the magic glue that allows all the vast sources of data and internetworking to now have real value through information sharing.

Summary: The Final Blend of Ingredients

So what does this all mean? We believe that without any significant investment, and little specialized training, virtually anyone will be able to interconnect pieces of data—data, created by prolific devices connected to us, over broadband and wireless interconnections—at blazing speeds. The data we collect in aggregate can be transformed—sometimes in real time—into information that yields new levels of business or personal value. This is the essence of Inescapable Data.

The key ingredients of Inescapable Data are communications, wireless networks, data, and data descriptions. The power of Inescapable Data is that both people and organizations with similarly scant resources can knit together divergent sources of information that yield new, highly valued capabilities, and create new sources of information that were once only available to those blessed with very large computing facilities, data archives, and specialized skills. Because we *can* interconnect data now, we *will*, and we will do so more and more in the future.

The Inescapable Data vision we seek to verify says that when a technology is good for both businesses and consumers alike, there results an exponential growth in the use of that technology as well as additional knowledge gains that were not previously anticipated, all driven by the massive ubiquity of data-producing devices. In this chapter, we brought the foundations of Inescapable Data together. Imagine every device in your home equipped with some amount of wireless connectivity, including your desk and chairs—with every device being able to emit information in XML format. Imagine every business machine and home appliance able to accept instructions and commands via human- understandable text XML, wirelessly. Imagine your supplier's inventory available (through a secure gateway, of course) in XML format, as are your MasterCard charges for the past 10 years. This represents massive amounts of data (some real time, some historical), and all physically (wirelessly) interconnected. Most importantly, however, all this data can be intelligently exchanged as "information" (rather than just raw data). We now ask whether this massive interconnectivity will usher in unprecedented and unforeseen efficiencies in our lives.

Let's explore.

CHAPTER FOUR

From Warfare to Government, Connectivity Is Vitality

One of the problems military leaders have in warfare is that they are overloaded with data—they have more imaging information than they have the people who can interpret it. Pervasive connectivity and distilling monumental volumes of data into tactical information locally is the new goal.

—Jay Bertelli, CEO of Mercury Computer Systems, supplier of massive processing systems

Introduction

The same data acquisition and management issues as in the commercial sector present themselves across federal, state, and local government agencies: data growth rates of 50 percent per year and greater, the requirement to network this data in real or near-real time, and the need to distill data from multiple sources into meaningful information. Fortunately, many of the same tools and technologies used in the private ssector are being used in the public sector as well. However, we found some interesting variations on these themes when we examined the rapid changes occurring in computing as applied to warfare and the battlefield, homeland security measures that are now

45

focused on surveillance, and challenges faced by state and local governments. Throughout, we found some common threads, including the following:

+ The need for more real-time intelligence
+ The need for better internetworking between agencies at all levels—from military intelligence sources at the federal level down to state and local government and government agencies alike
+ The distribution of command and control functions to gain reactive immediacy and battlefield advantage

Instant Messaging: Changing Command and Control in War

Instant messaging (IM) has become the cornerstone of many business messaging systems because it enables information-sharing immediacy and hence real-time decision making. It has also become a fundamental military messaging system, and its first battlefield deployment has already occurred: the Iraq War.

We interviewed Robert Nesbit, general manager of the Mitre Corporation's Bedford, Massachusetts, operation. Mitre is a large government "think tank," and Nesbit shared with us some interesting details about the impact IM has had on military command and control:

> You have to understand how wars are run. Typically, there are large command centers on the outskirts of the war zone with perhaps a 1,000 people. They are very hierarchically organized, largely due to hundreds of years of history. Everything is very formalized regarding approvals. The generals sit up on top (of the war room) in a booth that is somewhat like the luxury box in a stadium. They look out over the whole war room floor and have these big screens around them . For this [Iraq] war, we introduced instant messaging and it completely blew away the traditional command and control lines the military had for the last 100 years.
>
> The average floor person would be in four or five "chat rooms" at one time. Now, these aren't the same type of chat rooms as your teenage daughter would frequent, but they are based on essentially the same technology. One room would be the tanker chat room, another would be the ops chat room, another might be the predator assessment chat room. People on the floor could completely "piece together" operations simply by coordinating key personnel and activities among the main disciplines. One captain could get everything coordinated, all by himself, by sitting in

front of a single computer screen with multiple chat sessions active. In the past, lay-
ers of control would introduce delays as commands had to go up and down the
chains of command. This now is a real-time war. [Not unlike the supercharged
competitive environments many businesses now face.]

So imagine, a new general comes in and goes down to the floor. He asks someone
on the floor, "What are you doing?" He hears, "Well, we just found this high-value
target and we diverted an F16, but he needed gas so we got on the tanker, then
took out the target, brought in damage assessment and imaged the area, and we're
now talking to the press leads." All of this took place via instant messaging.

Mitre developed its own instant messaging software for military applications
that has one special and critical capability: real-time foreign-language translation (idiomatically correct). Nesbit explained that coalition forces in Iraq speak
and operate in many different languages—Polish, Spanish, and Ukrainian, to
name just a few—and therefore need to communicate in real time without
built-in translation delays (which would be considerable if manual translation
were required). "I'll admit, I was skeptical at first, until I saw it in operation. The
system is quite clever. It is very difficult to translate a given language's various id-
ioms, such as our 'whazup?' to something sensible in the target language. But it
worked; it really did, and was critical to the success of the war." Here is real-time
translingual text messaging at use on the battlefield. Imagine the barriers in our
world that could be broken down through the use of Inescapable Data devices,
networking, and IM with real-time translingual text messaging. Such a technological achievement could be as monumental as the invention of the printing press.

IM in the private sector is used for exactly the same purpose—bringing people together, shortening the time it takes to get problems resolved, and facilitat-
ing decision making, *virtually*. It is not uncommon in business to have a half
dozen "chat" sessions going on simultaneously. Because the medium is perceived
to be less formal than e-mail, messages tend to be short and to the point (and
may even contain multiple typos and grammatical errors that would be unacceptable in more formal written communication). Many people approach writing an e-mail just as they do with more formal written communication,
following the rules of correct spelling, punctuation, and syntax. Some people
take as long to compose an e-mail message as it would take to make a brief
phone to accomplish the same communication. IM circumvents that formality
while preserving the asynchronicity of e-mail. IM messages are expected to be

concise and not saved (and thus not scrutinized later). IM brings a "freedom" of communication and an associated efficiency. Perhaps even more importantly, however, it conveys a sense of virtual togetherness. Add real-time text translation and language barriers fall, and we all take a giant step closer to becoming members of a single world community.

"There are over 250 million IM users today," says Ken Kuenzel, CEO of Covergence, a start-up focusing on various real-time communication solutions. "This is expected to soar to 500 million by 2007," Kuenzel continues. If Kuenzel is correct, there will be half a billion users of a text-messaging technology within two years. Verizon alone processes more than 23 million text messages per day, and that is only a fraction of the traffic volume experienced in Europe and East Asia.[1] Two billion messages a month is the norm for some countries.

Battlefield Connectivity

Modern battlefields require far greater local data processing and connectivity than battlefields of the past. These needs are driven by the increase in the use of Inescapable Data collection devices that produce abundant real-time and critical battle and intelligence information. Just as business is being transformed by a plethora of new data sources, so too are military decision-making processes being transformed. Battlefield operators now have access to much "wider" (sources and types of) data that they can factor in to decisions that must be made locally as they integrate the distributed data with myriad other streams of knowledge.

"The rate of increase of the data being generated is greater than that of Moore's law (doubling every 18 months), so there is a need for more processing and a need for large systems," describes Jay Bertelli, CEO of Mercury Computer Systems, supplier of massive embedded processing systems. "In the military, commanders want to keep the data 'in theater.' The data streams off of an unmanned aerial vehicle (UAV), but they need to process it nearby and send it back to someone who can act on it, which drives a need for supercomputer–style processing power in very constrained and harsh spaces, in addition to highly connected networks."

---

1 *Boston Globe*, June 7, 2004.

Barry Isenstein, general manager and vice president of the Defense Electronics Group of Mercury, explains why battlefield processing requirements are so extreme:

> *The figure of merit isn't how big (in terms of processing power) of a system you can deploy, it is how much processing power can you fit into a tiny space. We are now stuffing a teraflop worth of processing into something the size of a milk box.*

What's a teraflop? Military processing typically requires a great deal of signal processing that uses computerized mathematical calculations known as floating-point operations, or flops. Years ago, the performance of a super-computer system was measured in megaflops—one million floating-point operations per second. Today, systems that perform in the gigaflop range (1,000× more than a megaflop) are needed for most of the sophisticated signal processing operations. The need for teraflop-scale processing power is becoming common as well (an additional 1,000× in performance or a million times more performance than a megaflop, if you can imagine).

All this computer power is being squeezed into ever-smaller spaces. According to Isenstein, "There is a major Lockheed Martin program, the Joint Common Missile program. Its aim is to replace a lot of the current air-to-air and air-to-ground missiles used by the navy and army. The processing space allotted to us within the missile is extremely tight, with a similarly tight budget for heat dissipation." The processing power, although nowhere near a teraflop, is still staggering considering that it is embedded in a missile, which is essentially a single-use product. In real time, the system has to process massive streams of data from many onboard sensors as well as onboard radar and two or three other classified sources of real-time intelligence...in a *missile*. In addition, targets are not always as stationary as a power plant, for example. Some of the more high-value targets are movable and might be in motion while the missile is in flight. "These missiles have to be very intelligent; you want to hit the enemy missile launchers and not the school next door," adds Isenstein.

Accurate target assessment just cannot be done with only one sensor consuming just one stream of data. For example, the missile's onboard radar—possibly the most modern Synthetic Aperture Radar (SAR)—could determine that a moving object is a "vehicle," but it could not determine whether the vehicle is an armored car or a school bus. Additional data from other sources is needed to more finely tune the image. For example, adding in a hyperspectral image of the area could help to detect the kind of exhaust fumes (e.g., diesel) emanating from the vehicle, which would narrow down the possibilities as to the type of vehicle. Other sensor data, such as detection of whether the vehicle itself is *emitting* data, would narrow the list of possible vehicle types even further (because school buses do not emit military signals).

In the past, military planners did not have real-time access to so many different sources of data and certainly never had the capacity to process the data into useful information in real time and in such tight spaces (e.g., as within the body of a missile). The ability to coordinate and fuse sensor data is now critical to success in the new battle zones.

"The data coming off of a Global Hawk UAV requires a tremendous amount of interpretation," says Isenstein. "In order to dispatch an F16 to drop a payload, commanders need trained personnel who can do the data interpretation—a very rare skill. The human is arguably the slowest link in the chain because of the amount of data to sift through. The more processing we can do in the air, the easier the understanding of the data." Analysis of historical data and trained computer programs that distill out the salient information can help to alleviate the problem of the shortage of trained personnel. As the military continues its never-ending quest to compress battlefield reaction time, some missiles will be designed with "loitering" capabilities. Loitering means that a missile can be fired at no target at all. It simply flies in holding patterns until digital imaging, radar, and other data sources point to a possible mission. In such cases, the missile's capability to process more data locally and derive intelligence from that data in seconds is critical.

Network-centric warfare is at the heart of the military's new real-time theater operations. Prophet Ground and Future Combat Systems are new programs driving communication, intelligence, and surveillance down to ground-level vehicles. Isenstein continues:

> Prophet Ground is putting SIGINT (Signal Intelligence) into HUMVEEs. Believe it or not, there is not much of that in the world today—a half a million vehicles that today are just vehicles, but in the future they'll all be connected. In this network-centric warfare. everything needs a COMs link and everything needs to talk to everything else throughout the theater. In contrast, the history of war until recently was to send an army out until they bump into something then back off and figure out what to do with it. Persistent surveillance and network-centric armaments allow commanders to know the enemy's position, direction, and intent. This is only possible by assimilating and digesting significant amounts of data, in real time, in the theater, as well as from stand-off platforms. The amount of

computer processing in a HUMVEE will rival what super computers had just a few years ago—and we only get the space of a milk box.

The general trend is to move more processing closer and closer to the soldiers in the field. Therefore, the need is for more intelligence "around the edges" of the battlefield network; commanders can no longer afford the informational latency introduced when field units have to reach back to some distant central command center for directions. As importantly, field units currently do not have the communications bandwidth to send all the raw data back to central command. First, it must be decomposed and digested locally. "They can't make reliable targeting decisions with just one sensor's data. Is it a bus or an armored vehicle? Before you blow it up, you need to coordinate sensor fusion *in the field*," Isenstein adds.

In the 1990s, a commercial technology used for tracking trucking-company vehicles was co-opted for military use. FBCB2 (Force XXI Battle Command, Brigade-and-Below) is a system used to support battlefield tactical missions. Specifically, FBCB2 provides real-time "situational awareness" for the commander, staff, and soldiers. In addition, it uses graphical displays and detailed target identification to provide a common picture of the battlespace. No more commanders and troops yelling coordinates to each other over the radio. The Iraq War exploited this new technology heavily; military networks were able to show battlefield conditions in real time.

FBCB2 is a mobile system of networked computers, radios, satellites, and software. Data from a wide variety of sources, including GPS, is blended together to form detailed knowledge maps of a combat situation, including landscape and positions of soldiers and targets. The knowledge is made available to all levels of the command chain, from field combatants to commanders back at central command. FBCB2 leverages Inescapable Data sources and its impact cannot be understated. It empowers the battlefield decision-making process through massive data correlation and fusing. It also breaks down the traditional military knowledge realms by allowing knowledge and decision making to flow up and down the chain of command.

Operations of all branches of military service are developing a huge dependency on key Inescapable Data themes: real-time information enabled by the use of Inescapable Data collection devices—both on the ground and airborne—locally processed into information with tightly compacted super-computer power, and coupled with many other streams of information to derive a new battlefield advantage.

Heads-Up Decryption

A growing problem in military and government operations is the proper dissemination of classified information. We clearly have technology that can allow documents to be transmitted between computers in a safe, encrypted fashion. The problem is that, eventually, a document has to be decrypted and presented for actual viewing. In any modern computer system, after the document is decrypted, there is a possibility that some flavor of it may stay decrypted longer than the reader intended.

The computer itself keeps the data in RAM and likely has temporary on-disk copies that might be hard to locate. Furthermore, the user of a document may inadvertently store it as a copy or e-mail it to someone else. The point is this: Once decrypted, it is nearly impossible to control who receives the "information" (including people looking over shoulders).

One possible solution is to never decrypt material until it hits the receiver's eye. With the advent of heads-up glasses and goggles (as discussed in Chapter 9, "Sports and Entertainment: Energizing Our Involvement"), a product can be created that decrypts material just prior to your eye seeing it. "We've been asked by a few different customers for goggles or eyewear that decrypts information at the last most possible inch," says Peter Purdy, CTO of Motion Research. "Such a device could have widespread benefit in military applications, filling a hole that has existed since the beginning of military communication."

We are entering an age when more and more sensitive data is stored electronically and needs proper protection, perhaps forever. Although this might at first sound a bit Jetson-age, the value of such a device is clear for military and intelligence agencies. There is a risk in having everything connected to everything else—specifically, that information could fall into the hands (and heads) of unintended recipients. Advances in personal-wear applications might help bring information to the right targets only, and the technology required is available today.

A "Connected" Homeland

The Department of Homeland Security (DHS) 2005 budget is $40.2 billion— an increase of $3.6 billion from 2004—and DHS has the fourth largest IT budget of civilian agencies (and the fastest growing one). More than $2.5 billion of the 2005 DHS budget is dedicated to BioDefense,[2] and approximately $3.4 billion[3] will be spent on information technology in general.

Arguably, the events of 9/11 could in part be attributed to disjointed government systems that did not communicate with each other. More than 40 separate information systems behaved as though they were islands of data unto themselves. Recently, the DHS started a program to introduce information sharing into the nation's intelligence systems infrastructure. A $350 million contract was awarded to Northrop Grumman to interconnect the U.S. departments of Justice, State, CIA, Homeland Security, and the FBI via systems that are compatible with each other and that can share each other's data. The goal, of course, is to leverage all the intelligence available in the fight against terrorism and other national security threats. The first, and now obvious, step is to have more pervasive networking and communications capabilities.

The U.S. federal government is now on the road to solving a problem that never should have existed in the modern computer age. However, a less-tractable problem is figuring out how to build automated systems that use electronic sensors—perhaps thousands of them spread over a specific geography—that perform real-time threat detection and analysis. Attacks from chemical or biological sources can be devastating and difficult to prevent. Even if some forms of attack are ultimately not preventable by these systems, the data they collect is of great value in determining what is going on when an attack commences (such as being able to track the progress of a chemical wave as it moves toward densely populated areas). Even afterward, the data can be used to determine how similar attacks might be prevented or at least dealt with better.

Thermo Electron's Environment division makes a variety of sensors for industry, and now for homeland security applications. Greg Herrema, president of the division, states: "If the probability of prevention (of an attack) goes down, then the capability in terms of detection and response has to be significantly greater." So, although DHS might not be able to prevent biological, chemical, or

---

[2] http://www.dhs.gov/interweb/assetlibrary/FY 2005 BIB .pdf.
[3] Federal Sources Inc., a McLean, Virginia, market research firm.

nuclear radiation attacks on the general populace, it can at least attempt to understand, contain, and deal with them should they arise. "Our new customers want smaller sensors with real-time data collection abilities that they can deploy pervasively," says Herrema. "Well-placed sensors located around choke points (e.g., bridges and ports) can support both threat prevention and response, in particular for radioactive threats that can be more readily detected from a distance."

The federal government is hopeful about its ability to deploy thousands of sensors across cities and suburban regions. There are many challenges, however. The number of different chemical or biological threats is large. In the past, sensors were built for a single purpose, for detection of a certain gas or chemical leak within a factory, for example. Building sensors with a broader range of detection capabilities will add significant cost and complexity. Another of the more daunting challenges is supplying power to these small and discreetly placed devices. "It might only cost $50 or $100 to produce a certain kind of sensor equipped with some sort of wireless capability, but if you have to run A/C power to each location, you dramatically increase the cost. Solar power and extremely long-lasting batteries will dramatically lower the need for expensive power circuitry, and alternative energy sources will aid in that challenge as well," says Herrema. Nevertheless, powering these sensors economically remains a short-term difficulty. In the meantime, real deployments of more expensive sensors are occurring, albeit in a somewhat less-pervasive manner.

ZigBee

What is ZigBee? ZigBee (www.zigbee.org) is an alliance of networking companies (including Motorola, Siemens, Philips, Honeywell, and15 others at last count) creating a new open standard for low-power, low-cost wireless networking. The goal is to enable the mass production of tiny monitoring and control devices that can wirelessly communicate with each other (and router nodes) using dramatically less power than anything presently available.

Instead of aiming at the market for faster and more capable networks, ZigBee is heading the opposite direction. To minimize power consumption, the distance between nodes is small and the internodal data rate is significantly lower than that of WiFi. However, the payback is greatly reduced size and expense, and much longer battery life.

Monitoring and control nodes are typically deployed in a star or mesh topology because they depend on each other to relay messages from one to another and on to router nodes. Early ZigBee deployments have occurred around industrial control and monitoring. However, ZigBee has obvious applicability for homeland security.

Does ZigBee compete with Bluetooth? In a word, no. ZigBee and Bluetooth are aimed at different uses and markets. Bluetooth devices require recharging and assume that deployment environments are more data rich. Consequently, Bluetooth is about seven times faster in terms of bandwidth than ZigBee and is aimed at more of a consumer- and communications-oriented market (cell phones, laptops, home audio/video), whereas Zig-Bee is aimed at automated, pervasive monitoring and control opportunities. Both have practical missions to fulfill in the world of Inescapable Data.

Millennia Net is one company making sensor products using the ZigBee protocol and has created tiny devices that can last several years on a wrist-watch–size battery. Its slogan is "Wireless Sensor Networking...Anywhere," and is targeting military/homeland and industrial opportunities. Their sensor networks can self-organize and self-heal, meaning that the network can automatically route communications around a failed node. Millennia Net is able to deploy large numbers of the sensors throughout a geographic area with minimal support requirements and high overall data/connectivity reliability.

The U.S. federal homeland security budget for fiscal year 2005 has a significant amount of money allocated for the detection of bio-related threats that are grouped under the general heading of BioDefense. Of that, $2.5 billion is allocated to a project known as BioShield. Another $274 million is earmarked for BioSurviellance. Another $118 million will be spent on enhancing environmental monitoring activities of such elements in a key subprogram known as BioWatch, a next-generation biosurveillance system. Between 2003 and 2005, the National Institutes of Health (NIH) sequenced genomes of all bacteria considered to be a possible bioterrorism threat[4] as well as viral and protozoa pathogens, and this data can now be exploited.

---

[4] http://www.hhs.gov/budget/05budget/nih.html.

BioWatch has been deployed to more than 31 major U.S. urban areas as of July 2004. In total, more than 500 sensors cover approximately half of the U.S. population.[5] These sensors are in use today for environmental sampling to detect biological agents. Currently, most of their data is collected manually, meaning that inspectors periodically visit the devices, plug into them, and download their data to some portable computer (such as a laptop), and then send the data off to analysis centers. Given the remoteness of some sensor locations, bicycles are used in some cases. One sensor is located up wind from the National Mall and somewhat resembles a telephone booth with an air sniffer and radio antenna.[6]

Part of the new BioDefense budget is to enhance automation and integration of the data. Approximately $11 million is earmarked to integrate real-time biosurveillance data gathered by sensors with information from health and agricultural surveillance and other terrorist-threat information from intelligence and law-enforcement agencies. Very much consistent with the Inescapable Data attitude, the federal government is moving in the direction of pervasive collection devices whose information is fused in real-time with other information streams. Clearly, post 9/11, we have learned that combination and assimilation of information streams is needed to extract real power from raw data.

Blanketing a wide geographic area with sensors presents new data processing challenges. Data must be analyzed in real time and correlated with other events taking place (perhaps from emergency-response vehicles, traffic-pattern sensors, communications traffic, etc.). The challenge facing the government is similar to that posed to manufacturers contemplating the use of radio-frequency ID (RFID) tags throughout a factory or warehouse. Tons of data generated in a short period of time must be processed as "complex events"; otherwise, the resulting information overload will render the data useless. Complex event handling is a new style of computer processing that brings intelligent understanding to rapid and seemingly unrelated streams of data blips—essential for certain sources of Inescapable Data.

DHS is equally concerned with monitoring and controlling U.S. geographical borders. The US-VISIT program, for example, is a new program designed to use biometrics—pattern-recognition systems using fingerprint and a digital photo data—to more accurately identify foreign visitors. As of January 2004,

[5] http://www.nationaldefensemagazine.org/article.cfm?Id=1467.

[6] http://www.nytimes.com/2003/11/16/national/16TERR.html?ex=1094011200.

more than 115 U.S. airports and 14 seaports were using the system. Foreign visitors traveling to the United States must submit to having their index finger on each hand digitally scanned to verify identity at the port of entry. The process starts overseas at the U.S. consular offices that issue visas. A traveler's fingerprints are taken and examined against a list of known criminals before a visa is issued. Travelers arriving in the United States are rescanned to verify their identity. In addition, a digital photograph is taken at the exit port and reexamined at the port of entry. Clearly, a global network built on massive data collection and communication processes is the heart of this system.

Similarly, $65 million will be spent on border patrol surveillance and sensor technology using remote video systems; $50 million for radiation detection for trucks and cars passing through various ports of entry, and $11 million for a new international trade data system, which is the first government-wide system for collection and dissemination of trade and transportation data, essential for more than 100 federal agencies. The trend is clear: more real-time data collection about individuals and vehicles, and more closing of some well-publicized gaps in overall homeland security by information sharing among government agencies.

Pervasive Public Surveillance

Video surveillance has quietly become pervasive. The annual growth rate for sales of video-surveillance equipment is now 15 percent (CAGR)[7] and increasing. Between government requirements, corporate initiatives, and our own public acceptance of the value of being monitored in the face of terrorist threats, the number of deployments is swelling. There is expected to be $1.6 billion spent on digital video *cameras* in 2005[8] in the United States alone.

Interestingly, the vast majority of surveillance cameras in use today belong to nongovernmental entities. An ACLU study of the number of cameras in New York City, for example, discovered that nearly 90 percent of these cameras were attached to private buildings. The perceived values derived from surveillance have become apparent to many businesses (e.g., protection of property and care

---

[7] http://www.visiowave.com/index.asp?index=intelligentVideo&S=sc13.

[8] http://www.usatoday.com/tech/news/2001-05-24-world-privacy.htm.

of a company's employees or an apartment building's inhabitants). The ACLU makes the point that an effort to restrict government use of surveillance cameras is probably a mute issue given their broad use in nongovernmental sectors.

Two key drivers are pushing us toward widespread deployment of video surveillance systems:

+ The cost of the equipment has dropped dramatically while at the same time ease of deployment (i.e., primarily, wireless devices) has risen.

+ Increased labor costs, a decrease in properly trained personnel, and a general worry regarding human safety require that we have more "eyes" on business and public property interests.

A manager or owner of a small 24-hour convenience store, for example, cannot afford to employ a security guard just to monitor the access points to the building. It is far more cost-effective to install a couple of wireless cameras and post a few strategically placed signs that alert potential interlopers to the fact that that security/management is watching all the time. Installation of video-surveillance networks is becoming easier and cheaper every day—moving this capability more into the mainstream and beyond the realm of high-value retailers, such as jewelry shops. Any and every store is worth protecting (as is any home or school, for that matter). But just hanging video cameras everywhere is not enough because there simply are not enough humans to intelligently manage and monitor the vast numbers of cameras. In the Inescapable Data world, camera networks become an everyday fact of life, but they must be linked to larger systems (possibly government systems) that can automate image analysis.

A building equipped with a large number of closed-circuit TV (CCTV) cameras typically has a control room that sports dozens of video monitors. Often, a given TV monitor screen is subdivided into quadrants, each showing a different camera's view. Often, any one quadrant cycles among many cameras. The control room is staffed with one or two control room operators stationed and (hopefully) continuously monitoring the cameras for suspicious activity. However, we all know that it is humanly impossible to sit in front of a TV screen for hours watching the same images flicker past over and over again.

"Black monitoring" replaces this highly inefficient method. Sophisticated new software allows analysis of video images to be more automated. The systems can distinguish normal activities for a given date and time versus suspicious activity.

At a minimum, the system can boil down hours of captured video images and dozens of camera feeds by identifying the most high-value scenes and events for closer human analysis. In the future, real-time indexing of images and far more sophisticated search mechanisms will enable security professionals to far more easily focus on evidence-laden video segments.

Chicago has installed a video system to discourage drug and gang activity as well as reduce the number of homicides. In high-crime neighborhoods, police have installed wireless, digital video cameras perched atop light posts. These cameras are protected themselves by a dome of bulletproof glass. Police officers in squad cars driving nearby can access these cameras using WiFi-equipped laptops in real time from their squad cars. The units can be taken down and moved to a new location within a few hours if need be.

The cameras themselves show the level of sophistication this technology has reached. The cameras can rotate a full 360 degrees and can zoom in on scenes up to four blocks away. Furthermore, they can "see" at night using special night-vision capabilities (a significant capability given that a large portion of the crimes occur at night and in low-light conditions). Unlike many video-surveillance cameras that are hidden, these are deliberately conspicuous—each is outfitted with a flashing blue light delivering the message that the city is serious about crime prevention.

The 2004 Democratic National Convention in Boston was also the scene of a landmark use of digital video and other surveillance technologies. More than 30 cameras were installed around the perimeter of Boston's Fleet Center where the convention was held. In addition, the coast guard used infrared devices and night-vision cameras in strategic spots around Boston Harbor, plus dozens more cameras throughout the downtown areas.[9] The digital feeds from these cameras were piped to agencies in Boston and Washington, D.C., so that, while sitting at their desks, security officials were able to zoom in for extreme close-ups. The cameras were sharp enough to pick out facial details or read license plates in some cases.

Interestingly, convention security officials were also able to leverage some surveillance networks already in place for other purposes. Boston's mass-transit system, the MBTA, had more than 100 cameras already in the area monitoring

---

[9] http://www.boston.com/news/politics/conventions/articles/2004/07/18/surveillance targeted to convention?mode=PF.

subway and bus stations. MassPort (the Massachusetts transportation organization) placed more than 900 other cameras at the disposal of security officials as well—a dividend that resulted from the massive downtown Boston highway project known as the "Big Dig" and from a variety of other public works projects. In a short order, more than 1,000 additional cameras were at the disposal of the convention officials—Inescapable Data monitoring that could be easily repurposed.

Part of the challenge convention officials had was that the Fleet Center is in close proximity to Boston Harbor. This greatly worried officials, who feared potential aggressors might enter the security zone via boats. However, a new coast-guard system named Hawkeye, especially designed for waterway surveillance, joined infrared, radar, and of course, digital video-surveillance cameras, together giving security officials a real-time total view of all harbor activity. So, total surveillance meant watching everything in and around the convention hall, including the vastness of Boston Harbor and the historical zigzagging streets around the convention center—a monumental task made easier by Inescapable Data networks and sophisticated digital monitoring techniques.

With thousands of cameras watching us in relatively small geographical areas for the purpose of public safety, we have become a "video connected" society without even asking. Who knows how many of those streams are saved to some disk and for how long? We presume such capture, storage, and later analysis is for our own good. That may or may not be a safe assumption Those thousands of "public" cameras stationed around a major political or sporting event are a small number compared to the building-security cameras already out there and sending their data somewhere.

The Republican National Convention

The Republican National Convention in 2004 also showcased some interesting use of video and networking on the part of protesters.[10] Organized protest groups used text messaging on their cell phones to send out broadcast messages of where the next protest would be staged. In real time, organizers could communicate with and control a large number of on-the-street protest leaders and participants with a few keystrokes. Essentially, the

---

[10] http://www.cnn.com/2004/ALLPOLITICS/08/27/wired.rabblerousers.ap/index.html.

protest network could be run like a military command and control center, with pervasive communication to each individual in real time using a commonly available device that most people already owned—the cell phone.

In the past, organizers would have had to use nightly meetings or Web sites to coordinate movements—which, of course, would not be as responsive or timely as instant text messaging broadcasts to the "troops." Furthermore, in an interesting twist on the "whole world is watching" theme, protesters were encouraged to capture police actions (such as brutality) via their cell phone cameras or PDAs and have those images uploaded to the main protest Web sites (as if having a 1,000 "public" cameras trained on us already isn't enough). Protesters who did not have a camera-enabled phone were encouraged to call their own cell numbers (or use their iPods) to make voice recordings of the events they were witnessing—essentially leaving themselves a message. A stunning amount of real-time communication, networking, and collaboration aided the protesters' rapid response to changing conditions (proving that it is not just Big Brother that could be watching).

Connecting State Governments...Together

As the tragedy of 9/11 made clear, the lack of connectivity and information sharing across government agencies were factors that impeded a more rapid response to the events of that day. The inability to share information is a problem for all governments from the federal level down to state, county, city, and town levels and stems from the way in which government information technology programs are funded. "All funding takes place on an agency-by-agency basis and has led to the creation of operational 'silos,'" according to Steve Quinn, CIO of the Commonwealth of Massachusetts. However, changing this approach to reflect a broader scope is not simple. "We're talking about changing the whole fundamental culture on how budgets have been done for years and years and years, and that is a very difficult and slow process to change. But if we don't change it, we won't change the silo effect," continues Quinn. Indeed, the "silo effect" is the essence of the intelligence problem pre-9/11.

In an odd way, Quinn is hopeful that in financially tight times, less state in-come resulting from lower tax income coupled with higher expenses due to in-flation will force governments to do more sharing, if only to save costs. Innovation is often driven by financial challenges, and where those challenges align throughout governmental levels and agencies, collaboration and project sharing could lead to better information sharing in the long run. The question is whether government officials will continue in their old established ways of budgeting or see the value of collaboration—uncomfortable as that might be.

Lessons from the Insurance Industry

The insurance industry has a similar information-sharing problem. The CIO of Safety Insurance, Dan Loranger, has had an interesting history as an IT administrator for large organizations across many different indus-tries. Loranger started during the pre-deregulation days of the airline in-dustry at a time when the spirit of cooperation (or should we say "coopetition") was vastly different from what it is today. "The airlines worked together. They would swap pilots and even aircraft when needed and, of course, allow each other's tickets," describes Loranger. "They wanted to share computer technology as well—even among competitors. Their healthy attitude was, 'If we're going to survive, we need to all help each other.'"

Loranger was part of the early team that installed the Saabre reservation system—a sophisticated reservation system that was developed by one airline and then opened up for use by all the others to share. The value of information sharing became obvious to all involved.

Loranger contrasts this with the insurance industry. "The insurance indus-try has been far too fat for too long," starts Loranger, "and any inefficien-cies were easily dealt with simply by raising rates or investments. The insurance industry has never really been in tough times that would force them to have to focus in deeply on the back-end IT side. The IT budget is quite small in comparison overall to revenue income. Any proposal to lower back-end costs was ignored. The insurance industry is driven by money-making plays not cost-saving back-end optimizations."

However, Loranger was not stymied in his desire to bring information sharing to the insurance industry. He saw the value the Saabre system brought to airlines and he had a vision for a similar back-end management system for insurance carriers. As times became a little more competitive, during one year that it was difficult to simply "depend on rate increases" Loranger pioneered the first true "connected" insurance business. Prior to his initiative, each agency of a carrier ran their business much like a silo—not connected to the carrier in any direct way and still very much dependent on phone and postal mail. "In the 1960s, American Airlines was online and productive. In the 1990s and early 2000, insurance agents are still using phone, paper, and mail as their primary communication tools. It was really ridiculous and ripe for a change," states Loranger.

State government needs a few pioneers. Now that funding is tighter and a new focus is on both IT costs and interagency cooperation, the ground is fertile for new approaches. Perhaps the open-source movement holds the key. According to Steve Quinn:

> We are deeply committed to open standards and open source. This is our best hope going forward for avoiding a repeat of the problems of an aging employee population and legacy software code. Open source has got traction in government; this could absolutely be revolutionary in terms of how software gets built and licensed. It is a different business paradigm. We donate code that we build and various companies become subject-matter experts in a certain area of government. The government is vast, and the opportunities for collaboration are enormous.

State governments are beginning to use information technology in novel ways, and we are headed toward "virtual" collaboration of multistate IT operations. Sharing data, software, and application-development practices is an important first step toward leveraging staff and resources among state agencies. Cost-reduction efforts, and data sharing and connectivity options now offered by the open-source movement, will further drive the connectivity of state and local governments.

Breaking down information silos and sharing data to realize new efficiencies and discoveries are goals that are consistent with our Inescapable Data vision; furthermore, the values realized are basically the same for businesses as they are for governments. The problem of governmental information sharing has been well publicized and may represent significant opportunities for commercial businesses to eventually participate in the vast shared-information space currently under construction.

Summary

We find it significant that military operations now exploit the same instant messaging technology that many teens, preteens, and twenty-somethings have become addicted to. Certainly, messaging has been a cornerstone of warfare forever, but real-time, nonverbal "instant" messaging *within* a given operations center can significantly alter historical chains of command in exchange for decision-making expediency. This expediency, expressed as real-time coordination of people and data resources, offers the same value to business organizations. The new battlefield vision is one of real-time gathering of massive volumes of sensor data, with wireless networks that weave the data streams together. Extracting real-time information from these data streams is now possible because of super-computer–like power packaged into tight and hardened in-theater environments. Without the proper and real-time distillation of the relentless data streams, operations would be paralyzed by the data or result in mistakes (possibly with horrific consequences).

On the homeland security front, a similar trend toward Inescapable Data gathering and real-time digestion and analysis is occurring. BioDefense initiatives are driving widespread deployment of sensors with wireless connectivity for centralized analysis and intelligence. The need for more comprehensive video surveillance, driven by a perceived need for greater homeland security, is now producing unprecedented volumes of data (data that has to be stored and analyzed by somebody somewhere). The pervasiveness of streaming image data-capture capabilities has brought with it a challenge to make sensible and ethical use of it. Imaging and wireless sensory technologies, honed on the battlefield, will find deployment in these newer and more homeland-security–focused venues, crossing traditional government and private-sector boundary lines. Finally, the historical silo'd approach to holding intelligence information is now turning toward full connectivity, not only to avoid another national catastrophe but to also streamline general governmental operations. For government agencies, connectivity offers new vitality.

CHAPTER FIVE

Pervading the Home

Throughout our homes and lives, we'll see our possessions and toys announce them-
selves wirelessly, and we'll find ways to exploit efficiencies, tightening our over
crowded lives and finally bringing back some gaps of time for ourselves and much
needed security.

—Mark Palmer, prominent RFID expert

Introduction

Our home lives are destined to become more "connected" with our appliances
and "toys" than we ever could have imagined. The charm of an Inescapable Data
world is that an acceleration of utility occurs as more and more devices become
data and network enabled. This chapter explores how the three most important
Inescapable Data technologies—radio frequency ID (RFID), wireless networking, and XML—will increase automation in our lives. This chapter also covers
the security role of video in our personal lives and how GPS-everywhere will
benefit us. There is a clear trend toward higher interconnection of a broad range
of gadgets in our lives, and the presumption that follows is that there is an accompanying amount of utility.

Key Foundation Technologies

The home-automation market has proved so far to be an elusive fantasy. For many decades, authors have been writing about automation throughout the home and the benefits it will offer us. However, the vision has yet to materialize. Why? Cost and complexity have traditionally been the primary inhibitors. "We currently use 10 different protocols to connect to 10 different systems," explains Jay McLellan, CEO of Home Automation, Inc. "It is straightforward to integrate security, temperature, and lighting, which we do for most of our customers. But beyond that, standards and critical mass are needed to have control over other appliances."

Some companies have tried to leverage A/C house wiring, piggybacking some level of functionality onto that preexisting infrastructure. However, all they wound up being able to do was control the power to something electrical (a light, for example) plugged into the A/C and at a cost of $20 or $30 per decoding device—not a real boon to automation. An alternative vision holds that homes of the future will be built with a separate Ethernet network throughout, providing a data path for far more functionality.

X10

X10 is an A/C wireline communication technology introduced in the mid-1970s. It is somewhat challenging to encode digital information onto high-voltage wires and to do so without affecting the appliances (in the form of "hum"). As a result, only a modest amount of information can be encoded and to only a fairly small number of target devices. X10 is quite useful for turning appliances such as lights on or off (or perhaps to dim them) and is currently the most popular home-automation network. Relatively inexpensive endpoint devices allow individual "power" control of appliances. Radio Shack, Home Depot, and other mass retailers have been selling X10 devices for two decades. Over the years, new devices have been created to allow your home computer to talk to the network and have more detailed program control over the usage. The newer desires for automation, however, stretch beyond basic A/C on-off control for appliances; we want to reach inside and control appliance/device operation and discover details of their content, usage, and maintenance, and we want to do this remotely with ease and low cost.

The Inescapable Data vision is different. It's not wired—its wireless. According to this vision, the number of conventional home devices that will come equipped with some amount of wireless networking and some simple self-describing set of capabilities via XML will be surprising. It will be as standard and ubiquitous as UPC codes—the critical mass of standard devices Jay McLellan wants to see. The Inescapable Data interface will be out there, waiting to be exploited by us (and a vast array of commercial enterprises).

Before diving deeper into the subject of Inescapable Data in the home, it is important to review the key technologies that will be at the heart of the Inescapable Data in the home:

- RFID tags and readers
- Wireless networking
- XML

RFID, Wireless, and XML

The three fairly new technologies of RFID, wireless, and XML are being integrated into home devices more and more and hold promise for advanced automation and lifestyle enhancement. Manufacturing and distribution applications already use RFID, and retail producers are starting to exploit its capabilities. The wireless computer networking in homes today (a number that grows daily) almost begs for other electronic products to join the networking fabric. XML is providing a mechanism for devices to expose their data in simple-to-understand and easily exploitable ways.

We believe that, ultimately, RFID tags will replace the ubiquitous UPC codes of today. Cell phones and PDAs equipped with RFID readers already enhance the consumer shopping experience. (Nokia and other manufacturers produce models with built-in RFID readers, primarily for field use in various service industries; these manufacturers are experimenting with in-store consumer retail information, too.) RFID tags come in a variety of forms and costs. The early tags were relatively bulky and cost up to a few dollars each—far too expensive for anything other than products or equipment with commensurately high price tags. However, large retailers such as Wal-Mart expect the technology to produce tags that cost pennies each and be tiny enough to be affixed to or embedded within just about anything. We fully expect RFID tags to be used on or in clothing, electronic appliances, toys, cigarettes, pharmaceuticals, and so on. The tags will also be part of any boxed food item. The RFID readers are more expensive and, as a result, will initially be found in the more expensive appliances in our home, such as washing machines and refrigerators. So, step one, having nearly everything being able to identify itself, is on its way.

Step two is allowing the data buried in objects to be extracted. Wireless networking will be key to the Inescapable Data home. Our love of the Internet drove computer networks into the home. Once they were there, we learned the value of wireless networks and the ability to stay connected almost anywhere. Wireless home networks are now penetrating an ever-increasing number of homes for general computer use, and now provide that missing backbone for home automation. It is expected that more than 50 million homes will have wireless home networks by 2007.[1] Although inexpensive by computer pricing standards, ordinary 802.11b wireless networking is likely too expensive to be added to tiny appliances, such as blenders (but may be perfectly suitable for more expensive items, such as refrigerators and washing machines). Bluetooth and other short-range schemes will offer more affordable solutions eventually, making home wireless networks truly pervasive, carrying data to and from nearly every electrified object in the living space.

Bluetooth

What is Bluetooth? Bluetooth[2] is a short-range wireless technology typically designed to span a distance of no more than 30 feet. Bluetooth is already in use by various cell phones to allow simpler hands-free communication to microphones and speakers. Some MP3 players use Bluetooth for wire-free ear buds. It can be used between PDAs and printers or GPS receivers and cell phones, and so forth.

---

[1] http://news.com.com/Study:+Wi-Fi+weaving+its+way+into+homes/
2100-7351 3-5136533.html.

[2] The name is taken from the tenth-century Danish King Harald Blatand. Blatand is translated as Bluetooth in English. King Blatand was instrumental in uniting warring factions in Sweden, Norway, and Denmark. In a similar way, the technology Bluetooth attempts to unite various manufacturers and industries in computing, cellular phones, and large-scale devices such as automobile.

Bluetooth is a radio-wave technology (like wireless Ethernet and cordless phones) and as such is not encumbered by line-of-sight issues that hamper other short-range communication technologies, such as infrared. It is designed to consume little power and can be implemented at low cost owing to the fact that its communication range is limited. Today, more than one billion suitable devices exist in the United States alone (cell phones, PDAs, MP3 players, gaming devices, and so on) that are targets for Bluetooth enablement, which will drive the volume-price curve downward. Worldwide adoption will drive the volume-price curve down ever further. As with any technology, it can take years before the adoption becomes pervasive. Bluetooth was first created in 1994, and now more than a decade later, we finally see accelerated deployment. Bluetooth may or may not be the final technology for less-than-Ethernet type of connectivity; some other sort of short-range wireless technology most surely might become prevalent and enable a new level of untetheredness in our lives.

Wireless provides the physical connection layer (so to speak). Step three, XML, provides the glue at the logical information layer. With XML, we no longer have to wait for costly developers to write specialty applications to exploit the pervasive physical connectivity and the data pervasive devices can generate. The "data" emitted will be easy for us to understand. We can use each other and leverage standard tools and technology because the "data" inside these various devices is easily readable by virtue of XML and easily utilizable by our wireless networks. These three technologies were not available just a few short years ago, but soon they will be prevalent. The combination of them will enable us to perform some exciting time-saving and life-enhancing tasks.

Whirlpool

Whirlpool has a new oven, the Polara, which is also a refrigerator controllable via a cell phone.[3] In the morning, you toss the lasagna in and set the device to keep it cool throughout the day. If the afternoon soccer game

continues

---

[3] *Boston Globe,* June 7, 2004.

Whirlpool *(Continued)*

runs late or you get stuck in traffic, use your cell phone to dial up your refrigerator-oven to alter the start time of the cook cycle. This is *not* quite the Inescapable Data way (although we are pleased that values are being understood). Somewhat like the faulty start of the home-automation industry, such devices are stop gaps until pervasive networks take hold.

In the coming pervasive world, it will not take a specialty device or a specialty phone call. Your PDA will have full access to all of your appliances *naturally* by virtue of XML and standard networking, and it will not matter whether you're in the living room or in Hawaii (because of the ubiquity of Internet connectivity). Already, we can be at work or on vacation and perform personal electronic banking and electronic trading transactions merely by having access to the Web. In any case, the fact that Whirlpool and other manufacturers are making such "connected" products is a positive sign, and such developments will help drive toward the bigger vision of seamless interconnectivity.

For Example, Refrigerators

Suppose your refrigerator knew better than you what was inside of it. "So what?" you might ask. Well, think about it for a minute. You're at supermarket and realize you do not know whether you need eggs, so you buy a dozen just in case. When you get home, you find that you already have more than a dozen. Now you have too many. It is no big deal, you think. It is Saturday, and you can make omelets tomorrow for breakfast. But, if there had been an *easy* way for you to know that you did not have to buy the eggs, you most probably would have made use of it.

The intelligent refrigerator—one that can tell you what is inside, how much of it, when you last bought it, and perhaps even when it is time to throw it out—has been a techno-vision since the advent of the "third wave." But until RFID appeared, smart refrigerators remained in the world of the Jetsons. In the near future, RFID tags built in to packaging materials will be able to communicate with RFID receivers built in to refrigerators. As you will read in the manufacturing and retail chapters, although RFID tags are today being used on more macro containers (pallets, cartons, crates), the direction is for them to go down into individual packages.

We will not have to campaign to have food producers put RFID tags on their products (so that that the items can report for duty once home and nestled quietly in your refrigerator or pantry). Manufacturers will do so themselves for their own benefit, including tracking facilitation, faster checkout times, loss control, and increased sales. Even without quantifiable benefits being immediately known, GE, Sub-Zero, and other manufacturers will include an RFID reader with a wireless interface in their appliances, mostly because they can. The technology will be inexpensive compared to the overall cost of the appliance, and will be worthy of major marketing campaigns (allowing the manufacturers to have some fun while seriously differentiating themselves from their competition).

Let's step through the process of endowing a refrigerator with intelligence as an example so that you understand how the process can be extrapolated to other appliances.

A manufacturer can (potentially) install a combination RFID reader with 802.11b wireless Ethernet, a processor chip, and some RAM into a refrigerator for less than $50. This RFID reader will run a rudimentary Web server application that allows your wireless home networking system to access the data inside. Therefore, a Web browser running on your laptop or PDA becomes a window into your refrigerator's contents, capable of reading the constant stream of XML messages emanating from the reader.

Many computer-type devices (such as your home wireless DSL or cable gateway) come with built-in Web servers to enable you to control or inspect them from your browser. Typically, the manufacturer tells you to "navigate to http://192.168.1.1" (or whatever) to then view and control the device. (Likely, your current wireless hub announces the exact address for you to initially configure it—try it.) Your refrigerator or other major appliance will be no exception. Without the manufacturer putting any effort into the interface, the "raw" XML output (available on a specified Web page) of a streaming RFID reader might look like this:

```
<RefrigeratorEnvironment>
    <OperatingConditions>
        <Temperature SetPoint="42.0"Current="41.5" />
        <DoorStatus MainDoor="Closed"F
        FreezerDoor="Closed"
```

```
            TimesOpenedToDate="1,204"/>
            <CompressorStatus State="On"PercentIdle="80"/>
            <OperationalStatus State="Normal"/>
        </OperatingConditions>
        <CurrentContents>
            <TopShelf>
                <Item Type="Eggs" Vendor="Star Market"
                Size="Large"/>
                <Item Type="Butter" Vendor="Land'O Lakes"
                Size="1lb"/>
                <Item Type="Yogurt" Vendor="Yoplait"
                Size="8oz"/>
            </TopShelf>
        </CurrentContents>
    </RefrigeratorEnvironment>
```

That might not be the prettiest display of information you have ever seen, but you could decode and make sense out of that fragment without a degree in computer science and would be able to "see" it merely by pointing your Web browser at your refrigerator's address. That in itself is a monumental step forward because, before XML and standard Web interfacing, to extract this kind of information from a processor you would have had to write a special program and understand some binary schema—far beyond the reach of the average consumer—plus, you would have had to know a great deal about networking and protocols.

Today, someone with a rudimentary knowledge of modern computing can easily pull this XML fragment out of the refrigerator's HTML page into a spreadsheet or database package or XML-processing package, and with a few simple macros sort, organize, and redisplay it. Someone with only slightly more advanced computing skill could build a customized, personal refrigerator Web page, complete with rich graphics, that pulls this data into a live display (perhaps laid out in visually attractive tables) and even reaches to manufacturer Web sites to pull in icon graphics of each food item. (Web pages today are commonly "cooked" from connections to other sites.) Building "neat" Web pages out of fundamental data elements and accesses to other sites is something many homeowners do today. For fun, go to Google and search for "our vacation" (in quotation marks) and you will get more than 306,000 hits, most of which are small-time ordinary people who have created personal Web pages (and posted pictures of their Grand Canyon vacation). If you dig through a few sites, you will be notably impressed by the talent of ordinary people and their ability to tie schedules and calendars and "blogs" together. Inescapable Data will leverage the power of the ordinary person; manufacturers will hopefully only have to provide the basics.

Aside from food contents, the previous XML fragment also details operational status and controls that could be presented on a maintenance Web page. Perhaps you will build a custom page enabling you to control the set point of the freezer from any Internet-connected computer that can reach your home network. Or a page that displays how often the compressor cycles on compared to how often the door is opened. Perhaps you will create a JavaScript program that schedules the refrigerator to a far lower temperature during the less-expensive energy hours and allows it to "warm" during the more expensive hours. If you cannot, quite likely, you or a neighbor will have a teenager who can. That kind of engineering help will only be necessary if you want to avoid buying software from your local supermarket or appliance provider. The value of standard interfaces and formats is that you can source materials and applications from a wide range of providers.

Now that the data from your refrigerator lives within your home network, it also becomes part of your "everywhere" network—that is, it is essentially available from the Internet itself (provided you enable such access and secure the access). You are then able to access it from any Internet-capable device, including the convenient-sized (and mobile) PDA. So while you are in the supermarket, you can glance at your PDA to find out whether you really are out of eggs (and with hardly any effort). At this point, you probably would not pay an extra $100 for a refrigerator that tells you how many eggs it contains. Over time, however, you probably will not have to pay anything extra at all for refrigerator smarts. (After all, do you pay extra for a computer-controlled carburetor or is it now standard in the industry?)

We believe that the capability will simply be there for us and for retailers to exploit because of the low cost of the base components and high use of standards and because interoperability allows for it—manufacturers do not need to invest much to bring the base capabilities to you. GE, for example, might put some cost into the actual electrical components, but no work into the interfacing and documenting. They do not have to work closely with the makers of the wireless or scanning products. They do not have to work closely with the cell phone companies, PDA companies, or the computer companies. Much like an owner's manual for an automobile is almost frighteningly small given the utility and complexity of cars, leverage comes from pervasive knowledge of how fundamental components and tools work—knowledge that a rapidly increasing number of us now have.

For fun, let's continue exploring the value of having our refrigerator know about its contents. Our dinner preparation can now be expertly assisted by our home-automation system. The system can suggest a wide range of menu items all based on actual ingredients contained within your house, perhaps factoring in the age of certain meats and vegetables. Perhaps it will make suggestions based on average meal price, or possibly based on total carbohydrate goals, or even based on your schedule.

You did not pay extra for this menu capability either. You either downloaded it from a supermarket Web site or your teenager did a little Java/XML dabbling and whipped it up while on the school bus. In the old world, to automate anything in the house you had to have expert understanding of a wide breadth of technology, and deep pockets to afford the materials and time. In the new world, you need only to be slightly on this side of the connectivity divide—an instinctive skill for future generations. RFID tags are not yet on our mass products, such as cereal, nor are refrigerators today equipped with RFID readers and wireless Web sites, but real advances are happening in that direction, lending credibility to that potential end state.

LG

Home automation is somewhat moving away from power on/off control and into more detailed appliance automation already. Your more expensive appliances, washers, refrigerators, ovens, dishwashers, microwaves, and so forth are already equipped with CPUs and some sophisticated processing power. LG, which is a large Korean company that makes a full range of appliances and electronics, has a vision of a fully integrated house. It has already begun shipping refrigerators and other appliances with built-in networks that can cobble a connection to the Internet. (The details are not published, but some sort of wireless networking between the devices ultimately can connect to your home cable or DSL modem.) It has committed to have all of its appliances networkable within a short time. It claims[4] that some Japanese CEOs expect "appliances without an

---

[4] http://www.lge.com/products/homenetwork/html/lge homenetwork.jsp.

Internet connection will no longer be manufactured." More than 100 different devices from LG such as DVD players, TVs, PVRs (personal video recorders...Tivo-like), and large appliances will be outfitted with wireless connectivity.

The value of Internet-connected appliances is possibly marginal (if there are only rudimentary on/off type controls), but then again, in the Inescapable Data world, many minor values join together to bring new and unexpected values. LG's refrigerator has a computer screen built in to it and potentially a capability to allow entry of desired shopping items (to then be picked up by your home computer or PDA or possibly directly into the store itself). Recipes can also be directly downloaded to their oven for easier reading via a built-in screen and automated setting of temperature. Other LG appliances, such as the washing machine, allow downloading of new wash programs that would perhaps deal with particular clothes loads specially. Of course, the basic on/off capabilities and device health monitoring are available—conceivably tied all the way back to a service technician. Not yet on their radar screen, RFID data combined with appliance intelligence probably offers the most amount of utility in home appliance automation.

We applaud LG's vision. Today, few of us would pay thousands of extra dollars for an appliance that could be observed via the Internet, but as stated previously, the "smarts" will eventually be included at nominal or no extra cost and the utility will quickly be incorporated into our everyday lives. For example, we have all experienced that moment of panic when we wonder whether we turned off the oven or stove before leaving home. We have probably all wished, at least once, that we could turn on the oven while at the soccer field, for example (if merely to get a jump on preheating). Some readers may even have wished they could, while at the office, send a video message to the refrigerator for the next person who walks by (similar to taping a Post-it note). LG is taking steps to making these capabilities a reality, although initially, it may be via some proprietary and custom interfaces. In the Inescapable Data world, manufacturers will use standard networking and XML and other interface standards to provide these features at a low cost and allow the general public to string the values together and deepen the values. The trend toward appliance networking appears to be here.

From Laundry and Home Inventory to Energy Systems

Whether you are aware of them or not, RFID tags are starting to be deployed in items of clothing—embedded discreetly in a shirt color or a waistband. The movement to wearable RFIDs is driven by both apparel manufacturers and apparel retailers. Both have a vested interest in loss control and providing a better shopping experience. The Gap, for example, is experimenting with in-store RFID-reading PDA-like devices that help shoppers match clothing with accessory items; these devices also receive well-targeted advertisements related to the merchandise. Gillette alone ordered more than 500 *million* tags in 2004, and Benetton ordered 80 million[5] for trials in various stores.

However, the utility of RFID does not end when you leave the store. It turns out that washing machines, like refrigerators, are also a good match for RFID readers. In fact, we can identify numerous values that come from having an intelligent washing machine that knows what is sloshing around inside. A smart washer could help people avoid the classic catastrophes, such as mixing colors with whites or using the wrong temperature or cycle or even the wrong detergent. In fact, RFID could eliminate the need to have any dials or settings on the washing machine itself...it should know how to produce perfectly clean clothes based on what it senses in the wash load. Come to think of it, though, we might still have to tell it how dirty the clothes are—assuming we want to divulge that information. Would you pay $100 more for such a washer? Probably not. Did you pay extra money for the end-of-cycle buzzer it has on it? Probably not. These capabilities will simply be there because the base cost of the raw components allows for it, and their utility will be far greater than a buzzer.

Interface-Less Appliances?

Might wireless appliances enable a new world of appliances that no longer have physical interfaces, such as buttons and dials? A great deal of cost goes into mechanical buttons and information lights and displays, all of which has to be manufactured to be rugged and withstand abuse (both of harsh hands and haphazard soils and spills). Manufacturers have always

---

[5] http://www.computerworld.com/managementtopics/ebusiness/story/
0,10801,79286,00.html.

had to balance how many controls to expose on a device against the direct costs and the indirect costs of support and confusion to the user. Software interfaces have a luxury in that they can present less-cluttered displays but still allow advanced users to drill down into more powerful controls or diagnostics.

Some appliance manufacturers have started using computer displays for those reasons. However, those displays add significant cost. If the manufacturer could count on users to have nearby wireless access (either a home computer but more likely an advanced cell phone or PDA), they could eliminate significant cost and produce a stronger appliance. If the trend toward home wireless computer networks continues, as well as wider adoption of PDA-like devices, we may very well enter an age where we control our appliances by pulling our PDA out of our pocket (which, of course, could be just as easily controlled from any remote Web location, further realizing efficiencies and convenience). Devices in the computer world, such as Ethernet switches and disk controllers, a long time ago migrated away from any front-panel controls to a completely Ethernet-connected interface.

Another value to RFID-enabled clothing is home inventory tracking. Assuming that you own or rent an RFID-enabled or "smart" living space, and many of the appliances in it are RFID-enabled, you could stop the seemingly endless searches for things. Are my running shorts in the closet, in the washer, in the dryer, or in the clothes hamper? It is perfectly reasonable to expect that dressers, bureaus, and closets will eventually be outfitted with RFID readers as well due to volumes driving RFID-reader component costs down.

A third value is creating the right "look" for a party or night out. A computer or PDA can help choose outfits for various occasions based on which items are truly available in your wardrobe. Tied back through the Internet to the manufacturer, an "apparel-selection" program could show you pictures or symbols of the various clothing items that could be appropriate. You can peruse your clothing inventory from your office chair or while by the pool. Neat little programs are available now that can visualize an entire outfit, allowing you to mix and match items like Colorforms (especially for finding the perfect shoes). Imagine combining one of these programs with data handed to it by your smart living space. Creative Inescapable Data users will find imaginative data sources to intertwine with the new information streams.

Another third-wave vision is of intelligent control of the living space environment—both from the comfort of your bed as well as from a remote location such as your car as you are driving home. Today, there are gadgets for your heating, ventilating, and air-conditioning (HVAC) system that enable you to remotely monitor and control your system, but those are specialty devices and have proprietary interfaces and likely require a dedicated phone line. Yuck—too snail-mailish. As with refrigerators and washing machines, your HVAC system is yearning to be connected to your *standard* wireless world and have easy-to-exploit interfaces.

Certainly, anyone driving back from a vacation can relate to the value and comfort of arriving home to a living space that is at an appropriate temperature (especially in the Northeast United States). We believe that consumers will want to be able to monitor and control the home environment (especially vacation homes) from any Web-enabled device and without any special hardware or hassles. The family calendar residing on the home PC could be easily tied into an HVAC system that could auto-adjust room temperatures at the proper times of the day. In the Northeast during the winter, for example, we often lower our thermostats a few degrees to save energy when we leave the house, and turn them back up when we arrive home. Using a PDA, we could tell our thermostats when we will be home (and without specialty and proprietary interfaces from our selected HVAC manufacturer). If it makes sense to have appliances such as refrigerators connected to the Internet (as in the LG case), it probably makes sense for HVAC systems as well.

As mass proliferation takes hold, we envision legions of renegade "open-source" programmers across the Internet spending significant parts of their nights writing the most bizarre things such as closet-optimization software— yours for free. Silly? How much time do the connected ones among us spend downloading the latest cell phone ring tones already, and for virtually no advance of efficiency? Or look at the proliferation of personal home Web sites created by Average Joe with rich graphics, interactive blogs, local weather insertion, and live video of their town center. History has shown us that people will dabble with technology if it is easy to access and offers just a modest amount of utility or fun. In the Inescapable Data world, a little dabbling for a specific value now has global reach and global value because of the pervasiveness of the devices and standard interfaces; we expect this to further accelerate ad-hoc usages and developments.

Intelligent Lawn Sprinklers

For years, more expensive homes have had automatic lawn sprinkler systems. Resource-conscious systems attempt to avoid watering if Mother Nature has recently done her job. Little collection tubes or dishes are located somewhere in the yard, and the system skips watering if there has been enough recent rainfall. Such systems are horrendously inaccurate and they have no concept of anticipated or forecasted rain. Some newer systems now use soil-moisture devices that are pushed into the ground and use wireless technology to transmit watering needs to the control box. The newest systems have satellite connections that receive local weather information, including humidity, rainfall, and expected weather and rainfall for the particular square-mile geographic area.

HydroPoint (`www.hydropoint.com`) is one company making such a system. Daily, its system receives weather information from National Oceanic and Atmospheric Association (NOAA) satellites gathering data from a vast array of weather stations across the United States. The HydroPoint system then analyzes the data and retransmits (via satellite) watering information to subscribers' watering controllers, achieving significant efficiency and conservation. Finally, this is moving in the Inescapable Data direction as multiple date sources are combined and turned into specific information (wirelessly). However, these newer advances are specialty devices and possibly proprietary technology. The Inescapable Data world will welcome standard wireless networking, and it should be straightforward to connect to Internet-based data sources and the watering controller itself without specialty technology or barriers.

As researchers looking for Inescapable Data in the home, we want to know whether these examples are the stuff of sci-fi or the requisite creature comforts of the not very distant future. We believe that those who suffer from extreme asthma, for example, will value a more intelligent HVAC system that is even tied in to the state weather-pollen forecast. Diabetics will value an overall food management system that tracks sugar and carbohydrate consumption. Homeowner's living in areas that can experience temperature extremes will likely enjoy optimizing utility usage to lower costs and extend component life. But we also believe that we enjoy end-of-wash buzzers on our washers, lighted refrigerator doors, and timed-bake ovens. In perspective, those are truly minor features compared to what will come naturally, and likely for free, in the Inescapable Data world.

We believe that manufacturers will detect demand for these kinds of capabilities, and that demand will come first from niche market applications and then blossom into mass adoption as the market matures and individual unit costs drop. After that, our vision holds that once everything in the living space is emitting data, and the conduits are in place to carry that data to processors that can intelligently decompose it and turn it into information, surprising new uses for these technologies will emerge. In much the same way that it does not take sophisticated programmers to create award-winning Web sites, it won't take programmers to leverage these technologies into the incredible improvements in our lives either.

Home Security: Video

The home security market is transforming into a video-centric, "U do it," market because of several factors. First, typical home security systems are essentially useless against the majority of break-ins—the "grab and runs." Perhaps your living space or that of someone you know has been broken into, despite the "security" stickers on all windows. As local detectives typically explain, thieves can pry open a back window and be in and out within the 90-second delay of the alarm system. This technique now accounts for the majority of all home break-ins.

Current home security systems leave much to be desired. It is expensive to wire every entry and window pane. They are notoriously bothersome to activate and deactivate, especially for those of us who are in and out all day long. They offer zero after-the-fact evidence to help get back your lost goods. Enter wireless video.

If we had just a glimpse of all cars passing by our house around a given time, and a glimpse of a person or two actually near or in the house, we would have a much better chance at both apprehension and conviction. (Often, thieves just ring the front doorbell and patiently wait for no answer; then they scurry around to the rear for their adventure.)

Until recently, video devices for home usage have been expensive, physically large, very low quality, and very difficult to operate (videotape-based, if you can imagine). However, technologies related to Inescapable Data, when combined with an affordable price point, have enabled a quantum leap forward in the effectiveness of living space security systems. These include charge coupled display (CCD) cells—the electrical component that "sees" the world and that is now prevalent in digital cameras—combined with and 802.11b wireless technology.

New video cameras today are wireless and can easily be squirreled away in places that make them difficult to be seen (and without turning the whole process into an expensive wiring project). Once connected to the home wireless network, the possibilities for intelligent surveillance abound. The video data produced by all these cameras can be collected on your computer system. A program that can detect periods of no motion can automatically delete these segments out of the stored video stream so that you can play back only the times when motion was detected, literally saving hours when you want to review what has been recorded. Once stored on your computer system, you could access it anytime while you are away via a PDA or remotely connected laptop. You could also forward the video file to a local police department as evidence, should the need arise. This is all available *today*.

How *inexpensive* is it to get started? Prices range from $25 per camera to $150 depending on resolution and size. (You pay more for those that are more discrete and hideable and less for larger or coarser resolution.) These prices are certainly well within reach for the average person, especially given that the cameras now easily interface to your home network and come with simple software. Linksys, one of the premier home wireless providers and a division of networking giant Cisco Systems, is now in the business of retailing wireless IP cameras—a statement of where the market is heading. Software ranges from simple still-scene elimination (to reduce disk space usage) to actual analysis of objects and motions (such as pets moving about at floor level). Some "indexing" software is also readily available to enable you to "search for all scenes with a moving object wearing red clothes," for example, although such capabilities are still somewhat limited to higher-end systems. The point is this: Prices, technology, and capabilities have propelled home video surveillance from an avant-garde tool to something as ordinary as a home Tivo or photo printer.

It is possible that, with a proliferation of digitized video-capture devices, we will become a society obsessed with the digital capture of anything in our lives. (The skyrocketing adoption rate of camera phones and now video phones is a testimony to this statement.) We do not necessarily need every room in our homes monitored; an outside view of the house and a kitchen view might suffice. While on vacation or at work (away from the home office), it is comforting to glance at your PDA or a section of your "home" Web page and see that all is well. Have you ever been out at dinner and had a panic vision, for no sane reason, of your house on fire? Comfort returns with a simple discrete glance at your PDA. Certainly "nanny-cams" received notoriety as cases of babysitters mishandling the children in their care were publicized. As a parent, you can now be virtually present while a babysitter watches your children in your home. You could monitor your house-cleaning people. What about your children, who might be home alone after school? With a date? Regardless of whether you will deploy pervasive in-home monitoring yourself, it is more than likely that at least some of the living spaces you visit will. (Still worried about those 1,000 cameras around the DNC now?)

Video camera systems have been available for some time, but it is a rare home that is video-graphed as of yet. Prices have now dropped dramatically, and the simplicity of integration has increased to the point where the Average Joe can set up a wireless monitoring system with a Web-viewable interface and know nothing more about computers and technology than was necessary to get his wireless home computer network functioning in the first place. This is what leads to pervasiveness and then the accompanied utilities. We are likely at the beginning of widespread video deployment of personal video monitoring (to say nothing of commercial and government monitoring systems).

GPS—Tracing Our Steps

Global Positioning Satellite (GPS) is the technology that enables you to know exactly where you are on the planet, down to the last square foot. "Years ago, the civilian use of GPS was limited to an accuracy of a hundred feet or so compared to the higher accuracy of military usage," explains Robert Nesbit, general manager of the Mitre Corporation (Bedford, Massachusetts, operations), a large government think tank. "The Clinton administration ended that disparity, and now we all have the benefit of near perfect accuracy."

We have all seen GPS systems in car navigation systems. What has changed is that the technology has been shrunk in both size and costs to the point that GPS can now be put into tiny and pervasive devices. Case in point,

Nesbit explains, "As a result of the E911 mandate, congress requires cell phones to have a GPS chip built right in to them, although not necessarily exposed to the average user." Nesbit continues, "Sony is the number one maker of embedded GPS chips"; so, you might imagine where this is heading. There's an old saying in the computer world—technology advances are driven by either gaming or porn or both.

More than 20 million GPS devices are in use today in nonmilitary capacities. According to Adrian Kingsley-Hughes, a prominent author on GPS technology, "The largest new growth area is in handheld devices." This includes cell phones and PDAs as well as sport devices for outdoor adventures, such as hiking. The technology is now so prevalent that Coke had a special promotion for the 2004 summer[6] in which 120 Coke cans were equipped with GPS-enabled cell phones and the recipient needed only to place a phone call (via the can) when they discovered the can.

"Think about this," Adrian quips, "the expression 'Where are you?' will disappear from our dialogues. This is the new equivalent of caller ID. Caller ID was essentially 'location' information, right? The display showed you that Sally is calling from work or Joe is calling from home. We lost that when we went all-cellular." Adrian's point is that, like caller ID, at first we may resist these new locator services, but in the end, we will accept and embrace it. Today, when your phone rings, do you not expect to see who is interrupting you? Might you now expect to also know *where* they are calling from as well?

Stalking via GPS

Not all uses of GPS are desirable. In August 2004, a Glendale, California, man was arrested for stalking his ex-girlfriend by using a GPS system. The man built a homemade device that combined a GPS receiver and a cell phone with a motion detector. He surreptitiously attached this device to the undercarriage of his ex-girlfriend's car. Whenever the car would move, the cell phone would turn on and periodically send GPS location information to a Web site the man was monitoring. The woman became suspicious when her ex-boyfriend kept appearing at places where she was

continues

---

[6] http://www.adrants.com/2004/05/coke-launches-gps-coke-can-promotion.php.

Stalking via GPS *(Continued)*

(such as the airport, bookstores, and elsewhere). She ultimately caught him when he was under her car replacing the cell phone battery. This case points out a new level of concern with being so easily connected (and thus monitored).

Tags or bracelets exist today to allow tracking of children. "Have you ever gone to one of those crazy amusement parks in the summer?" Adrian asks. "Too many people packed into a 500-acre section of the earth. It's every parent's nightmare. I for one would value an amusement park that offered free tracking bracelets to all young children where my PDA could constantly navigate me toward them. In the UK, we're exploring bracelets for child abusers as well. Safety or privacy risk? When pushed, most of us would come down on the side of safety and security."

Nesbit explains that there is a significant recent enabler of this GPS craze:

> GPS uses satellites, and a device has to lock on to four or five satellites before it can get an accurate reading. This process can easily take minutes and consumes a great deal of power (and thus battery size) as the system hunts for suitable satellites. This is particularly problematic indoors or under heavy forest cover where signals are weak. GPS was thus relegated to vehicle navigation systems. More recently, cellular and GPS technology have come together in a synergistic way. The local cell sites retain accurate satellite information and prebroadcast this information to cell-GPS enabled devices. The devices are now able to near-instantly lock on to the correct satellites and do so with minimal power consumption. This is why we'll now see GPS-enabled devices be pervasive.

Many of us seem to have an insatiable appetite for details. Inescapable Data could turn this appetite into an obsession. We do not want to know that it is the Smith's house calling us, we want to know that it is Tom Smith. We want to know where he is when he is calling us. (After all, he's interrupting our life; why should he need to hide his whereabouts?) We want to know whether a spouse is still on the tennis court or in the lounge and able to tolerate an interruption. We want to know whether our child is in the movie theater or behind it. We want our cameras to superimpose landmark and geographic information onto our photographs automatically. (Ricoh's Caplio Pro G3, for example, is a camera with a built-in GPS that automatically watermarks photo's with location information.)

On the other hand, there are more productive uses of personal GPS as well. Our Inescapable Data thesis states that it is the coupling of a pervasive technology with other pervasive technologies that results in greater gain. Look, for example, at where the business or leisure travel world is heading. We visit our favorite travel Web site and book a trip to Orlando. The XML output from the travel site is automatically digested by our PDA-based calendar tool and correctly blocks off the appropriate days. The same PDA then automatically traverses XML-based airline schedules. And, as we pass thru DFW on our way to Orlando, using GPS it guides us from gate C21 to gate B18, all the while sensitive to the last-minute gate-change information. A connected relative who we expect to meet at the airport knows our whereabouts as well. Never once do we call to say that we have been delayed an hour, and, of course, we would never discuss where to meet. The relative simply knows where to be, and when. Knowing exactly where we are at all times and advertising that through networks to trusted targets is an Inescapable Data component.

Theme Parks and RFID

A new theme park in Fort Lauderdale, Florida, uses RFID bracelets to help parents keep track of children.[7] Wannado City is a theme park designed around children's future career aspirations. The park's slogan is "America's First Real-Play Park," and children get to experiment with being a doctor or a paleontologist or a variety of other careers. The park is large, about 140,000 square feet, mostly indoors but divided in to a tangle of "stores" or locations for interaction, somewhat like a sprawling shopping mall. All visitors to the park get special wristbands that have embedded RFID chips that wirelessly transmit the wearer's identity to the park's various sensors. Kiosks located throughout the park enable visitors to locate members of their party.

---

[7] http://news.com/Theme+park+takes+visitors+to+RFID-land/2100-1006 3-5366509.html?tag=nefd.hed.

Summary

The charm of the Inescapable Data world is that multiple data sources can now be easily hooked together for new values. We are entering an age that will be filled with devices emitting data, most notably RFID tags on our consumer products, but also streaming video sources and other devices. Wireless Ethernet and other wireless technologies are already being adopted at astonishing rates, and we (collectively) expect our data devices to be wirelessly enabled now. XML and related technologies are paving the way for data-emitting devices to be easily understood by us, while enabling us to rapidly knit their data into higher-value settings. Quite possibly, we soon will see our appliances come more Internet-accessible and perhaps even have an understanding of exactly what items are in them. Wireless video will offer us improved personal and home security, and GPS will provide that desired detail of knowing "where" we are (or anyone else, for that matter). In the meantime, we are seeing the beginnings of appliances reaching outside of their enclosures, the steady deployment of wireless everything, and the early stages of new data-emitting products.

CHAPTER SIX

Connecting Medicine

With massive databases of real-world responses to things where we do not at first envision a mechanism, we find a pattern in the data that implies a mechanism and then work backward to discover it...Scientific inquiry in medicine is being fundamentally changed by the availability of large and ubiquitous data sources.

—Dr. Thrall, chief of radiology at Massachusetts General Hospital

Introduction

The medical, health-care, and life-sciences industries are experiencing data growth and now connectivity at phenomenal levels, a circumstance that promises solutions for some of our most worrisome problems. From cancer cures to better infant disease prevention to improvements in service and quality of care, the lifeblood of the new medical world is data, and wired and wireless networks are the blood vessels. Inescapable Data devices will generate volumes of interconnected data, and then processing power (prohibitively huge only a few years ago) will tease out relationships and automate interactions.

DNA—Massive Data, Massive Value

DNA is *the* information molecule of life. "Interestingly, the DNA of any two individuals on Earth is actually 99.9% alike," says Dr. Phil Reilly, CEO of Interleukin Genetics. "There are 3.1 billion base pairs in the human genome," continues Dr. Reilly, "yet a mere 0.1% of 6.2 billion is 6.2 *million* differences, which explains our remarkable distinctions." The study of those variations leads to the discovery of genetic predisposition to various diseases, and hence the great interest in mapping the human genome and studying it intimately.

"Suppose you and I compare our Gene A," adds Dr. Reilly, "and we find that two or three places out of 30,000 bits [for a gene] are slightly different. Perhaps you have a greater incidence of heart disease, and it is related to those bit differences affecting the functionality of a protein that is coded for that gene and now has a different efficiency of some metabolic pathway downstream." Through extremely computer-laborious number crunching and cross-analysis, key associations are learned that in turn lead to new drug therapies or treatment protocols, only possible through the power intrinsic in the data and the ability to analyze it.

DNA Analysis and Anti-Spam

In a rather odd twist, computation biologists at IBM's Watson Research Center have created an anti-spam filter based on tools and techniques used to analyze genetic sequences.[1] E-mail spam is a growing and annoying problem for most everyone. Companies and people creating the spam are becoming increasingly clever in how they create e-mails to avoid the commonplace filters. Part of the challenge is that it is considered a far worse problem to erroneously block valid e-mail. Therefore, spammers attempt to add extra text in messages and subject headers to make their e-mail seem legitimate and desired. IBM's Bioinformatics Research Group started adapting some of their bio pattern-matching algorithms for e-mail analysis back in 2003. The anti-spam algorithm grew out of an algorithm called Teiresias, which researchers were using for protein annotation. Determining the properties of a protein (such as function and structure) turns out to be similar to analyzing and understanding e-mail messages.

---

[1] http://news.bbc.co.uk/1/hi/technology/3584534.stm.

The researchers trained the algorithm on nearly 100,000 messages. Over time, the algorithm learned similarities of a dollar sign ($) and the letter (S), because spammers will often encode messages like this: "$ave big on new enhancing pills." In tests, more than 97 percent of true spam e-mails are recognized through this new and unconventional approach. The advances in computing and algorithms for gene sequencing and analysis turn out to have a valid deployment in more commonplace areas. Inescapable Data and networking allow such cross-uses to be made and the values applied to broader areas of our lives.

Sequencing of the human genome cost approximately $3 billion and took nearly 15 years. The amount of data this project produced is staggering. There are approximately 25,000 genes hidden among the 6 billion bases to express the "generic" human genome. The first step was to acquire the data. But, that process provides only a generic set of data for a species (useful, to be sure, for detailed analysis of individual genes and events). However, genetics researchers now project that within as few as 5 to 10 years, they will be able to map an individual's personal genome and do so at a cost of as little as a $1,000 per individual.

What is the value of handing someone $1,000 to map your own personal genome? Some medical researchers believe that knowing your personal genome—carried with you, perhaps on your PDA or ID card—will allow your doctor to prescribe customized medication regimens to more effectively treat specific diseases.

"There is a particular drug for lung cancer, Iressa, that for most of the people taking the drug it is of little or no value," Dr. Reilly explains. "But, for a small number who have a particular gene variant, the drug is of great value for some reasons of protein interaction that we don't fully understand. If we could merely identify ahead of time which people would react perfectly to this drug, we have achieved a major advance in medicine. We could now choose a drug that matches your particular genome and we enter an age of personalized medicine." Reaching this conclusion was only possible through massive information sifting.

"We should soon be able to screen for gene variants which will signify risk for many more disorders. This would allow early interventions to avoid becoming ill at all," exclaims Dr. Reilly. Dr. Reilly believes that with fast mapping and identification of individual genomes, people could potentially avoid contracting thousands of diseases and that this could be done at a very early stage in life, but we need many more genome mappings and analysis (without waiting 15 years and spending another $3 billion).

Today, individual computers available for use in clinical settings do not exist that can process massive quantities of data in any reasonable amount of time. Your laptop, for example, has less than half a terabyte of disk space, and it would take your computer three hours just to read and digest every byte of your 3.1 billion base pairs before it could even begin to process it. To exploit this gene-centric therapy opportunity, the computer world will have to embrace many changes. One such discussed change is the move to "federated computing," where a great many computers work together on very small parts of a large problem and then make the results generally available. In the Inescapable Data world, the value of information is in its sharing.

Fortunately, there is a slow but steady movement in the medical field to allow data to be shared as information (in self-describing XML or other techniques). As a citizen concerned about your own longevity, would you be willing to make available your genome—in its totality or in pieces—for analysis by a large faculty of university-based researchers, or even a young but promising college level pre-med student with a theory on the best way to quantify prostate cancer risk? Would you make available a fraction of your computer's CPU time and resources as a participant in a global federation of computers dedicated to finding genetically linked cures for certain diseases? In the world of Inescapable Data, both are distinct possibilities.

Simply restated, our Inescapable Data view is that, while analyzing relationships among data elements themselves is an interesting and useful endeavor, it is the analyzing of relationships between disparate data sets that nets new and possibly more significant values. Suppose, for example, you correlate the electronic records of your visits to the supermarket with your genome and with the genomes, diets, and disease histories of 2 *billion* other people. You might discover some hidden dangers lurking on those supermarket shelves that could be avoided. What then happens when you correlate those results with the frequency of your visits to the health club? (Okay, we already know that answer.) Impossible? Right now, today, yes, it is not possible due to our lack of total electronic record keeping. But the data is starting to be gathered today, and the connections are being made today that will allow such analyses to be made in the near future.

Data Collected About You

How farfetched is it that someone today could analyze your food consumption against your workout schedule? Nearly every supermarket now accepts bank debit and credit cards for purchases. With the high prices of food, a typical family weekly shopping trip costs more than $200. Many people are reluctant to carry such cash with them and opt for the convenience of bank cards. As such, your weekly shopping market knows your name and every box of cereal and loaf of carbohydrate-laden bread you purchase. As for the health club, even YMCAs today are using electronic ID badges for daily entry, and these badges track every time you enter and leave a facility. Furthermore, newer workout machines also enable you to swipe your card through the exercise equipment itself to better track or help you adhere to your workout schedule. So, there is already a meaningful amount of health data being collected about you that through analysis could be correlated to a variety of other common databases, such as geography, socio-economics, prevailing weather, and perhaps now your personal medical information. The valuable difference the Inescapable Data world brings is the interaction of personal and detailed databases that allows for new insights.

The famous Framingham Heart Study took 20 years before researchers who studied and gathered data from thousands of individuals produced their findings. That data is now available in some electronic form for other researches to exploit and attempt to correlate with other data streams. Such studies are taking place continuously in the medical world, and increasingly their details and results are increasingly being made available for wider exploitation. Web connectivity and standard electronic records for describing the data (such as XML-expressed information) allow for more rapid integration into other research. What once would have taken a team of programmers weeks to decode via a proprietary database can now be done nearly instantly and even by average citizens (much like average citizens can look up real estate values in their town or search for a blender at WalMart.com). Furthermore, just finding the interesting databases is dramatically simpler due to search tools and a new emphasis on sharing within the medical communities. In the world of Inescapable Data, it is highly likely that the data needed to do meaningful medical research already exists somewhere. As a researcher or even as an individual, you can tap into it and make correlations.

Bioinformatics/Pharmaceuticals

"The pharmaceutical industry can no longer count on blockbuster drugs," says Kris Joshi, global strategy executive for IBM's Healthcare and Life Sciences division. "The model has to change from hunting elephants to hunting game. $800 million today for drug discovery brought through to market is far too high and needs to come down to the $100 million arena. Most of the large-scale diseases have drugs (to treat them with) now, and so the shift needs to be to somewhat narrower opportunities. Technology and changes to how technology is used will get us there."

Following the runup in the bioinformatics industry in the year 2000, analysts started predicting that data-driven drug discoveries would come easier and faster. "People saw so much data from genome-scale work that they figured with that vast amount of data there must be answers," Joshi explains. The reality was different. No doubt that bioinformatics is heavy on data and data analysis, and that is why most of the premiere research has been done using large super computers. However, big data plus big computers does not necessarily equal bigger-than-life results. "Two things need changing and we're starting to see the beginnings," explains Joshi, "a move toward federated computing and a move to openness and self-describing data."

Computers have never scaled linearly with regard to cost complexity against performance. That is, a single CPU computer costs a mere fraction of a four-CPU one. The cost disparity gets even larger as more CPUs are added (and memory and disk). Part of the reason is related to the interconnect technologies (between the CPUs) and partly because the market audience is far smaller. Bioinformatics has been a solid consumer of the highest horsepower machinery around, which has also positioned the opportunities only toward the largest bio players and around the largest elephants. A trend that, according to Joshi, needs to change if we want to see a broader set of solutions for medical problems.

Federated Computing

What is federated computing? The pioneer program in federated computing was the 1996 SERENDIP (Search for Extraterrestrial Radio Emissions Nearby Developed Intelligent Populations) project

continues

that originated from the University of California, Berkley. Thousands of Internet-connected enthusiasts volunteered part of their computer's time to searching massive databases of accumulated signals from space in an effort to find a minute signal in a monumental sea of static hiss—a signal that could be identified as originating from some form of extraterrestrial life. Volunteers were sent portions of radio-emissions data and specialized software to analyze the data. The results were then collected back from each individual volunteer and aggregated. Although only a hint of a possible extraterrestrial signal was subsequently identified, the success of this initial SETI project gave rise to many other large-scale distributed computing projects.

More recently, Stanford University inaugurated the Folding@Home project[2] to model protein "folding." Understanding how proteins fold (or misfold) can lead to discoveries related to specific diseases and related medical treatments. The largest super computer available today would still take 30 years to complete a simulation. Fortunately, the process of simulating protein folding can be fairly easily broken up in to separate pieces, making it ideal for federated computing. The Folding@Home project currently boasts that more than one million CPUs throughout the world have participated in their folding simulations; people simply visit the Web site and download the software to their home PC. Each PC then processes each piece in its "spare" time, transparently, and transmits the results back to the main organizing system. With Inescapable Data comes pervasive computing. Federating literally millions of individual computers into a huge processing complex is a technique that we think will bring solutions to some of medicine's most daunting problems.

Computers are used for primarily two different major contributions in the bioinformatics and pharmaceutical space. One common use is in massive data analysis, collection, and reduction. Terabyte data sources are common and need to be combined and analyzed with other similar-sized sources in processes that take days of super-computer computing. The second common use is for actual simulation of biological activities, known as *in-silico modeling*, that can save years of experiments and costly and dangerous field trials. Although many problems

---

[2] http://www.stanford.edu/group/pandegroup/folding/.

in either category can exploit federated computing, many other problems cannot and require computing power that challenges the imagination. Tightly coupled clusters are a common approach wherein high-end servers from IBM, Sun, SGI, or HP are tied directly together as a single large machine, often with 2,000 processors working in concert. As large as those systems are, they are still not powerful enough for the more daunting data-based problems. A teraflop (a trillion mathematical floating-point operations per second) is not enough, and the industry is looking for petaflop-size machines (1,000 times more powerful than a teraflop).

Enter the much-talked-about grid computing, which connects together groups of machines within or between various institutions and across different computer manufacturer models. Part of the challenge of a commercial or research institution is in balancing their spotty computer needs against their bank account. Typically, institutions under-buy their computer horsepower because there are gaps in usage. As a consequence, many analyses take months instead of perhaps a week (a week if they had access to the highest-power machinery during the needed interval). Sun's Sun One Grid Engine (among similar offerings from competitors) enables organizations to pool various high-end computing resources under one management umbrella and more efficiently exploit the power. It is this sort of cooperation and sharing that is fundamental in the Inescapable Data world and nets us faster time to important discoveries.

The pharmaceutical industry is changing, driven partly by the lack of elephants and partly by more ingenious and enterprising players. Keep in mind that because we now all live far longer than ever before, we are less likely to die from some common mass-scale disease (for which drugs have been discovered) and will instead die of a more narrow element of a disease or combination of diseases. This is propelling the industry toward change, and several elements are in place leading to a synergy:

- The ability to combine separate computers for a single task (federations, clusters, and grids) on an unprecedented scale
- Open source in bioinformatics and related arenas
- Data sharing via descriptions

Although part of the industry is very much proprietary, secret, and closely guarded (due to the historically high value of elephant-level drug discoveries and the costs of getting there), we will find such companies are more the dinosaurs than the norm going forward. Universities and smaller research institutions are finding power in banding together and working common elements of different problems...somewhat of an outsourcing model but with a bit of a research flavor. To the participating companies, they get to leverage hardware infrastructure and some core amount of analytical analysis. This then frees them up to focus on their particular drug-discovery details.

The open-source movement in the bio/pharma spaces is particularly interesting. Typical bioinformatic commercial software can cost as much as a million dollars or more for a site license. As a result of this extreme cost, as much as 25 percent of all software used in the life-sciences field is now created in the open-source (free) community,[3] far higher than in any other discipline. Quite likely, the adoption and use of open source will continue. The heart of bioinformatics is data, and data is being collected and discovered (via analysis) at historically high levels. Shifting to a model of higher cooperation and information and tool sharing should yield more discoveries.

CDISC, Clinical Data Interchange Standards Consortium (www.cdisc.org), is a nonprofit organization supported by major industry players to allow for better information sharing and exchange. CDISC is based on XML and other standards and allows a wide range of data related to clinical and nonclinical work to be readily available for consumption by the FDA and other interested parties. The formats, like with any XML implementation, are vendor neutral and both machine and human readable, allowing for faster integration and usage. In the Inescapable Data world, more and more intercompany groups are forming for the purpose of paving faster pathways to information usage and sharing, particularly if some government approval or regulatory step is involved. We should expect such a level of cooperation, openness, and standards in other industries as well for the same economic and time-efficiency reasons.

---

[3] http://www.lifescienceit.com/biwaut02secrecy.html.

Radiology

Dr. James Thrall, chief of radiology, Massachusetts General Hospital, talks about the digital divide in medicine and how some hospitals have begun to cross it. The process of reading breast, colon, and other high-volume scans "manually"—i.e., by a trained radiologist reading them one after another—can become tedious and error prone if done for long periods of time. By contrast, computers never tire, seldom complain, and can now be fantastically accurate based on "training" from analysis of massive historical data:

> *Departments of radiology that have crossed the divide behave differently than those that haven't. We used to think that reaching the divide was the goal, because we could envision all that could be better. In reality, the goal is the exploitation of data, not the collection...We currently save all radiological images, of everything, indefinitely. Why? Because of the mining value...We recently went beyond our 100-millionth digital image captured, and at the rate we're going we will have a billion images before long. We're adding a terabyte of disk space every other week, because we need massive numbers of cases in order to get good inferences and correlations. [X-rays and other radiological data can easily be many megabytes of data per image or even from a single "slice" of part of an anatomy—heavy data to store and more hefty to sift and search for patterns.]*

Radiology, and medicine in general, is gravitating toward computer-aided diagnostics. However, doctors need years of digitized data to make this process effective. This is particularly true in radiology. "We can show that 5 or 10 years later what was predicted at diagnosis time was actually true," continues Dr. Thrall. "There is a *time* enhancement of the *verity* of the diagnosis now as a result of the medical image histories." An important characteristic of Inescapable Data is to have enough data and over a long enough time period that valuable inferences can be discovered. The data, at least radiological data, is now being collected.

We expect to see a huge increase in computer-aided diagnostic usage coming, made possible by having petabytes of historical image data and analysis already collected. Note that a petabyte is equal to 1,024 terabytes—an amount of data that would have filled a warehouse with disk drives just a few years ago. It can actually be argued that the data becomes the hypothesis. "The data is screaming at you that there is something going on here in addition to whatever hypothesis you started with. You have all the data. Now figure it out," exclaims Dr. Thrall.

In fact, with massive repositories, some purely data-oriented analysis techniques can distill meaningful patterns without specific medical background. A hope of the Inescapable Data world is that unrelated industries will derive techniques and tools applicable to other industries, as we saw with bioinformatics analysis being used for e-mail spam prevention.

Radiology data is an Inescapable Data *natural* given its heft and pure digital format. Although sharing and having easy-to-exploit formats allows for better care, some worry that it raises privacy and security concerns. To that point, Dr. Thrall states, "With paper or film records, there was no security; folders of records were left lying around, and anyone could observe them. At least with digital forms, you need authentication, passwords, and access activities are logged and audited."

Other hospital patient records are not quite as far along as radiological data. "The history of hospitals tracking patient data and charts is abysmal," continues Dr. Thrall. "When the data was on paper and film, there was simply no practical way of sharing it. Now, even if it's in digital form, sharing remains elusive. I can travel to Europe and find a bank machine that effectively has my bank records and allows me access to my money. If in that same town I have an accident, there is no ability to get access to my medical records." Barriers to interinstitutional sharing still exist, but like airline reservations and electronic banking, the industry will mature and learn that connectivity at the patient record level allows them to leverage the world rather than just their locality.

We *will* get to the point where there is a massive fluidity of all patient data so that if you get sick in a different state or city you can get to the information. Today, individual hospitals have crossed the divide, but are not linked, an opportunity for the Inescapable Data world.

Hospitals

Hospitals are complex social organizations and are managed very differently from the top-down style of commercial businesses. The hospital's medical professional staff provides services to patients. On the other hand, presenting, storing, and managing patient data is the job of the hospitals IT administrative staff—not the medical professionals delivering services. As a result of this and a number of other factors, hospitals have been typically slow to automate their patient records processes. However, the impetus to create the electronic patient record has given doctors and administrators reason to come together.

Other parts of our lives are already chronicled and recorded electronically, and as the Inescapable Data movement progresses other missing parts will get filled in. If you call many nonmedical service providers for assistance—say your automobile dealer—you typically hear a keyboard clicking in the background as someone retrieves an electronic record of your account that contains your addresses, phone numbers, car purchase date, car make and model, service history, and important tie-ins to manufacturer-recall information, safety information, and perhaps even some information that allows an opportunistic salesperson to make a pitch. By contrast, if you call your medical provider, an attendant may put you on hold while he or she *physically* retrieves your record from an aisle of color-tabbed folders. If, perhaps, your eye specialist has some of your patient data online, you can be sure that he has no interface to your cardiologist.

Dr. Peter Slavin, CEO of Massachusetts General Hospital, understands the importance of both having electronic patient information and of sharing it:

> *Electronic patient records are a huge advancement in the world of hospitals and clinical care, enabling a whole new level in better patient care. This is long overdue, and there are many contributing reasons to the delay. Part of it is related to cost. In the profession, we tend to prefer to put money into actual equipment, medicine, or professionals. Another part of the reason is due to most doctors operate independently and as such have independent systems, either electronic or manual, that meet their specific needs and uses. These two elements are changing. For one, as a group, we're realizing the absolute cost and efficiency benefits of increased electronic records and connectivity, primarily through speedier care and record keeping, but also in better safety. Second, the size of various HMOs and health groups have been growing steadily, which affords efficiency gains and has provided the new opportunity to have consolidation and integration of back-end resources.*

Slavin admits he is a bit of a pioneer in this field. Another one of the challenges he faces is that hospitals can differ greatly in the ways they track patient and lab data versus the ways this data is handled by individual medical practices. Both sides have been slow to evolve their patient records automation processes and have typically done so independently of one another. This leads to disparities that require integration of data sources.

What is the value of a paperless medical record? Aside from the obvious benefits of faster service and more complete per-doctor histories, the real value comes from the ability to integrate a number of different data sources. "Any doctor in the Partner's network can understand the various history and treatments of a particular patient," explains Slavin. "This can have dramatic benefits. A doctor treating a patient for a routine eye examine will now have his cardio record directly at his disposal, which could very well have important relevant information such as blood pressure history." Slavin goes on to explain that the benefits run deeper and include a more accurate understanding of prescription drug usage and interactions, because all that data can referenced automatically when needed, helping doctors avoid a great many of the preventable problems. This is squarely an Inescapable Data vision—interconnection of many different sources of data to derive far higher values than any single source would produce on its own.

One of the most interesting hospital settings that Inescapable Data technology is showing up in is the operating room. Slavin describes some pioneering work Partners is doing designed to greatly improve the utilization of operating rooms and patient care. At the heart of the new OR is RFID in the form of tags placed on patients. Currently, every patient admitted to a hospital wears a plastic ID bracelet—a practice unchanged for many decades. Bar codes on bracelets have been in use in some hospitals, but those are cumbersome and slow in comparison to RFID tags that can be instantly detected.

How might RFID be exploited in an operating room setting? "As a patient is wheeled into the OR, the operating room computer systems will know that this is John Doe and what are the scheduled procedures. Furthermore, the system will know what machinery and tooling and medication is needed and can verify that only the proper items are in the room. All of this greatly cuts down on the time to verify everything and most importantly a reduction of preventable mistakes and higher utilization of the room, the staff, and the machinery."

Beyond the OR, RFID usage can be expanded to other areas throughout the hospital. RFID in the operating room can become a model for in-room patient care, for example. Whenever a medicine is dispensed in this setting, the hospital's internal system can wirelessly and remotely scan RFID tags on the medication containers to verify that it is the proper prescribed medication for *that* patient. Too often, well-meaning nurses and aides will administer the wrong medication because of any of a number of reasons, such as room turnover (to a new patient) or the doctor not informing all the floor personnel.

Separately, a new concept has emerged that specializes in augmenting the life-critical task of monitoring patients in intensive-care units (ICUs). VISICU,

Inc., a Baltimore-based company, is the innovator of a technology system, the eICU solution, which addresses patient safety like never before. "From a central location, a hospital system links critical-care physicians and nurses to ICU beds across multiple hospitals for remote monitoring patients 24 hours a day," describes Frank Sample, CEO of VISICU. He continues:

> The same data available in the patient's ICU room is connected to our remote system, and also incorporates live video feeds, and a direct hotline to both the patient's doctor and the nurse or physician in attendance. The remote eICU facility is tied into the patient's care plan established by the attending physician and can deal with unforeseen situations extremely fast. Many problems are controllable if caught early enough but can rapidly become acute otherwise. In fact, Sentara Healthcare of Norfolk, Virginia, documented a 27% reduction in hospital mortality along with a 17% reduction in overall hospital length of stay using VISICU's eVantage system.

Sample goes on to explain that modern ICU medical equipment is not only computer based but also designed for connectivity to other systems for sharing data or monitoring. The addition of high-quality video cameras provides important visual patient information and is only accessed when needed. Network speed and associated decreased communications costs now allow for transfer of all this data, thus enabling the success of such efforts. The technology, business values, and client benefits are adding up.

Although there are indeed significant cost savings for hospital systems that employ the eICU solution, the driving factor in remote ICU monitoring is truly improved patient care and outcomes. Often, small problems that develop with an intensive-care patient can swiftly deteriorate into critical conditions. Even a well-staffed hospital ICU may not detect or may miss the early opportunity for correction because the attending physician is off site or with another patient, hence the need for an augmented monitoring process. What hospitals are using this new approach? Currently, larger hospital networks are early adopters due to the size of their ICU operation. The hospital provides the physical location for the remote facility and staffs the eICU center with *their* critical-care doctors and nurses. VISICU provides the eICU technology, methodology, and system training. The dramatic cost savings come not from reduced physician and nurse staffing, but rather through a decrease in outliers—patients who spend more than six days in the ICU—and hospital mortality. Overall, this represents a pretty good win for everyone, enabled by high-speed networking, hardware and software interoperability, and data assimilation.

Scheduling Care Delivery

"As the owner of a thriving general dentistry practice, we deal daily with a simple but significant problem: scheduling," says Dr. Jeff Tocci, DDS, owner of a Boston-area dental practice. "Without a doubt, advances in client connectivity to data from appointment schedules to dental records will reshape the business of any primary-care physician or specialty doctor and greatly increase the satisfaction of the care recipient." What's the problem with the seemingly simple issue of scheduling?

Outside the world of hospitals, a family's principal home-care organizer (PHCO, which in many cases, is Mom) is the chief interface to the doctor's office, primarily for scheduling and keeping appointments. Putting aside the increased challenges of dual-working families, home schedule orchestration has reached new levels of stress. Statistically speaking, the average family with 2.7 kids plays two sports per season, takes piano lessons, and attends drama classes and numerous birthday parties, not to mention holidays and vacations away from home. In turn, this makes scheduling and keeping doctors appointments challenging. Often, the primary health-care giver, such as Doctor Tocci, bares the cost and trouble for any scheduling snafus.

"I don't mind working part of my Saturday. I don't mind working Tuesday evenings and taking appointments until 8 or 9 P.M. Offering extended hours allows us to better meet people's scheduling needs. What is excruciating is when an appointment doesn't show up or cancels hours before the scheduled time," continues Dr. Tocci. "This costs me significant lost money and increased levels of aggravation, but most importantly it detracts from another patient who could have benefited from that time. Many doctors have begun charging customers for missed appointments, and this then leads to poor patient sentiments and usually an irate phone call or two. What we need is a better conduit of contact to the primary home-care organizer so that we can be flexible, accommodating, and punctual."

UK Loses $300M Due to No-Shows

The United Kingdom's health-care system, the NHS, states that missed appointments are costing it about $162 million pounds (approximately $300 million) annually.[4] More than one million appointments are missed each year in the UK (between general practitioner and nursing appointments). Of these missed appointments, 55 percent are blamed on the client simply forgetting the date or time. Missed appointments also rob a needy patient of an earlier time and more prompt service and greatly add to stress and costs. Worldwide, the cost of missed appointments could easily be more than $2 billion. NHS is exploring the use of electronic messaging to improve scheduled appointments and gaps in service. Ealing Hospital in West London is one of the hospitals (among others) using short message service (SMS) (text messages to patient's cell phones) to remind patients of routine outpatient and MRI scan appointments.[5] Text reminders are automatically sent directly to the patient's cell phone some amount of time prior to the appointment. The fully connected Inescapable Data world is all about minimizing or eliminating gaps.

Here's how the typical dentist appointment is scheduled: As the PHCO leaves the dentist office (often with 2.7 children in tow), he or she haphazardly agrees to the next visit date suggested by the office staff without verifying suitability against the paper-based, kitchen wall-mounted calendar at home, but fully intends on taking the folded appointment-reminder home and reconciling it later. Other distractions—a soccer pickup and a list of phone calls to return when back at home—follow the office visit. Soon, the PHCO has long forgotten about recording the appointment. In an effort to achieve higher appointment success, doctor offices often deploy the laborious and costly process of calling patients 24 to 48 hours in advance. Often, this is far too short of notice for the patient and the doctor to properly accommodate any changes. No-shows and stress abound. Although a small handful of techno-savvy PHCOs carry electronic personal organizers, such devices are far from pervasive. There is fertile ground for change, change enabled by convergence of pervasive technologies. Two years ago, the average PHCO did not carry a cell phone or even use

---

[4] http://www.pharma-lexicon.com/medicalnews.php?newsid=12446.

[5] http://www.cnn.com/2004/TECH/08/12/hospital.texts/.

the Web for e-mail communication. Today, many adults carry a personal communication device 100 percent of the time and use the Web at home to completely keep current with soccer schedules, schoolteachers, and myriad other life-important schedule-related events. Medical businesses can count on many clients possessing a cell phone and can appropriately exploit noninvasive asynchronous (but immediate) messaging for both parties' benefit.

Today, the majority of airline and hotel reservations are either made via the Net or researched via the Net (and then booked by a short phone call). Airlines and hotels are large industries with a relatively small set of big players. Whatever competitive feature one offers, such as online booking, the others naturally follow to keep pace with the competition. The community health-care delivery system, in contrast, is highly fragmented and run essentially by proprietors. However, small, fragmented businesses can offer services equal to the big players by using Inescapable Data technologies and leveraging large outsourcing firms for non-value–add services.

Dr. Tocci elaborates on the opportunity:

> We [doctors] are more willing than ever to outsource various aspects of our non-value-add business. I don't need to be a Webmaster; I have an outside firm that manages my Web presence. In the same way, I don't need to be in the business of scheduling appointments. It's mechanical. Moreover, customers want self-service. They want to scan the schedule themselves. They want to find a day and time where they can get both kids in at the same time based on what procedure is needed and the availability of my staff against their busy schedule. They want to do this scheduling dance late in the evening, long after my staff has gone home, from the comfort of their home computer table or from their PDA on the soccer field.

Most community health-care providers now use PC-based scheduling software. Some are even capable of exposing their scheduling tools through their own Web pages. Scheduling can also be outsourced and managed by service bureaus that can provide the technology interface at high speed and low cost through scale (quite likely the same providers of the doctor office Web presence today). So, when we combine these services with Inescapable Data devices we have the makings of an advance. Reminders can be automatically sent both by e-mail and text messages at recurring intervals prior to the appointments (one week, day before, four hours before, and so on). In addition, the PHCO can be in direct contact with the provider's office and can monitor current office conditions. Are appointments running half an hour late, an hour late? Has the doctor been called out on an emergency? Has an earlier appointment opportunity opened up due to a cancellation?

"It seems simple and obvious," observes Dr Tocci. "The values are very high for both my practice and my clients." As technology has advanced and grown into our environments, we develop certain life-efficiency expectations, such as being able to find an automated teller machine (ATM) within a short walk from *anywhere*. So too, as Inescapable Data technologies advance, we may well come to expect "connected schedules" for all consumer businesses. Those not offering these kinds of services will lose out to competitors that do—and, not just dentists and pediatricians, but every health-care provider, car repair shop, and hair stylist. Those who have crossed the connectivity divide will look for connectivity and scheduling efficiency in their service providers—connectivity made possible by the growing pervasiveness of personal communication devices (cells and PDAs), combined with digital cellular and/or WiFi services connected to care providers using the Web-based services for self-scheduling.

Online, personal services scheduling is still in its infancy. It is not here today. But this will change with astonishing speed, driven primarily by the fact that almost every adult carries a cell phone (much like they carry keys) and cell phones are now PDAs as well. Faster than the adoption change from VHS to DVD in the household, we will see the average person rapidly become 100 percent schedule-connected because the value is high for all busy people, and we're all busy people now.

Trite as it may seem, the cost savings and personal productivity gains from online personal services scheduling could be enormous over time for both service providers and consumers. When your doctor's schedule is electronically connected to your personal schedule, everyone wins. The more your personal scheduler knows about your life, the better it can help you pack for the trip, alert you to your child's homework schedule, and remind you to take your medication. Oh, and don't forget the dentist appointment.

Pediatric and Personal Health Care

Until the advent of self-help books and the Internet, information regarding personal health care was largely in the domain of the health-care provider. We now live in an age where health-care information is everywhere—some of it worthwhile, some of it misleading at best. Nevertheless, once connected to the sources outside the physician's office, we cannot seem to get enough information about our own health and that of our loved ones.

Most parents use "baby monitors" that enable them to listen for their infant while they are somewhere else in the house or outside. This monitoring brought significant freedom (albeit for one hour at a time) to apprehensive young parents. Baby monitors are mostly a simple one-direction communication device that provides remote audio monitoring plus a visual-audio bar graph representing sound levels in the baby's room. Beyond sound monitoring, simple devices could record other useful and possible critical medical metrics, such as body temperature or blood sugar level. Body temperature is a good indicator of stress in all species[6] as well as general physiological status. In addition, a sick child's temperature can spike during the night without anyone ever knowing about it.

"As a pediatrician, one of the most fundamental diagnostic metrics we have is accurate body temperature," explains Dr. Meyerson, a local pediatrician in suburban Boston. "Unfortunately, many parents do not take a child's temperature accurately, and instead call us saying, 'My child is very hot and we're really worried.' If we, as doctors, simply had accurate measurements of current, recent, and historical body temperatures, we'd be better able to diagnose and treat problems confidently. Is the temperature 101.2 or 102? What was it an hour ago? What is the child's typical temperature at 10 P.M. at night when this child is healthy? Has it spiked in a very short period of time? These are simple but important questions, and having accurate and detailed historical information can make a huge difference."

Chip Implants

Here is an important Inescapable Data question: Are small, wireless electronic implants that measure a few but nevertheless fundamental body metrics possible and even practical?

Let's first look at more extreme implants to bound our expectations. Cyberkinetics is a firm that makes a brain implant chip that is the size of your small fingernail and attaches to 150 neurons that control major limb

continues

---

[6] http://www.teagasc.ie/research/reports/beef/4806/eopr-4806.htm.

Chip Implants (*Continued*)

muscle movements. "Our device is clearly invasive, and so our first target audience is disabled citizens who need a mechanism for using a computer and the freedom that brings," explains Timothy Surgenor, CEO of Cyberkinetics. "The chip is placed on a key location of the brain and wirelessly transmits to an external transmitter and then is amplified and turned into computer mouse and keyboard inputs. This sounds extreme to many people now, but consider Lasik surgery. Ten years ago, if someone said to you 'Let me peel back the surface of your eye and use a laser to burn and reshape your cornea and then re-glue the surface of your eye,' what would you have said? The point, quite simply, is that seemingly dramatic alterations to small parts of your body can eventually become commonplace and accepted. More than 50,000 people today in the United States have chip-implants that control epilepsy and other similar diseases. It is entirely within reason to expect dramatic growth of lower-cost less-invasive implant devices."

There are a variety of less-extreme and noninvasive body-monitoring devices. Measuring livestock health is a major concern among cattle raisers and health-safety guardians. Several different systems exist today for real-time monitoring of bovine (cattle) body temperature. One system is a sort of "capsule" inserted into the first stomach of the cattle, and the other is a device inserted deep into the ear near the eardrum.[7] In either case, the system consists of some battery source, a microprocessor, a receiver, a transmitter, and a temperature sensor (in an extremely small package). Once per minute the system wirelessly transmits body temperature information to some collection device. The information can then be stored or, if out of normal range, be relayed to a cell or PDA device. Rapidly controlling and containing sickness in livestock is a serious health concern.

In October 2004, the FDA approved use of an implantable chip in patients to pass on medical information.[8] Delray Beach, Florida-based Applied Digital Solution's VeriChip is the world's first implantable radio-frequency identification (RFID) microchip for human use. About the size of a grain of rice, the device is inserted under the skin in a quick

---

[7] http://www.teagasc.ie/research/reports/beef/4806/eopr-4806.htm.

[8] http://www.boston.com/dailynews/287/economy/FDA approves use of implantabl:.shtml.

procedure. The goal is to allow doctors access to patient medical records, speeding care. They are currently targeting patients with chronic diseases such as diabetes, cardiac conditions, and Alzheimer's. The linked data could alert doctors to allergies or other important treatment and care needs. In a more unusual use, VeriChip devices have been in use in the trendy Baja Beach Club in Barcelona by VIP members for easier identification and payment for drinks and food.[9] Implantable devices for either medical care or for fun seem to be coming our way.

Whether we use an implant device for baby body temperature, or some sort of more acceptable bracelet or finger ring, the opportunity for more detailed and continuous body monitoring is possible due to microscale devices, Bluetooth and similar short-range wireless options, and RF and WiFi connectivity to higher-order devices such as your household computer. Let's explore the value chain of such technology. From the doctor's point of view, recent and historical trending is invaluable. (Not everyone's base body temperature 98.6 degrees Fahrenheit, for example.) For the parent, in addition to simple audio, the parent can now monitor and be alerted to important body temperature changes and catch problems before a temperature spikes to a worrisome 104.2 degrees.

The Inescapable Data interest is not so much in the creation of such devices (they will be created no matter) or even in the vertical utility of the device (the value directly to the patient or care giver), but rather the accelerated benefit of interconnecting the data. Indeed some of the value will be realized by the pediatrician for better care of the patient based on the patient's accumulated data. Other values will come from broad sets of data being amassed and then potentially analyzed by far-away people (due to networking and self-describing data sets) for potentially some important values. Is there a relationship between the number of early infant fevers higher than 102 and a later tendency to develop ear infections? As a group, do Asian Americans average a lower body temperature when living in Northeast urban America? Does average body temperature in specific geographic regions correlate with local weather in any interesting fashion, and is that then a predictor for some regional economic condition? Silly? Perhaps, but with vast data available, Inescapable Data users will tease-out relationships that are reminiscent of what the financial analysts have done for years to gain even the most modest edge in a market. Today, we have scant

[9] http://www.prisonplanet.com/articles/april2004/040704bajabeachclub.ht.

(if any) personal medical data collected, but in the Inescapable Data world, the data will be there and more readily mined.

Something as simple as an accurate body temperature sensing and recording device could have tremendous unforeseen value. Imagine if a device could also measure sucrose or salinity levels how the values would be notably higher. We could envision devices that measure electrical and chemical signals as well. Should your toilet have a built-in Ph sensor (along with salinity), because there could be valuable inferences to your health, especially if networked with your body temperature, time of day, and calendar (key stress source)? Is this silly (as silly as using a laser to reshape your most precious field-input device) or essential in the new world? Similar to Massachusetts General amassing petabytes of digital images for more than a decade, once information is collected, trended, and cross-correlated with other vessels of historical and real-time information, the values abound.

Summary

The medical and life-sciences fields are huge and notorious for both the volumes of data they create and the value in proper analysis of that data. It is clearly an area for Inescapable Data, especially because these industries are producing more data than ever before and at an accelerating rate. As computer horsepower and strategies such as federated computing improve, we could enter an age of personalized medication made possible by knowledge of our personal genome. Drug discoveries will migrate to more specialized drugs (because of more specialized diseases) made possible by pervasive computing and wide data sharing. Petabytes of radiology data will provide for automated diagnosis of some of our most worrisome diseases. Doctor-office scheduling will finally meet the needs of overly busy people and improve everyone's efficiency. Our own home health care will embrace continuous personal monitoring of a variety of our bodily metrics. Data will abound, networks will drive real-time connectivity, and we will leverage the world's soldiers (us) to tease-out critical relationships and values. As said earlier, the magic occurs when the number of machines and people manipulating the data rivals the size of the data itself—this is possible in our Inescapable Data world.

CHAPTER SEVEN

Work Life: Oxymoron No Longer

It is 3 P.M. and you are at the office. You start a conference call on your cell phone, go to your car, and proceed to drive home, perfectly multitasking, giving your employer your travel time as work time. In return, your employer lets *you* greet little Johnny as he gets off the bus. The call finishes up at 3:50 P.M. and you have 10 minutes until your next appointment. If you were at work, a fellow employee (likely) might distract you during this time. Instead, you use these 10 minutes to season the roast and toss it into the oven alongside large Idaho potatoes. Slow cook at 300° for 2 hours; after all, there is now no rush.

The 5 P.M. call is moving along normally—a typical irate customer and you instant message back and forth with your boss and fellow co-workers deciding to discount the customer's next order and pushing them ahead in the delivery queue. Around 5:45, still on the call, the new soccer schedule comes across your computer and you realize that there is a field conflict. You spend the next 5 minutes composing several e-mails to various team parents and soccer officials straightening out the near catastrophe. The call has now ended, and you get up to get something to drink.

Question: Were you working?

Answers: (A) Yes
            (B) No
            (C) Not sure

If you answered C (not sure), you are in the ever-increasing group of people who have seen their work lives blend with their personal lives to the point of being confused about what and where is work.

Introduction

Technology clearly changes the way in which we work and live. We think that in the Inescapable Data world, technology will actually define how and where we work in an intricate blend of both. This chapter explores the ways that the same technology can be used for work as for sport or pleasure. Let's examine just how pervasive technology allows us freedom, flexibility, and efficiency in the workplace...if not some confusion.

Converged Connections—Of Conference Calls, Cell Phones, and WiFi-Enabled Laptops

Prior to the year 2000, we were a business world in love with our office spaces and corporate travel. We traveled to work (the office) every day. We traveled away from the office for customer meetings, for internal meetings, for conferences, for awards ceremonies...we traveled because we could and we believed that it was necessary for the competitive advantage. That all changed rather quickly with the economic downturn of the early 2000s and, of course, 9/11. In short order, we relearned how to do business remotely by first re-igniting the "conference call."

The obvious intention of increased dependence on conference calls was to reduce corporate travel and its attendant expense. The less-obvious downside of this trend was that although these admittedly low-tech calls resulted in high-value efficiency, they also produced an increased rate of stress-producing multitasking.

The corporate payroll compression of the early 2000s specifically meant that we were all tasked with far more work than a single individual could perform adequately. To help make us more efficient, we introduced cell phones so that we could make calls while traveling and WiFi-enabled laptops that enabled us to take our work anywhere and exchange messages with anyone (provided a "hotspot" could be found). Conference calls, cell phones, and laptops have pushed personal multitasking to unparalleled levels. For example, workers are now able to process the relentless stream of e-mails and instant messages as well as review financial and marketing documents, all while supposedly being active during a conference call. (It should now be clear why videoconferencing has yet to catch on.) The experience of Mark Bregman, CTO of Veritas Software, is becoming more and more common: "I was on a call the other day and realized half way through that four of the people were physically at the same site but separately dialed in. Why? Because we need to work on 10 things at once now."

Does this sound unsettling? It is not for some. In fact, for those able to do three things at once, it is a stress reliever. Prior to this work style, employees who were required to be physically at meetings (even on-site) would worry about e-mail that was piling up as well as a half-written product presentation due the next day. Stress would slowly build as the meeting drew long. The productiveness of a conference call definitely suffers because multitasking participants are only slightly paying attention. But no matter...overall efficiency is increased for those who can draw the connections together and somehow manage to stay engaged in the call at the same time.

Unexpectedly, the preponderance of conference calls and portable office accoutrements has gained workers a new degree of personal freedom: nonoffice hours. Suppose you have conference calls at 2 P.M., 3 P.M., and 4 P.M.—each one booked for an hour. Does it matter whether you take those calls physically at your office or your house? So, you can be home for a child who gets off the school bus at 3:30 P.M. and even get the roast into the microwave defrost cycle. In any given conference call, the majority of participants are on mute. When they need to speak, one often hears the ambient sounds of home life—dogs barking, children screaming, or the sounds of bathwater sloshing about.

Growth of Teleconferencing

In 1997, the teleconferencing industry introduced reservationless self-serve conference calling setup (not requiring an operator) systems. This significantly accelerated usage, and the industry grew by double digits for years.[1] The stagnant voice phone market suddenly became a growth market. From just before 2000 (and before 9/11) through 2003, the market grew 40 percent and continues to grow at nearly that pace,[2] driven by several

continues

---

[1] http://www.bizjournals.com/atlanta/stories/2001/03/19/focus3.html.

[2] http://e-meetings.mci.com/confnews/20030506-a.php.

Growth of Teleconferencing (*Continued*)

factors: a need for more expedient business transactions, minimizing travel expense, avoiding contagious diseases (the SARS outbreak), and dealing with a more geographically diverse workforce. Add in rapidly falling voice communication costs and Internet-based voice conferencing (plus Internet-augmented e-meetings and video capabilities), the industry will continue to grow. Teleconferencing compresses time for us.

For some, the flip side of this new freedom is that calls can often take place at midnight when dealing with Asia, or 5 A.M. when dealing with Europe, or 10 P.M. when in Europe dealing with the U.S. The reality of the global economy for most of us is that the workday is now completely ill-defined in terms of start and finish hours.

Conference calls, cell phones, and laptops all enable a level of freedom nonexistent in the old corporate world. We can now work anywhere...and everywhere. Proportionally, they de-emphasize the value of the physical corporate office cube. In large multilocation companies such as IBM, a project team typically consists of people spanning three to six different sites (and maybe as many countries). Out of the 300 people who may be in your physical building, virtually none of them have any relation to you or the work you do anymore. You are now knitted together by a virtual thicket of project blogs, e-mails, instant messages, and, of course, conference calls. Does it even matter whether you physically go into work anymore? Often, it does not.

Work@Home

Mark Canepa, executive vice president of Sun Networking, says, "11,000 out of our 33,000 employees now work from home and have no office in any building. I myself have no office, nor do most executives at Sun. We have these banks of executive-style offices, and we may reserve them in advance much like a hotel room at the Marriott. In fact, we have eight-tenths of an office per employee for those who need to physically be here. We've invested heavily in an adaptive work environment and have neatly virtualized every employee's office with Smart-Card technology." Sun's SmartCard is a credit card–like device that once swiped through a reader renders the adjacent computer to the last full configuration that this user previously desired. SmartCard resonates well with Inescapable Data because it exploits common hardware by virtualizing individual environments, enabling its users to be rapidly comfortable regardless of location.

The cost savings of work@home are substantial. From the employer's perspective, the cost savings come from many different sources. IBM, for example, will save from $8K to $14K for each employee who elects to give up a permanent office (dependent largely on local real-estate rates). The productivity gains can be substantial, and employees become more willing to work through their morning and evening "drive times" and are perhaps even more willing to take a 10 P.M. or 5 A.M. conference call. Equally important, employee morale and happiness typically improve because the employee is less often caught in the middle between work and home-life demands.

From the employee side, the cost savings can be substantial as well. Commuting costs drop to near zero because employees go into the office only occasionally (a significant benefit given the sky-high price of gas and the average commute in the U.S. being more than 40 miles round trip). Daily trips to the coffee shop, the corner deli, and to the company cafeteria can be eliminated as well. Add in the value of being there when your child gets off the school bus, the value of a family dinner ready at 6:30 P.M., and the value of seldom missing a soccer game, and we are building happier employees.

But office buildings still exist. "We call it the Edifis complex...a lot of companies still feel they need to have a building in order to feel like a real company," states Jack Nilles, owner of JALLA, a long time tele-work consultant group. "It takes them a few years, and then they realize they might not need as big of a facility," continues Nilles.

Sun's view of the office building of the future is refreshing. "We see a large cafeteria-type area, much like food courts you'd see in a mall, courtyard-type setting. Surrounding this area are various conference rooms for more private meetings, but by in large, people will meet right there in the social atmosphere of the food court, peppered with 'wireless everything,'" describes Canepa, who explains that Sun is already doing this in some locations. The need for company buildings will still exist, at least partly because we do indeed need to work face to face some of the time and we personally value the importance of human contact. The advantage of the new world is that at least some significant part of our daily office lives can be conducted outside of the office setting and equally as effective (given that the tools and technology are now pervasive between the home and office). A bit more control and flexibility has been given back to the employee in exchange for more work hours, typically.

During the course of our interviews for this book, we met with more than 45 senior executives, and it was surprising to see a clear division between managers who understood and embraced the move toward work@home and those who did not. Primarily, the division was along age lines. Those over 50 would look at us like we had three heads, typically saying something like, "How do I know they are working?" Younger managers are far more likely to embrace work@home probably because they are living it within their own organizations. They would often recite with pride just how many different geographic territories their teams spanned. Nilles explains that the underlying resistance to work@home stems from lack of training. "Managers panic when they start to have employees work at home. They have never been trained to manage remote or nonoffice employees. They need to understand the various tools and tactics that can make it a fabulously successful experience for both sides."

For what it's worth, youngsters of today (college kids) will be our work force of tomorrow, and they are growing through times of remote work themselves. Most, if not all, colleges offer e-learning style classes wherein students do not even have to show up for classes physically. The lecture, homework, and even tests are administered online. If not, the class is at least significantly enhanced by companion Web materials. The point is this: The new worker generation is ready to accept nontraditional methods of accomplishing tasks because they are living it.

Job Moves to You

Two decades ago, IBM insiders used to joke that the letters I-B-M stood for "I've Been Moved." Job offers often came with an expectation to relocate at the whim of the corporation. In contrast, now IBMers have a new meaning for the old acronym: "I'm By Myself." In an Inescapable Data world, work moves to the person rather than the other way around.

Here's an increasingly common scenario. You're a manager in a Boston office of a mega-size systems and services company. A job requisition opens up and allows you to fill a position you have had vacant for months. However, because the company is trying to maintain a level head count, you must first attempt to fill the job from within before looking outside. With 160,000 employees, there is a good chance that one of them has the right skills matrix you desire. However, there are 1,000 office locations around the globe, so the odds of the right and best person for job within your current facility are extraordinarily slim. So you look for, find, and hire Dick, a well-qualified candidate out of San Jose because he is the right match for the job. No matter that Dick is 3 time zones and 3,000 miles away. You're comfortable because you have high-speed Internet, instant and text messaging, good ol' e-mail, and a cell phone to keep you in constant touch. He can even afford working in some additional "boundary hours."

Here's another increasingly common scenario: Another of your employees quietly mentions she is having trouble getting their youngest off to school in the morning. Similarly, being home to help care for her husband's aging parents later in the day is also becoming increasingly important (a theme excruciatingly familiar to a large number of people). She states that she actually has plenty of hours in the day to do everything, including her demanding job, but she is having a hard time working around these family issues. Too often, she has to take sick days, but most importantly, her stress level is elevated. When in the office, she spends a significant amount of time just checking in with everyone at home to be sure things are under control.

Finally, she pops the question: "Because Dick is working productively out on the West Coast and we only ever see him 'virtually' through conference calls and e-meetings, do you think I can work from home, too? I'll be sure to put in even more hours saved by no commute and I'll be more efficient balancing my home and work life. I have DSL at home, and with the VPN, I can access every server as if I were here, in the same way Dick can. Can I telecommute?"

So the dominos fall. As a manager, it is incredibly hard to justify how one employee can be remote and part of the same group doing the same work and not allow others to exploit the same flexibility. So it is best to embrace the opportunity and learn how to properly manage such a situation because it is simply inevitable. Work@home can also reduce stress—a serious concern for young families trying to raise children and maintain two income streams at the same time.

Nilles is enthusiastic about multiple levels of "wins" in the telecommuting model:

> We can demonstrate conclusively that people actually work more and accomplish more work when they work from home. The typical office workplace is no library. The level of distractions and interruptions is very high. For the at-home worker, the level of personal home activities roughly matches what they consume for time by calling home and trying to patch-together babysitters and other care givers. There are three huge gains: 1) They don't rigidly end their workday at 5:15; 2) they have

far fewer distractions from people coming in and chit-chatting about the weekend and TV shows; and 3) when they are doing focused work, it is finished earlier and with higher quality.

There are 80 million "information workers" in the U.S. (people who work in typical office settings primarily using computers for their work). According to JALLA, typically 20 percent to 30 percent of those people are what is called *location dependent*—that is, they physically need to be in the building to perform their job (receptionists, many medical-related jobs, and so forth). Doing the math, there could be as many as 60 million people who currently have "cubes" in some undifferentiated office building who could be more productive and happier working from "anywhere" in the Inescapable Data *connected* fashion. We are not in the business of giving out investment advice, but it sure looks like a good time to sell your office real-estate holdings.

Instant Messaging

Let's review some of the new tools of the twenty-first century. Not everyone is using these tools, and a brief overview while highlighting their utility and importance in the connected world is worthwhile.

Instant messaging (IM) is a computer-based technology that enables you to send a quick message (typically short written text) to another computer running the same IM package. (As IM matures, the need to run the same IM package on all interconnected computers will disappear.) The IM software is typically loaded when your computer boots up and runs unobtrusively in the background, all the while advertising to everyone else within your IM group that you are online. A small panel insert on your screen presents you a list of all people in the IM group, often called your *buddy list*. The panel insert shows their online status (online and recently typing, online and not typing, or offline). People can be added to your buddy list at any time, and you can maintain several different lists—perhaps one for Project A people, one for family and friends, and one for the soccer team. At a glance, you can tell who is online and whether they've been recently typing (which means they should be near their computer). Some IM packages enable you to attach "objects" (files, music, pictures, databases, and so forth) to messages, and some even enable you to add a voice recording just by clicking the microphone button. IBM's new package, for example, is a reasonable attempt at blending e-mail, IM, and voicemail all into a single package. To send an IM, you just click the target's name, type a short message, and click Send. This action opens a chat window and starts a "chat" session. The chat window remains open, displaying a scrolling history of your conversation for as long as you keep the window open. Others can also be invited into a chat in progress. In fact, it is easy and common among younger users to have three or a half dozen people chatting in a single view.

As much fun as all this sounds (some teenagers find IM addictive), it is also an extremely practical business tool. Questions get answered in moments with IM. Receivers of messages now receive far fewer e-mails and feel less stressed. People lower in seniority ask questions of superiors with ease, and superiors go directly to subordinates for answers without worrying about chain of command. In short, problems get resolved far faster. IM has become the great leveler of corporate hierarchies.

IM

IM usage is soaring and has gone mainstream.[3] Although teens and young adults still dominate the landscape, usage in the workplace is rapidly growing. Some interesting statistics: 90 percent of teens and young adults use IM, 50 percent of age 55 and older use IM, and 50 percent to 70 percent in the middle age groups use IM. Nearly one-third of IM users use IM in and for work purposes. AOL states: "It is clear that instant messaging has gone mainstream." With more than 250 million regular users and 80 million messages sent per day, IM has established itself as a solid communication medium. An interesting change took place during the recent IM adoption years: always-connected computers. Prior to 2002, the vast majority of nonwork users were dial-up, and so e-mail was the proper asynchronous communication method. Post 2002, the rapid adoption of DSL and cable in the household meant computers were routinely tied (online) to the Internet and thus suitable for an interactive message.

---

[3] http://media.aoltimewarner.com/media/newmedia/cb press view.cfm?release num=55254160.

Some believe that IM was the single biggest business productivity tool introduced in the past five years and that any company that is still using e-mail as their "fast communication" method is living in the dark ages. As mentioned in Chapter 4, "From Warfare to Government, Connectivity Is Vitality," IM has the ability to completely change command and control, and the effect is that problems are now resolved down-rank and accordingly much faster due to less waste of time. What started off looking like a trendy toy for bored teenagers (at least to us) has turned into a critical business application for many corporations.

Admittedly, we started off protesting against IM when it first made its way into the business world. Given the stress of multitasking, conference calls, and the nonstop barrage of e-mail, the last thing we needed was to be more reachable. As we watched the way others used IM, however, we asked ourselves whether we really wanted to be less reachable. If the boss is on a call at 8 P.M. with an irate customer of mine and needs immediate answers, do I want to be less reachable? If my teenager is about to get in a car with the "cool kids" to head into the City, and wants to check in with Dad to see whether it is okay, do I really want to be less reachable? What we really wanted was to be *more efficiently* reachable—hence our discussion of the various attributes of communication mechanisms in the earlier chapters. IM provides a "quiet" and instantaneous method of reaching someone in a minimally invasive way.

Like so many technologies, IM had little utility until it became pervasive. Teenage users made IM pervasive—not the business community. The business world is far more bifurcated. We currently see reasonable penetration in the very large companies that span many offices and time zones—those that mandate IM usage because of the efficiency it offers and the benefit from the reduced e-mail strain. Mandating IM usage makes it pervasive. You can count on reaching someone anywhere within the organization as long as that person is in front of a computer screen or PDA and using the tool. Some companies have even gone so far as to even eliminate office phones, relying on wireless Ethernet, IM, and cell service instead. This results in initial and continuing reduced monthly costs when building out a new office facility—for those companies still building office facilities.

IM, and its cousin text messaging (à la cell phone), enable pervasive communication and exchange of data and information—critical tools for the connected employees.

Groupware and Virtual Office

The groupware concept is older than IM (at least in popularity). The groupware vision was that project results could be accelerated if a shared repository—software-defined areas that hold all the electronic documents and project management data—was created that could be accessed and updated by all group members. Currently, groupware is an effective collaboration tool used for large project management by equally large companies. For smaller companies, ad-hoc usage of a shared file server often suffices. Small Web servers are also now used by more physically diverse groups.

Groupware, despite early hype, has remained somewhat hidden, deployed appropriately by those large multiregional companies but avoided by the rest of the world. A trained administrator is usually needed to set it up and typically, it requires an additional capital investment in server and storage hardware and administration. Groupware also focuses heavily on managing shared document repositories, making it vulnerable to competing products with a broader vision.

The vision of virtual office software is different. Groupware is currently being replaced by virtual office—a groupware-like application with far more functionality. Virtual office software was born as a result of our increasing work mobility and an increasing need for groups to work on projects jointly while spanning locations. Customers and suppliers outside the company can also be included.

Groove, an example of virtual office software, combines the attributes of a shared file server, an IM function, and project-management tools (e.g., calendar and others). It can be deployed in minutes by users of the application themselves and does not require an investment in additional hardware. (It cleverly uses the participating member machines as sort of a distributed repository, thereby eliminating the need for a central machine.) The fact that virtual officeware (VOware) sets up instantly and securely without installing specialized hardware or calling in a technician means the utility of virtual officeware extends well beyond businesses. It is a practical tool to be used for school clubs, soccer team members, and even authors writing a book such as this one. (We use the Groove software.)

VOware adds a new level of "awareness" to communication. A bit like IM on steroids, VOware has the concept of a "workspace" (i.e., a project) with group members, digital assets such as files, and tools such as whiteboard sharing and calendars and so forth. However, it is the combination of these elements that allows for a much deeper insight into what your fellow peers are doing without actually being in their presence. In fact, you can be more aware of what they are doing at any given time than you could if you were all working in the same office complex. From a simple glance at the application, you know who is currently "in the workspace" as opposed to merely being online (and whether they are active and using their computer or have been idle or away for a bit). You know which documents they are currently updating. You know which documents have been updated recently by someone else and not yet read by you.

Chat sessions for the whole group are built in to the software, including voice. It is straightforward to hold an ad-hoc virtual meeting wherein you are broadcasting a portion of your computer's screen to all other participants. By using your voice and mouse, you can direct a presentation electronically— known as *whiteboarding*. Microsoft Word users can also allow multiple people to be simultaneously editing the same document in a coordinated fashion.

Think back to our outline of important communication attributes in Chapter 3, "Inescapable Data Fundamentals": asynchronicity, immediacy, awareness, utility, and happenstance. VOware goes a long way toward wrapping together our most valued communications requirements and is one important tool for enabling successful remote workers. In an Inescapable Data world, you have the freedom to work whenever and wherever you want, without compromising quality or efficiency. Nor should there be remorseful feelings for loss of physical proximity to your fellow workers. The tools, the data sources, and the network all say that you can successfully work this way.

Text Messaging and Convergence

IM and VOware are wonderful tools that bring our remote employees and friends back into a tighter circle. Unfortunately, those tools require at least a laptop to function. However, many times, we are in a supermarket or at a bus stop during bounded work hours—or at least what used to be bounded work hours—and are not carrying our bulky laptops.

Text messaging, also known as SMS, was invented by cell phone companies, not computer companies. Thank goodness for that, because phone companies have always better embraced interoperability among their competitors. (Could you imagine if your AT&T cell phone could *only* call other AT&T customers? The computer world thinks nothing of having such restrictions, at least among end-user applications, unfortunately.) Now that cellular networks are all digital, it is pretty straightforward to combine text messaging with voice. Text messaging is disproportionately used by teenagers currently, partly because they are more often away from a computer (and therefore away from IM) and partly because it is cool. Text messaging is far more rudimentary than IM. For one thing, you lose the "awareness" of who else is on. (There is neither a buddy list nor a suitable display that could even show one.) Furthermore, you are relegated to typing messages by using a phone keypad that has only eight useful keys. It is very cumbersome to type a message of any length.

The good news is that more functions are coming to your cell phone thanks to convergence. The cell phone manufacturers are getting creative and making mobile phones smarter—more like PDAs. In turn, the makers of and PDAs are now carrying cell services. It is pretty clear that the future will bring us pervasive, simple, cell-enabled devices that allow nearly the same set of messaging capabilities that our bulky computer counterparts offer. As a result, a new challenge will arise: how to receive the right message on the right device.

Ken Kuenzel, CEO of Covergence, a start-up that specializes in message routing among various technologies, states, "It is a significant problem now getting the right message to the right tool for the target user. People want to see a given message as soon as possible. That could mean they want it delivered to their cell phone as a text message if they are on the soccer field, or to their computer via e-mail if they are flying in an airplane. They don't want to process a message twice, and they don't ever want to miss one either. Couple all that with the fact that the back-end business systems for these various technologies are all different and don't mix well. This is turning out to be an important problem to solve." Companies such as Convergence are now appearing to help solve some of the management, interoperability, and integration problems. The future holds hope that we will properly receive messages on our various devices in some coordinated fashion.

The New Employee: Independent Consultant

As a result of less "face time" (time in an office among project peers), employers have started amassing databases that contain the skill sets for the company's employees. The amount of detail put into these databases is stunning. In the engineering world, for example, every skill and realm of knowledge that an engineer develops while working on a project is summarized within the database. It could be a new computer language, such as C#, mastery of a new Java library or a new computer platform, or even use of some end-user application such as an accounting package. The goal is to better match employees to tasks across a large, geographically dispersed company.

Many times while running a project, the need arises for short-term assistance or consultation from a "subject-matter expert." Working inside of a company with more than 100,000 employees, for example, one can be relatively certain that there is at least one person somewhere in the organization who has the *exact* knowledge needed. Without a detailed database of skills, it is impossible to find the right person and as a result, the project costs more to complete. A "Google for employee skills" allows the employer to finally mine their own most precious resource. Companies historically have incorrectly identified their employees as one of their main assets; the real assets are the specific skills and the ability to find and exploit those skills.

Employees also win in this new work-management scheme. They are more likely to have a queue of work in front of them than ever before, work that is satisfying and broadens their own exposure (as a result of working on a broader range of projects). The value of being connected to "just the right person who can solve my problem" is just the sort of efficiency that comes in an Inescapable Data world.

Are we heading toward a world of independent consultants? We are all subject-matter experts in a particular area. If it is valuable for our own employer to better connect our skills to business problems, won't it also be better for a broader range of companies? Might such a cross-company skills database allow companies to run even more successfully with far fewer full-time employees? As you will see in later chapters, one theme in the Inescapable Data world is for large companies to become smaller as components of their work get "teased-out" and sourced in a broader market.

Social Implications

Nicholas Christakis, notable Harvard sociologist, has an interesting view on the changing and more fluid work environment many of us are now experiencing. "It is an atavistic phenomena...it's a throwback...we're going back to home as the center of our lives, like when we were farmers," explains Christakis. The view is shared by many of us living in world where the work life and the home life are blurred. "I started work the other day at 4 A.M., corresponding with my peers in the UK. I later got wrapped up in more situations with remote peers and never actually made it into work. At 1 P.M., my kindergarten daughter comes into my home office and asks, 'Daddy, do you still have a job?' I explained to her that I simply work everywhere, which caused an odd smile."

Technology and connectivity have truly allowed a great many of us to work anywhere and everywhere. Everywhere. At the beach. At the soccer field. After dinner. Before breakfast. Even during professional sports events. As a reader of this book, your position with regard to your "connectedness" falls into one of two camps: It's you, you get it and you do it or, from the sidelines you watch others doing it, perhaps even shaking with fear and praying it's not so. We call this the connectivity divide.

If you have children, you know that they are growing up on the connected side of the divide and bringing that with them into their future work lives. The changes in technology and connectivity are giving us back large packets of time while borrowing our attention during idle moments. We will see our kids more. We will see our spouses more. We will travel for pleasure more. We will indeed be working more as well—and on more productive and enriching tasks. Technology is allowing work to be more pervasive and, in return, our lives are less rigid.

Summary

So now you have had a rather broad look at a variety of technologies that can, if we want them to, dramatically change our work lives. Conference calls, which are admittedly low tech, enable a significant percentage of the work force to be more work@home than ever in the past, creating in turn a new demand for increased technology and automation during our nonoffice hours. Proliferation of IM, VOware, and text messaging dominate and now blur our work versus home lives. The reality is that the business tools used in the office (e-mail, messaging, phone, file servers, the Internet, etc.) are *exactly* the same tools now available in our homes, and with no compromise of service or efficiency. The Inescapable Data point is this: Business and citizen tools are perfectly aligned, and both teams win. Those of us who have crossed the divide hopefully have more freedom than in the past (and hopefully, our employers are receiving additional work from us at the same time). If Inescapable Data (and communications) is not enabling such luxury with freedom, perhaps we need to reconsider its value.

CHAPTER EIGHT

Real-Time Manufacturing

The solutions to the challenge of an 80% improvement in efficiency mandate are not within our own factories, but rather intertwined throughout the now real-time value chain and unleashed by innovative and direct connections to each other's data and operations.

—Brian Jones, CEO of Nypro

Introduction

In the Inescapable Data world, the ability to compress product manufacturing time, tease-out inefficiencies, and increase product personalization combine to create significant new values made possible by omnipresent wireless networks, data exchange, and, most importantly, a willingness to tear down business walls.

For the past few decades, manufacturers have taken an incremental and inwardly focused approach to improving efficiency. Upgrading a machine with an engine that has slightly more horsepower yielding 10 percent more units per day, higher plant utilization, or fewer operations to perform—such upgrades represent incremental and inwardly focused changes. Manufacturers are now beginning to see that if they want to effect radical improvements in efficiency, they must look outside the walls of the factory. They must also develop a willingness to allow very deep and direct relationships with suppliers, distributors, customers, and even competitors (called *coopetition*). The *value chain* as it is now called, forms the linkages that tie together manufacturers with suppliers, distribution channels, retailers, and finally, consumers.

Serious gains in efficiency can come from making value-chain linkages high speed and transparent. To do so, manufacturers must be willing to break through the comfort barriers that have existed for decades. In short, the value chain, from raw materials supplier all the way through to the customer, has to operate like a single, well-oiled machine—a machine that needs a minimum of human intervention and exhibits near-zero latency. Such process optimizations are possible and can yield up to an 80 percent end-to-end efficiency improvement. What makes this possible is the ability to harvest a wealth of data from many different but interconnected sources all along the value chain, and then analyze and exploit the data in real or near-real time.

The Changing Manufacturing Landscape

To get a sense of how the manufacturing landscape is changing at a rapidly accelerating rate, we spoke to Brian Jones, CEO of Nypro, Inc. Nypro is a 50-year-old leading global provider of precision plastics injection molding and related manufacturing solutions with more than 12,000 employees, 40 manufacturing facilities in 17 countries, and nearly a $1 billion in sales annually. Nypro makes a wide variety of plastic-molded products from syringes to cell phones to computer parts. "During the past three years, the way in which we conduct business has been turned upside down, driven by extreme demands for efficiency that will separate out the new winners of the manufacturing world," claims Jones.

Historically, different manufacturing companies, even in the same industry, have chosen different operational models to serve their customers. Some companies have used a supply and distribution model that relies heavily on centralization and concentration of resources in fewer, larger locations—a pattern that resembles the "hub" structure used by today's airlines. The assumption was that the scale of a larger, more centralized operation could offer better value to the customer than a less-centralized, more distributed model, mostly through resiliency to increasing demand.

Nypro took a different approach. In contrast, Jones points out that, "At Nypro, we had more of a services-business mentality. We would find a location near one of our largest buyers and set up a facility there. The general rule was that we had to be close enough to the customer that their head engineer could drive out to our facility in the morning for a meeting or inspection and be back before lunch," explains Jones. "For 25 years we operated this way and were very successful. We were able to service our customers with extreme diligence."

Then, things changed dramatically. "Three years ago, the world turned upside down. The drive for efficiency and simplification was like a large explosion. Those of us that saw it had to first understand it, then embrace it, and then redesign to match it. After just three years, the competitive, supply, and customer landscape is almost unrecognizable," continues Jones. "Our major customers were on a rampage to wipe out as much as 85% of their supply chains. We saw one major cell phone buyer first drop from many hundreds of suppliers down to 100, then down to a mere 20 as of a couple of months ago," explains Jones.

Jones believes that what large customers want is dramatically reduced supply chain complexity, and that one way to achieve that is to reduce the number of links (or kinks) in the chain. Typically, this means that their suppliers must either learn to accommodate them, or get out. "You now need to supply customers from multiple factories all around the globe but as a single concerted organization."

"You want to hear about the instantaneous always-connected business? Try having a meeting with a large cell phone manufacturer, arguably *the* most connected set of humans alive. While you're in the meeting explaining the status of a project, good or bad, they are immediately keying into their personal communicator your status and instantly everyone back at their headquarters knows your situation. A few years ago, you at least had the time it would take for them to get back to their hotel and fire up the laptop. In the modern world, we're intertwined with our partners and our status is their status; there is no hiding," states Jones.

Essentially, what has happened is that the large buyers have forced the best of both worlds from their suppliers like Nypro: They want the nimbleness of a small services-oriented, nearby supplier yet with the heft of a broad and scalable one. These two entirely different manufacturing models have now been forced together as a result of the efficiency demands of customers, both in terms of product cost, but even more so in terms of time to market.

An effort to streamline operations and reduce overall time to market is driving another important trend: the outsourcing of an increasing number of manufacturing process steps. Nypro not only builds, it is also now engineering more of Motorola's cell phone line. "Within the last three years, Motorola has outsourced about two-thirds of their work. The new concept is *original design manufacturer*. We do the market studies and iterate products and study consumer needs and values and then we build and manufacture and assemble as much of the product as they will allow. The only projects left back inside such companies are those that they truly believe are their intellectual property or define their much more forward-looking businesses. This change has raced in and altered business models up and down the chain, and within a mere few years."

Nypro's large customers are driving this with unprecedented energy. Gone are the days of just aiming for a 10 percent improvement. In Nypro's new world, customers are expecting that manufacturers implement radical new redesigns of their processes by leveraging real-time communication, collaboration, and shared data. They have insisted on an unprecedented 85 percent improvement in time and money savings. How can that be achieved?

Value Stream Mapping

Value stream mapping (VSM) is a concept popularized by the book *Learning to See* (Rother/Shook). VSM (and lean manufacturing) essentially says that customers are only willing pay for the "value-add" parts of any process. Everything else is "Muda," the Japanese word for waste. In VSM, the theory is that 85% of any process is Muda. Eliminate that, and you've achieved your improvement goal. The trick, therefore, is to first learn how to identify Muda and then eliminate it.

"The general feeling among manufacturing managers is that this concept of 85% waste is heresy. We've been so conditioned to simply look microscopically and inwardly at our own processes, searching for 5 or 10% improvements here and there. When someone comes in and says we're going to redesign for 85% improvement, they are incredulous," explains Jones. "Many times there is passive resistance. They don't 'see.' You first have to learn to see, and then once you 'see,' it will drive you nuts; you'll see massive improvement opportunities throughout everything in your life. In our business, we're now like the Pac-Man game, eating up value chain dots, because our customers need us to take on larger sections and without increasing durations. Internally, we call this high-velocity systems and we run around preaching this to our own suppliers and customers. If they want to play with us in the 85% improvement game, they have to learn to see what we see, and then they have to build their business directly in to ours. It is the only way."

The overall philosophy in the new world is that efficiency can only be significantly increased if we reach beyond our own finite element control and optimize processes and steps across major businesses and business systems, and real-time communications and data and information exchange is the key. This is consistent with the Inescapable Data mantra that businesses will be driven by efficiencies goals more than immediate bottom-line profit and that the new efficiency realizations will only occur if the breadth and depth of business operations spans organizations. This means opening up key internal aspects of your own operation and allowing your customers and suppliers to tie into your systems and processes to an unheard of depth. "Most North American companies would turn inventory 10 times a year. We now have customers that turn inventory 1,800 times a year, 5 times a day. Do you think a month-end inventory report to them now has any value? You can't get from 10 to 1,800 by squeezing. You have to start over and be willing to tear down walls of control and knowledge. Our customers want to know exactly the current inventory levels of any single part we're producing as well as its dependencies. This is unprecedented yet required in order to reduce that 85% of Muda," extols Jones.

Automotive Resequencing, Wirelessly

Automotive manufacturing is notoriously a floor-space-intensive operation. Building a Hummer aggravates assembly-line floor-space issues given the heft of the major components, such as those bulky seats, which make for local inventorying and staging nearly impossible. AM General manufactures the Hummer for General Motors out of its Mishawaka, Indiana, plant and the new H2 has extremely aggressive sales (and thus production) goals. Without being able to physically expand their plant, AM General had to redesign their operations to meet a much increased production load and lean manufacturing analysis led to innovative deployment of wireless networking technology. AM General deployed products from WhereNet and GE Fanuc Automation (CIMPLICITY) to build a novel real-time parts replenishment system.[1]   *continues*

---

[1] http://www.managingautomation.com/maonline/magazine/read.jspx?id=1605638.

Automotive Resequencing, Wirelessly *(Continued)*

Because of competitive pressures and plant closings, automotive manufacturers are forced to new levels of flexibility such as moving several different models of a vehicle down a single assembly line as well as line-time customizations of vehicles. Naturally, this creates significant challenges with coordinating parts at various line-staging cells. Wireless on-the-line devices and RFID allow a line to be rapidly reconfigured without restringing wires and to be real-time tied into the supply network. In the H2 case, AM General uses special wireless "WhereCall" buttons affixed to each operator work location (and easily moved around). Instead of having a cache of Hummer seats queued up at each cell (of various colors or other details), the operator is able to signal a forklift driver to retrieve the next-needed seat by pressing the appropriate WhereCall button.

Similarly, each H2 has affixed to it a "WhereTag" (RFID), and as it passes out of each manufacturing cell its location and status is real-time updated in the central manufacturing system, CIMPLICITY. This data is amassed in various databases and continuously examined, trended, and managed for exceptions—which are wireless sent out via Nextel to manager's pagers. With such technology, a given assembly line can be "multi-tasked" (if you will) to build several different model cars as well as better handle customizations, greatly reduce floor space, and nearly eliminate transient inventory...all Muda.

Is there really 85 percent Muda in an operation? Many factory owners would be inclined to think differently. They look around and see their 1,500 employees running around trying to keep up with machines and forklifts and even working overtime and weekends. Their common mistake is that busy-ness does not mean value-add from a paying customer's point view. (Customers will only pay for the values they receive.) Let's examine a simple hypothetical metal-stamping plant. The customer has ordered 10,000 units of some brushed-steel custom emblem. The manufacturer first buys the raw steel and because the customer ultimately receives steel he is willing to attribute some cost for this step. The manufacturer "receives" the steel, which is a process of coordinating a delivery, inspecting the raw goods (that should be exactly what was ordered), keying some payment system, and then moving the goods into some holding area. All Muda. The steel sits in inventory for some number of weeks and, when it is needed, it is first located by some floor personnel and then transported to the work machine. More Muda. At the machine, the material is re-inspected. (Is this the right raw material? For which customer? Which process steps must be performed?) Muda. Finally, the metal is cut and stamped and brushed, all values the customer is willing to pay for. On the outbound side, nearly the same set of operations take place with additional staging, delay (inventorying), and shipment to the buyer. Muda again. Indeed, there is at least 85 percent of nonvalue steps, time, and labor applied to the product creation.

Traditional factory optimization techniques would look at a single narrow activity, say that of transporting the raw material to the work area, and try for a 10 percent efficiency gain. Perhaps this year, they use propane-powered drivable forklifts instead of human-pulled hand-pumped ones. Inward focused, "squeeze" approach to improvement. Having the courage to "see" revolutionary approaches can be challenging. The revolutionary approach, in the metal-stamping example, would be more along the lines of: no inbound inspections of material quality because we're tied to the suppliers quality-control records, no inbound inventory holding because our supplier delivers the raw goods the moment we need it because he was tied into our "build schedule" records, no "what steps do we perform to this piece" at the machine because the piece comes with an electronic record of instructions, and so forth throughout the completion.

Another hypothetical example: ATM machines. Suppose a given regional bank wants to increase usage of its services and machines. It plans, like it always has, to add 10 percent more machines to a given large territory every year, year after year. If the bank steps far enough back, it's not machines that people want. People want an ability to buy things with the ease of cash without being encumbered to carry a large wad of cash. Eliminate the machines altogether. Instead, start a campaign to have the bank's ATM card accepted "as cash." Dramatic difference in capital and operational costs (and hence why we see a rapid adoption of debit cards at all retail locations).

ATM: Rise and Fall

Once upon a time, ATM machines were few and far between. One often had to drive to find one. Not now. One finds them in every conceivable location. The first proponents of ATMs were banks that realized that at 27 cents per ATM transaction, paying $1.07 per transaction at the teller window was less than cost-efficient. Next, retailers started installing them in the belief that easy access to cash translates to more money spent in the store (hence the proliferation of ATMs in convenience stores, malls, and markets).

However, debit cards challenge all that thinking. ATM use has fallen to 57 percent of U.S. households in 2003 from a peak of 65 percent in 2000[2] (source: Synergistics Research, Atlanta). This is attributed to the rising use of debit cards, and is influenced by several factors:

+ Consumer rejection of ATMs fees (considered too high by consumers)
+ Perceived safety of carrying less cash
+ Speed plus convenience of using the cards that act like cash

Even gas-station convenience stores accept debit cards today (or Speed Pass or other noncash fast-payment devices). The point is this: Adding ATM machines was solving the wrong problem—people are not looking for easier access to *cash*, they are looking for easier access to *purchases*.

Many new tools are available to help various companies interconnect their systems. Although e-mail, faxes, and even Web pages will continue to be useful for human communication, those are not the tools of the new trade. On the engineering side, virtual office and groupware allow for real-time collaboration on designs and documents through shared repositories and instant messaging. Asynchronous collaboration yields far higher efficiency and smoothes out time-zone bumps between manufacture and buyer and serial approval processes.

As wonderful as e-mail has been, it has a natural electronic boundary that solidifies the separation of two parties. Shared workspaces are an opposite mentality that essentially advertises that separate teams are virtually co-located without the barrier that a message-exchange mechanism introduces. On the manufacturing and fulfillment side, software exists today that directly attaches

---

[2] http://www.mlive.com/news/grpress/index.ssf?/base/news-17/
1095087375314090.xml.

multiple companies' business systems together as a result of XML and Web services. The inventory level is directly known. The product location is directly known. The order quantity can be directly changed. Product options can be directly changed. No delays and no human-to-human involvement. Our point is not to detail any particular type of solution, but rather the more general notion that all the electronic streamlining you have grown to look for within your walls can now be done across your chain, if you're willing to take the walls down. Tie the business systems directly together.

Changing a business operational mentality can be tough. Let's examine inventory tracking for an example. If you want to know an inventory level in your supply chain 150 years ago, you wrote a letter and waited. Fifty years ago, you picked up the phone and queried. Twenty-five years ago, you might receive a fax on a regular schedule. Five years ago you might receive the information via an e-mail. Today, you might dial a special Web site and self-serve. All are incremental improvements but completely miss the real objective. Like the ATM example, the real objective is not to learn about inventory levels. What is even done with that information? Skip the intermediary step of discovering inventory levels (which is Muda) and jump directly to automated fulfillment, procurement, and receivables. Don't get cash to buy goods, go directly and buy the goods. Getting inventory knowledge was not the goal, and so improving the speed (of getting inventory knowledge) was missing the larger opportunity. The new opportunities are created by driving business systems together directly at an automated electronic non-human–involved level—barreling through traditional walls.

RFID and Real-Time Insight into the Supply Chain

Eliminating Muda is now of paramount importance to manufacturers, and RFID technology is one of the key technologies that can be applied to reduce waste. At the heart of this new approach to supply-chain management is real-time tracking and monitoring of every crate, pallet, and box through exploitation of RFID.

"RFID will impact the entire build-to-order segment of the manufacturing industry very quickly, and will eventually impact all of manufacturing and the supply chain," says Jim Kirkely, CTO of QAD, a leading provider of applications for global manufacturers. RFID will help manufacturers reduce the time it takes to deliver products, and make their processes leaner and more efficient through the gathering and sharing of data in real time using the Inescapable Data sources we have been discussing.

One of the early applications of RFID in manufacturing will be the tracking and tracing of goods through the supply chain to reduce shrinkage due to theft, mismanagement, and fraud. As products are manufactured, and finished goods are transported on pallets and cases, they are susceptible to loss as they move through the supply chain—losses that can be minimized using RFID.

Shrinkage is as big a concern for manufacturers as it is for retailers. According to a National Retail Federation Security survey, retail organizations in the U.S. lose 1.8 percent of their total revenues to shrinkage. European and Australian organizations report losing in the 1.75 percent range. However, shrinkage is not just a retail issue. A conservative estimate by IBM's business consulting services says that manufacturers typically lose close to 1 percent of their revenues to shrinkage. Gillette alone estimates that it experiences a 5 percent shrinkage rate for razors and blades. This translates into a loss of $180 million sales annually.

Bioterrorism and Handling Product Recall

Managing manufacturing information and tracking data has moved from a competitive advantage to a business requirement to now a government mandate in many cases. The Bioterrorism Act of 2002 requires "one-up, one-down" traceability of food and similar products throughout a manufacturing supply stream. Operations centers must have full accounting for all materials and goods received, the processes applied to them, and the next destination. Companies are mandated to produce detailed product-flow accounting within four hours of a request. By mid-2005, all companies with 500 or more employees must comply with Section 306 of the Bioterrorism Act. The better the tracking of goods, the more efficient (and more narrow) a product recall can be. Real-time data collection and integrated computer systems are at the heart of compliant manufacturers. The cost of noncompliance or archaic tracking systems can be exceedingly high. ConAgra, for example, in 2002 had to recall more than 18.6 million pounds of beef suspected of E. coli contamination rather than 354,000 pounds because they could not produce sufficient evidence of tracking detail.[3] ConAgra subsequently left the beef industry.

---

[3] http://www.rossinc.com/kiosk/Food and Beverage/Make it, Pack it, Trace it, Track it 6.04.htm.

Manufacturers are now moving to establish e-commerce connections to their suppliers as they automate their internal production processes at the same time. These processes have historically been dependent on many manual operations. Accuracy and productivity suffer as a result and more automation through data connectivity promises to close those gaps.

For the past decade or so, inventory and work-in-process data have been gathered by personnel using bar code scanners. These largely manual processes are expensive for three reasons: First, there is the obvious direct labor cost involved with performing manual processes versus automating them. Second, manual processes are notoriously error prone. It can take only seconds to generate an error, but hours to correct it. Third, manual processes elongate the time during which products live in the supply chain rather than on showroom floors or in consumers' homes.

As previously pointed out, the ultimate buyer will pay only for the value-added parts of the process. Inventory and tracking operations do not (in themselves) make a product better for a customer; so they are Muda and must either be eliminated or 100 percent automated. RFID technology, along with the back-end computer systems and intercompany communication conduits, allow for dramatic efficiency gains.

Twenty suppliers to Metro, the fourth-largest retailer in the world, are already placing RFID tags on all shipment pallets. As pallets move around facility locations and through doorways and onto or off of trucks, wirelessly and discretely nearby sensors make note of the passage. Metro plans to ramp RFID usage to include 80 more suppliers in 2005, and swell the ranks to more than 300 by 2006. As products move from warehouses to other distribution points and finally to a store loading dock via truck, goods are automatically tracked by Metro's automated distribution system. No human intervention is required to scan or inspect a shipment. The location of a shipment of goods can be determined instantly at any given point in time without the old costly process of calling around and checking multiple sources. Metro estimates that they'll reduce their truck unloading time by half simply because pallets never need to be inspected to learn of their contents—which is both slow and error prone. Wal-Mart, despite significant resistance among its top 100 suppliers to its mandate that those top suppliers be RFID compliant by January 1, 2005, has also seen more than 40 suppliers *voluntarily* sign on to comply with RFID.

These early stage pilots are only the beginning. By January 2006, Wal-Mart expects all of its approximately 10,000 suppliers to be RFID-enabled. At the same time, a supply chain estimated to be four times larger than Wal-Mart's, the U.S. Department of Defense (DoD), has plans to RFID enable more than 43,000 of their suppliers. Obviously, that is going to have a widespread ripple effect throughout many industries.

Why all these mandates and initiatives? The ability to know where every item is within the supply chain and on store shelves could save retailers billions of dollars per year. Here's an estimate from Sanford C. Bernstein & Co, a New York investment house, of what Wal-Mart might save annually when RFID technology is deployed throughout its operations:[4]

- $6.7 billion from a reduction of manual processes. Eliminating the need to have people scan bar codes on pallets and cases in the supply chain and on items in the store reduces labor costs by 15 percent.

- $600 million from the elimination of out-of-stock conditions. Even with the most efficient supply chain on Earth, Wal-Mart suffers out-of-stocks. The company boosts its bottom line by using smart shelves to monitor on-shelf availability.

- $575 million from better control of shrinkage. Knowing where products are at all times makes it harder for employees to steal goods from ware-houses. Scanning products automatically reduces administrative error and vendor fraud.

- $300 million from better tracking of the more than one billion pallets and cases that move through its distribution centers each year produces significant savings.

- $180 million from reduced carrying costs. Improved visibility of what products are in the supply chain—in its own distribution centers and its suppliers' warehouses—lets Wal-Mart reduce its inventory and the annual cost of carrying that inventory.

- $8.35 billion in total annual savings from the use of RFID—greater than the *total annual revenue* of more than half the companies listed on the Fortune 500.

Accurate inventory tracking—tracking without gaps and disjoint business systems—is critical to realizing gains in overall supply-chain efficiency. RFID aids in tracking a product (or pallet, or box) accurately throughout a plant or warehouse. Add-in GPS transceivers on all shipping trucks and the goods can

---

[4] Source: CIO Insight, Sanford C. Bernstein & Co.

now be tracked 100 percent of the way through the process, from raw materials to finished goods, to distribution channels, and onto the showroom floor. Tightening the end-to-end tracking of a product, through pervasive networking and data collection, enables manufacturing cost savings and time efficiencies.

New Computing Architectures Driven by RFID-Type Sources

RFID is a powerful new tool. But to use it effectively, manufacturers might have to build new computing infrastructures. Why? RFID deployments can generate enormous amounts of data and flood an existing business's system with more data than it can handle. New computing architectures will be needed by all participants in the value chain to provide information to each other in real or near-real time. It is estimated that Wal-Mart's in-store implementation of RFID alone will generate as much as 7 terabytes (7 trillion bytes) of data per day. Use in the supply chain will generate even more. As a point of relative magnitude, consider that the entire U.S. Library of Congress contains 20 terabytes of data. Wal-Mart could therefore generate as much as the equivalent of a Library of Congress' worth of RFID data every three days. Obviously, such a volume of data could cripple business systems not equipped to handle data volumes of this magnitude and defeat the very purpose of deploying RFID in the first place. What is needed is an advanced technology infrastructure designed to handle this Inescapable Data.

"The good news is that large-scale, real-time computing architectures are not new," claims Mark Palmer, ObjectStore's vice president of complex event processing and RFID. "Instant decision making on high-velocity data streams is a challenge that large trading systems have faced in the financial services industry, military command and control systems have faced, and network management applications have faced in the telecommunications industry." One example of a large-scale real-time architecture is Amazon.com, whose used book and CD system handles real-time inventory updates from hundreds of thousands of third parties, but caches it in a real-time data-management system that services up to 50 million inventory queries an *hour* during the Christmas season. "Many technologists hear about Amazon.com's system and say: I don't have their problem," continues Palmer, "but even a fraction of the Amazon problem is a huge problem, and the challenge is approaching more and more businesses faster than they realize."

RFID is driving Amazon-like data streams into manufacturing and retailing information systems, which, for the most part, are presently not designed to handle the barrage. "Traditional data management approaches using conventional databases like Oracle cannot handle this new load," claims Palmer. By contrast, real-time computing architectures have ways to handle large volumes of fast-changing data and are now being used more frequently by information technologists. The first RFID Reference Architecture proposed at the MIT's Auto-ID center in 2003 prescribed a real-time, in-memory event database (RIED)," continues Palmer. "The reason for the RIED was simple—physics: Memory is 1,000 times faster than disk, and in-memory event databases are 1,000 times faster than relational databases for RFID data. Although commercial implementations of event-driven databases have been available for years, their deployment has not been pervasive—until now."

Complex event processing (CEP) is a new field that deals with the task of processing multiple streams of simple events with the goal of identifying the meaningful events within those streams. An example of a stream of simple events could include a church bell ringing, the appearance of a man in a tuxedo, and rice flying through the air. The related complex event is what one infers from the string of simple events: A wedding is taking place. CEP helps discover complex, inferred events by analyzing other events: the bells, the man in a tux, and the rice flying through the air.

CEP's pioneer David Luckham of Stanford University, the author of *The Power of Events, an Introduction to Complex Event Processing in Distributed Enterprise Systems*, defines a complex event query language that treats event time and order, in addition to event data, as the basic elements of data processing. According to Gartner, CEP will become a common computing model within 5 to 10 years. But developers aren't sitting still—you can build CEP systems today in languages such as Java or C++.

One of the main elements of CEP is a new language, the Event Processing Language (EPL). An EPL query is like an SQL query in that it looks for relationships between objects. With and EPL query, the objects are events and the main query metaphor is time and causality, not relationships between data objects. That is, EPLs answer questions such as: "Let me know when these 2 events happen, in this order, within 30 seconds of each other." SQL is not designed to handle those types of queries. So, this is both a new type of language, but also a new style of computing: event-driven computing.

Event-driven computing will become more prominent as Inescapable Data technologies are integrated into mainstream computing infrastructures. CEP is one of the key elements that extracts intelligence from Inescapable Data streams. Combinations of CEP, event-driven architectures, real-time data management, and federated, distributed middleware, can all be combined to unlock intelligence. In many cases, intelligence cannot be gleaned in real time from Inescapable Data streams without all four.

Real-time event databases are designed for *streams* of data not sets of data (a fundamental computing paradigm shift introduced by the availability of Inescapable Data). Associations and relationships between objects contained within event streams are based on time and proximity, not primary and foreign data keys. Event databases are designed to store dynamic data, not static data. The difference is fundamental and significant, hence the need for new architectures. The developers of event-driven systems will need to adopt these techniques to keep up with Inescapable Data sources such as RFID.

"While the problem isn't new, the tools are new to many, and evolving quickly; venture capital in the United States is heavily investing in them, innovators are beginning to adopt them, and systems are being deployed more quickly because of them," said Palmer. It would not be prudent to force-fit traditional processing architectures to this radically new stream of data. Fortunately, the computing industry wrestled with similar data streams recently and has developed new tools that can now be applied to RFID and other Inescapable Data streams.

The Shipping Business

The shipping business, in particular UPS, has understood the supply-chain efficiency message, too. For many decades, the large shipping companies were mainly in the business of moving packages from one endpoint to another. As a result, they built up massive physical traffic networks, distribution centers, and service locations. In parallel, most large manufacturing companies had their own distribution centers and logistics operations. Distribution centers are arguably one of the most capital-intensive steps in an overall supply chain.

Observing the redundancy, UPS and other large shipping companies have been successful in teasing-out this costly, nondifferentiating, common denominator of all manufacturing companies—Muda as far as the paying end customer is concerned. UPS claims that they can take from 2 to 20 days out of a company's distribution process,[5] which classifies this program as a revolutionary improvement and not merely an evolutionary 10 percent gain.

---

[5] http://www.ups-scs.com/solutions/white papers/wp distribution bypass.pdf.

As alluring as this efficiency gain sounds, getting there will require some effort. The manufacturer will typically need to know the final destination of a finished product as it rolls off its production line so that shipping information can be mated with the product at that time—far sooner in the process chain than many companies can presently accommodate. Thus, back-end IT systems have to be streamlined, and key front-end sales and customer databases need to be integrated with manufacturing process systems so that data is shared among all systems involved. (In general, data sharing is a key Inescapable Data capability.)

How Are the Shipping Companies Doing?

So, how are the shipping companies doing? Let's look at a simple metric: the stock values and trends of FedEx and UPS. FedEx stock has grown from $5 in 1995 to more than $85 in 2004, a nearly 20-times improvement in less than a decade, and at a very even, constant rate. UPS stock value has grown from $50 in 2000 to $75 in 2004—a 50 percent increase in four of the toughest recessionary years.

For 2005, FedEx will increase capital investment to more than $2 billion because of strong demand.[6] The emergence of online retailers (e-tailers) such as Amazon.com, drugstore.com, and many others, have driven the need for direct-to-consumer shipping. As successful as such stores have become, they are extremely dependent on their shipping vendors who link them with their customers. The shipping companies are also becoming more of a partner with the manufacturing companies by tying their own businesses systems closely together with their manufacturing customers.

Moving goods across international borders is especially troublesome and adds significant time to product delivery, typically taking several months for a product to go from factory to store. UPS has launched a new service, called UPS Trade Direct, which takes an end-to-end approach to moving goods from factory, across international borders, and ultimately on to the retail store or customer. With UPS Trade Direct, packages are individually packed at the point of manufacture and then consolidated by UPS as a single freight through to customs for faster clearing. Then the consolidated shipment is broken back up (a process known as deconsolidation) once in the U.S., and then rapidly processed

---

[6] http://www.thestreet.com/pf/stocks/transportation/10179573.html.

through UPS's extensive handling network. All throughout the process, individual packages are traceable by customers and suppliers. Although this might sound sensible and reasonable, it is a significant departure from how shipping usually occurs between countries and one that reduces elapsed shipping time from six weeks down to two or three in many cases.

It is also not hard to see how technologies like RFID will become essential to the shipping industry. When a box rolls off the manufacturing line and is tagged with product and customer information, the shipping company truly becomes the partner of the manufacturer, sharing production and information databases. The box is no longer faceless, with only a destination address. Rather, it is now part of an order, for a particular customer, likely coupled with other products and boxes, and routed and billed to the customer. Never does the box stall in motion or need rotation or alignment for a bar code scan. Never does it need to be opened and its contents visually inspected. It can even be returned by the customer directly through the shipping company with financial credits occurring automatically. GPS, RFID, and integrated computer systems sharing data enable revolutionary improvements in efficiency.

Customized Through to Consumer

There is a new market trend toward customized products, no matter how big or small a product may be. Toyota, for example, has a new saying: "We'll never build the same car twice." Shopping for a vehicle online now offers the consumer the ability to customize to the smallest detail without impacting the delivery date.

"It's the scalability of one," observes Nypro's Jones. "Our buyers want very individual products from us now—lot sizes of one—but they insist on not bearing either additional cost or duration." In some cases, we as consumers will also expect a degree of personalization of many major purchase items. For commodity or nondifferentiating products, we may not expect customization of the product, but rather of the process to procure it coupled with the ability to buy it 24/7 and receive it the next day or sooner.

A supplier could not "scale lot sizes of one" without the automation enabled by end-to-end connectivity. In the past, custom and small quantity orders would require special management attention that was an exception to a standard shipping process. Flags, paper notes, or special handling instructions would be affixed to boxes or parts, and supervisors would have to periodically shepard the "custom order" through the process. Receiving status of such an order at the other end would be an exercise in human networking.

Today, order customization can no longer be treated as an exceptional condition. It must be built in to the process. The product or part carries its instructions electronically (perhaps RFID tag referencing the build-to-order database record). The system processes these instructions on a per-part basis (e.g., paint this one blue) while real-time databases are updated seamlessly. Successful manufacturing companies can use Inescapable Data technologies to adapt to such a scheme.

Build-to-Order Manufacturing

We have seen the need for specialty or custom manufactured goods for decades. "We're continuing to see a trend of moving away from a make-to-stock strategy in manufacturing and fulfillment to a make-to-order or configure-to-order strategy," says Mike Dominy, a senior analyst with the Yankee Group.[7] Black Model-Ts no longer retain customers in a world where buyers value form and fit along with competitive price. Vans, Inc. is an example of a company that marries customer's desires for custom shoes with manufacturing operations thousands of miles away in China.

Through the Vans.com Web site, customers can click on every piece of material that goes into a particular shoe, specifying the color and potentially other attributes. Between 5 and 10 materials (or sections) are commonly used in building a shoe and, using the Vans.com order process, each one can be customized.

There were many challenges for Vans to overcome to get all of its business systems tied together and produce "one-off" custom orders that didn't incur unreasonable delays or costs. Web services integrate Van's Web site with its MRP system as well as a unique purchase order that is then transmitted to China. Innovative supply-chain software from J.D. Edwards was key as was compute machinery from IBM that provides "capacity on demand," allowing Vans to easily handle unanticipated demand peaks.

---

[7] http://www.webservicespipeline.com/trends/46800394.

Many operational changes were driven by this need for customized product. Instead of batching together monthly purchase orders (which is normal in the shoe industry), purchase orders are now created and transmitted nearly continuously and for individual shoes. Distribution centers that normally hold and queue batches of one-style product now had to be equipped with specialized automated handling machinery to zip the custom orders through. Vans used UPS's WorldShip system, which handles all the shipping data, and the China factory is able to print domestic shipping labels for each individual box and affix the labels at the moment of manufacture. Transoceanic shipments are first aggregated into larger containerized groupings to clear customs faster. When they arrive in California, the containers are broken down into groupings for individual destinations and cross-docked[8] back onto UPS trucks for delivery directly to the customer.

Higher customization can be more easily achieved by deferring the final assembly step to the last possible moment. Some shipping companies now understand this and, in an effort to do more customized order fulfillment, have taken on the some final kitting, assembly, and integration tasks. This is a trend that is expected to continue (reminiscent of Jones' Pac-Man eating up value-chain dots imagery).

There is not just a single step or single change to enable customized manufacturing. Rather, the end-to-end process has to be rethought and refactored to allow for the process and electronic infrastructure changes. Data exchange technology and networks and business services are all available now that can come together to essentially stretch a wrapper across the global design, manufacturing, supply, and distribution chains—many of which are completely separate companies (if not competitors some of the time). Once in place, the new tightly coupled integration allows for customization to be a nondisruptive event.

An interesting outcome of value-chain integration—for manufacturers, suppliers, and shippers—is that all become more impervious to economic downturns. As Motorola, for example, outsources more and more of its production and engineering to tightly coupled partner firms such as Nypro, Motorola be-

---

[8] Cross-docking is a technique where packages come in on one loading dock and are immediately routed to an outbound dock and a different truck for delivery without any holding or queuing time.

comes physically smaller. This allows Motorola to become more nimble, more able to respond faster to market changes, and more tolerant of market down cycles (primarily from having to invest in much less capital and labor-related resources). At the same time, a manufacturer such as Nypro achieves more resiliency as well because it has scaled to meet diverse needs of a broader customer base—a rebalancing, of sorts, in the manufacturing world.

Video-Controlled Production

We see video being used as an Inescapable Data gathering technology more broadly than ever before, and across a wide range of applications. Certainly, video is used for surveillance (both in homes and across public areas), and we will later examine how video can be used by retailers in ways that now go beyond monitoring for security purposes—ways that allow retailers to gather customer data that was previously unavailable.

In the manufacturing sector, video is becoming a key element in process automation, rapidly optimizing many activities. What has changed recently is the move to the use of all-digital video, which in turn allows for process examination and analysis by systems as opposed to eyeballs. Use of digitized video analysis driven by manufacturing needs will in turn drive significant advances and availability of digitized video as a surveillance tool in more pervasive ways (crime, antiterror, and home security).

The coming pervasiveness of digitized video has been enabled by several factors, including the following:

+ High demand for consumer charge coupled display (CCD)-based gear (primarily consumer cameras and home video camcorders) has driven up production volumes and picture quality (pixel densities) while decreasing costs of the primary component, the CCD cells.

+ The integration of wireless network interfaces with digital cameras has recently become more practical.

+ Advances in image-processing techniques, largely made possible by increased single-chip CPU speeds and decreased component sizes, allow a camera to do most of the digital processing "locally"—i.e., within the camera itself.

Cognex Corporation is a leading supplier of video-based machine vision systems.[9] Dr. Robert Shillman (better known as "Dr. Bob"), CEO of Cognex, describes the changes taking place in the machine vision industry:

> As few as four or five years ago, the largest application of machine vision was in semiconductor manufacturing, where the manufacturing speeds and the physical tolerances were beyond those of human vision and attention span. Today, however, machine vision is used in a wide variety of "everyday" factory applications ranging from ensuring that labels and caps are properly placed on medicine bottles, to ensuring that all of the seat mounting bolts are present in the floor pans of trucks. The drivers for machine vision on the factory floor are the need to reduce errors, to reduce scrap, to reduce liability and, and in general, to reduce manufacturing costs, all while increasing overall product quality and increasing production speeds.
>
> The advances in the past five years in both digital signal processing hardware (DSPs) and in image-analysis software have made machine vision systems both highly capable and affordable. Prices of under $5,000 per unit—complete with camera, illumination, processing hardware, and intelligent software—are typical. Vision systems, for example, now are used to analyze all of the labels affixed to a product or to its printed box and adjusts, in real-time, the process to ensure that every item produced is to spec. Prior to the availability of affordable machine vision systems, human inspectors were stationed up and down each production line to "baby sit" multimillion dollar production machines. These are difficult and mind-numbing tasks for humans to accomplish effectively, but they are perfect jobs for machine vision systems, which never blink and which never get bored.

Dr. Bob goes on to describe the challenges that machine vision had to overcome to be useful in the "real world":

> It is quite easy for a person to determine if the cap on a toothpaste tube is screwed down properly, but it is very difficult to design image-analysis software that will work reliably under all possible factory-floor conditions and product variations. For example, it might be relatively easy to write software that could reliably determine the position of a red cap on a white tube, but it would be far more difficult to create software that could determine the exact position of a white cap on a white tube.

---

[9] Headquartered just outside of Boston, Massachusetts, in 1981 has shipped more than 120,000 vision systems having an aggregate value greater than $1.2 billion.

And, when you add to that the complexity of "real-world" manufacturing—the fact that the tubes are moving by at rate of 10 per second, that they are vibrating, that they don't always appear the same (for example, some tubes might be dented), that they are not always in the same position, that the designs of the tubes and caps are often changed by the marketing department (often, without telling the production department!)—you realize the technical challenges that designers of machine vision systems faced. And, adding to those technical challenges, machine vision systems also had to be low in cost and easy to use in order to achieve widespread acceptance. Given those challenges, is it easy to see why there are so few successful machine vision companies today?

The good news: With modern CPU horsepower and years of work improving the associated algorithms, machine vision can finally solve these complex challenges.

Five or so years ago, the machine vision paradigm was to communicate the raw analog signals produced by standard video cameras through coax cables back to a remote computer system that performed the analysis of all the images. These early machine vision systems were too expensive and too difficult to use for all but the most demanding applications. But, because of the increasing power and decreasing cost and size of digital signal processing chips (DSPs), modern machine vision systems can now be about the same size as a cell phone, and contain a camera, illumination, vision software, and image-processing hardware. And, because they are low in cost and compact, these "vision sensors" can be placed at every point of the production line where value is added. They automatically snap images of each product moving by, and then they communicate pre-processed results (not the images) back to the factory control systems, which take the necessary corrective actions.

Much of the data gathering and processing challenges are akin to those of RFID—tons of packets of information snippets that must be stored (cached) and processed using complex-event processing models (e.g., mis-cappings on toothpaste is increasing while another system is detecting mis-feeds in the cap-loading line). And, as vision systems become more and more prevalent, more real-time information will be made available for correlation with a wider set of processes in the manufacturing complex.

"For example, today, an executive at a paper products manufacturing company can now sit in his office and literally 'watch' 10 different manufacturing plants around the globe and compare their production results," explains Dr.

Bob. "In today's world, it is not good enough to wait for the end-of-week manufacturing report. A business executive needs to know the exact status (including quality metrics) of all of his production facilities so that he can optimize them." In the new world of higher intercompany tie-ins, the data and images could also be made available to both suppliers and customers, in real time.

Imaging is data-intensive and will strain back-end existing systems. Thankfully, the costs of key enabling technologies (disk space, processing power, and 10Gb Ethernet networking gear) are all trending downward. As a result, image data gathered from a manufacturing operation can now be "mined" more economically. Engineers can sift through millions of images and look for trends, correlations, or deviations against time, or against established specifications for components that are sourced from outside suppliers. Historically, the manufacturing segment has never had this kind of data available. Moving forward, we can predict that, because of their affordability, these systems will be used, and that data correlations will emerge that have not yet been anticipated. As in the usage of Inescapable Data technologies in the medical and commercial segments, the mining of image data will have extraordinary value to manufacturers as well.

Summary

The forthcoming changes in manufacturing are centered on dramatic performance improvement goals. Many manufacturers have invested heavily in historical processes that will rapidly become obsolete. *Seeing* the revolutionary new approaches is sometimes difficult for manufacturers, because they are often myopically focused on existing facilities and operations. Use of Inescapable Data technologies can, however, help them break out of focusing only upon achieving the "local maximum."

Real value can be gained from optimizing the entire product supply organism from end to end. A desire for faster fulfillment will develop among customers that will force the need among suppliers for the transparent tracking of all events occurring in the supply chain. Technologies such as RFID, wireless devices, and digital video are at the heart of the new track-everything-everywhere mentality, and when these technologies and the data they generate are tied to back-end business systems, supply-chain and manufacturing optimizations soar. The increase in data volumes and accelerating need to move these burgeoning data volumes from one end of the value chain to the other will tax the capabilities of existing business systems. However, the technology required to accommodate the new value chain models is now becoming available. In the Inescapable Data world, the need to compress product creation time, reduce line operation costs, tease-out Muda, and increase product personalization combine to create even higher joint value made possible by pervasive networks, data collection, data exchange, and most importantly, a willingness to tear down business walls, to achieve manufacturing in real time.

CHAPTER NINE

Sports and Entertainment: Energizing Our Involvement

Most sports I have been involved in, especially today's "extreme sports," involve a reasonably high level of risk. At 230 miles per hour, real-time technology not only gives you a competitive edge, it saves your life.

—Dominic Dobson, president of Motion Research and former Indy 500 racecar driver

Introduction

In the world of sports, technology is becoming more and more of a critical factor, for both the advancement of the player and for the enjoyment of the fan. One trend is clear—having real-time data equates to a competitive edge. Data is being collected and exploited by Inescapable Data devices in real time across a wide variety of sports, and is being used in creative ways. Combinations of communication and computer technologies come together, giving participants new levels of competitiveness, and bringing spectators closer to the event. Inescapable Data is infiltrating a variety of sports events from the highly "mechanized" ones such as racing, to individual sports such as swimming, through to team sports. A new breed of sporting events is emerging that mix the real with the virtual, propelling sports head long into a new world of games that often reward mental agility over physical prowess.

Auto Racing by Numbers

"Mechanized racing events, racecars, motorcycles, speed boats, and so on are driven by technology to a stunning level," explains Dominic Dobson, former racecar driver and now CEO of Motion Research. "In these mechanized sports, the major costs are in capital equipment and easily into the tens of millions. This is what's driving the extreme use of technology—to decrease the time to analyze data, to therefore increase the competitive advantage, as well as to increase the fan's and sponsor's experience."

In the early 1990s fans could rent "pager" devices at Indy 500 events and receive continuous lap-time updates. Today, you can rent small video devices similar to a Game Boy and pick up the real-time camera feeds from any of the live cameras positioned around the track and in the pit areas. The popular racers will have cameras mounted in the vehicle's interior and even have cameras mounted on helmets. The fans at the event are now "in the driver's seat" (visually, at least) and can control which car and which video stream they want to observe.

The amount of technology and data traffic now in use by racing teams is astounding. A cadre of vehicle-mounted sensors stream channels of data back to pit crews in real time. Crew members are in constant touch with a car's engine temperature, RPM, brake pressure, ride height, steering, and tire pressures to name just a few. The instant the car rolls into the pit, the crew knows exactly the status of the vehicle and what changes are needed.

With the exception of NASCAR events (which have historically precluded the use of remote, real-time vehicle monitoring), all of a vehicle's data is collected and analyzed in the pit area. Questions such as the following can be answered as the race is in progress:

+ Did the new synthetic oil have the desired reduction in engine temperature?

+ How many rotations has the left-front tire gone through and is it time to resurface or replace it?

+ Is there a relationship between time of day and this racer's success rate with the higher-octane fuel?

Data-Laden Cars

Much of the same data is actually being collected today by commercially available automobiles. As a vehicle owner, when you take your car in for service, special computers and interfaces absorb that data to help diagnose problems. It's not that the auto industry is trying to hide this data from you, the owner of the vehicle. Rather, it just has not been historically practical to expose the data to end users. As a driver, trying to monitor a lot of data as you are driving can be distracting as well.

There are some end-user devices available for a few hundred dollars, such as the EZ-Scan 6000 from AutoXray, that allow at-home vehicle diagnosis. These PDA-like devices plug into the same under-the-hood connector that the repair shop uses to access all of your car's runtime metrics and history.

Looking ahead in time, your vehicle may be wirelessly enabled (using Bluetooth, 802.11b, or both) and its runtime data will be made available to you via a Web browser interface, accessed by a nearby PDA or laptop. Some of the information may be useful to you (various fuel-efficiency metrics, for example). However, data locked up in the vehicles onboard computing system could be far more valuable to the manufacturer.

The manufacturer, for example, could frequently get real data regarding the type of driving conditions (as evidenced by various speeds and brakings), typical amount of idling time, typical warm-up time, frequency of trips during rain, hours driven when the temperature is below freezing, and so on. Such data could have monumental value to the manufacturer who is desperate to know details of product use for future competitive improvement opportunities. As we move toward greater product customization enabled by Inescapable Data, the vehicles we buy will fit us better because they and their developers will know us better.

Incidentally, who owns data collected by your car? Is how you drive and take care of your car your dirty little secret? Or, does the next buyer have some entitlement to that data? Currently, your car has an odometer. Both the manufacturer and federal regulators have gone through some trouble to ensure that it is accurate and tamperproof. Is that data as valuable to

continues

Data-Laden Cars *(Continued)*

the prospective used-car buyers as excessive braking habits, excessive vehicle loading, or unsafe turning speeds? If you bought a car from a supposed
little old lady with mild driving habits, would you not want proof and assurance of the actual driving patterns? When you buy a mutual fund, do
you not look closely at the fund's history and various managers' performance? Inescapable Data allows our more sophisticated devices to carry
with them rich histories of their travels and usage patterns...and that data
is available to be exploited.

"The car racing business is truly a business, and everything about the operations side is easily as sophisticated as any other business back end," explains
Dobson. "Building and maintaining race cars is exceedingly expensive. We
RFID tag our costly pieces and track inventory with meticulous scrutiny and
we have direct real-time connections to the engineering teams of our sponsors.
We may not appear like Wal-Mart from the spectator view, but behind the
scenes we have the same real issues and we're just as driven by efficiency as any
other business." Dobson knows of no other sport where the collection and re-
distribution of data is so complete. The racing industry was born as a result of
technology and will drive technology to advance. "At the heart of racing is data,
and exploitation of the this data builds the winners."

Heads-Up Sports

"Heads-up" displays are particularly interesting Inescapable Data devices that
are starting to be used in some sports and could also be driven, by wider adoption, into our business and personal lives. Heads-up displays have been used for
decades to train the pilots of commercial airliners as well as space shuttle–borne
astronauts. However, the heads-up display technologies used in these applications are expensive, require a lot of power, and are physically heavy, and thus
nonsuitable as sports gear. To be suitable for sporting applications, they must be
small in form, lightweight, run off battery power, and be wireless-enabled.

Heads-up displays have typically used a head-mounted visor to display some
amount of data or an image that is superimposed on the view seen by the wearer
of the device. This data is typically presented in text form, or as small-scale

diagrams, and is projected in a way that does not require the viewer's eyes to constantly refocus as they move continuously back and forth between the view ahead and the text or image projected onto the visor. So, instead of moving your head around to see dials, charts, screens, etc., you simply shift your eyes.

Think of what you experience when you drive your car. You often have to move your head in order to focus your sight on the radio, for example, taking your eyes off the road. It can take up to two seconds for your eyes to refocus and re-interpret the new view. In sporting events where a tenth of a second can separate winners from losers, such time is an unavailable luxury and quite dangerous.

Peter Purdy, a former competition skier (among other sports) and currently CTO of Motion Research, developed the first patented, athlete-mounted Doppler speed-detection system—heads-up display *goggles*. "We developed technology that was sufficiently small and lightweight, and could be operated off of a small battery that fits entirely within the skiers racing goggles." However, unlike heads-up displays that use a visor to reflect an image back to the eye, Purdy's technology projects small amounts of an image onto the retina of one eye, at a perceived distance of 13 feet ahead, while the view as seen by the other eye remains completely unobstructed. A skier, competing in a downhill slalom event, for example, can see elapsed time and speed while continuing to focus on the course ahead.

"By allowing one eye to take in the display image and the other to see the real-world image, the brain superimposes the display image automatically over the real world," explains Purdy. "The issue with any heads-up technology is that you have to balance the value of cluttering and confusing the user's overall scene view. In the fast world of racing, there can be no distractions. The beauty of heads-up technology is that your brain can process simple images such as short text or speed graphs without any compromise."

Purdy goes on to explain that the technology required to produce "in-glasses" style of heads-up displays is quite advanced in terms of development, although its most practical and productive uses presently remain out of the reach of most consumers. Nevertheless, Purdy developed heads-up goggles for the engineers of a large aircraft manufacturer who wear them as they walk through an airplane shell as it is being assembled. As engineers glance around the inside of the shell, they see the full wiring schematics superimposed on the surface of the shell. The view is dynamically adjusted based on view angle and position within the shell.

Such devices require a display/projection resolution closer to that of a real computer and hence have high cost and higher power consumption. Motion Research is currently focused on developing consumer-level data-projection eyewear for use in high-speed sporting events that require a continual focus on the view ahead.

SportVue

Motion Research's SportVue is a $150 to $300 consumer-grade, heads-up display system targeted at the average bicyclist or motorcycle rider. Unlike goggles, the SportVue uses a tiny one-inch-wide display that attaches to the edge of any helmet near the top of the user's field of view. The display is wirelessly connected to a data collection device elsewhere on the bike or motorcycle that monitors speed, gear number, and body metrics such as heart rate. (Bicyclists attempt to attain a particular cardio-saturation level and maintain that level throughout a trip.) Although the amount of information displayed is purposely modest, the point is to augment visual reality with a careful amount of pertinent information without compromising safety or enjoyment of the experience.

In the world of sports, heads-up displays will be used initially in events where helmets are normally worn. One can imagine, however, the utility of such a device to a broader range of sports events and even in our daily lives. As we become inundated with information from PDAs, wearable computers, and cell phones, we will need to find ways to more easily and more rapidly assimilate the information and make it useful.

Although currently available consumer-grade heads-up displays do not offer a fantasy-like full-immersion virtual viewing experience, they are a significant step forward toward our Inescapable Data vision where multiple data sources are converged and made readily available to us in real time. Going forward, we will see eyewear that is both innocuous and unobtrusive, that can enhance our life experiences by adding data, text, and graphics without so much as a turn of the head, and that is within the economical reach of most consumers.

Inescapable Data and the Individual Athlete

The use of Inescapable Data gathering devices can also enhance the performance of participants in a wide range of "personal sports," sports where there is typically a single athlete as opposed to a team, and where advances in skill come from excruciatingly detailed examinations of style and motion. Devices are now being created that provide real-time data about a variety of different aspects of the individual's performance—data that can be analyzed, trended, and cross-correlated with other Inescapable Data sources, both during and after the event. Use of such devices will become prevalent among the celebrity competitors, in turn creating consumer demand that will eventually drive their widespread adoption and mass-market availability.

The Swimmer's Edge

Historically, it has been hard for swimmers to understand the details of their motion through water. A coach is needed to walk alongside of a swimmer while trying to see a swimmer's movements both above and below the water line. Dr. Rod Havriluk, president of Swimming Technology Research (STR) explains that "until recently, the best option available to a swim coach was the use of underwater and surface video cameras. At least he could then make a *qualitative* analysis of motion. What has been missing is widespread use of *quantitative* data."

Havriluk's company manufactures a system (Aquanex) that measures the forces on both hands throughout the swimmer's entire stroke cycle via sensors that are worn between the middle and ring fingers. These sensors transmit continuous force data via wireless connection to a nearby computer that calculates peak force, average force, impulse, pull time, recovery time, stroke rate, and stroke length. The data is then stored in the computer for later review or analysis. A graphical display of a particular force curve can be compared to a hypothetical optimum curve, helping swimmers to truly understand what to improve.

"For the past 100 years, many swimmers have relied on the Olympic champ as the model for technique. But, even the fastest swimmers have ineffective elements in their style. That's why there needs to be an emphasis on quantitative data. An increased use of quantitative data will help make technique improvements over the next 100 years."

For swimmers, the lack of force data has been a critical missing piece of competitive information. There are many aspects of a swimmer's stroke that can be improved with a force analysis. "For example, even in breaststroke many swimmers do not exert the same amount of force with both arms. Once we show them the data graphically, they understand it and can focus on minimizing the difference. Similarly, in the crawl, we often see technique limitations in both the 'pull phase' and the 'push phase.' Many swimmers waste motion on the pull and then fail to take advantage of their strength on the push. Once they see their force data, they understand how to make the technique changes that will increase force, and therefore, make them swim faster."

"From the deck of a pool or even with an underwater camera, it is impossible to determine force variations. Once we have the data in digital form, we have great opportunities for additional analysis, such as tracking the progress of a single athlete or correlating performance with body measurements and training regimens." Connect the data points together and discover new and unforeseen relationships that can be used to improve performance—Inescapable Data in action.

Connected Swim Meets

Although the swim sensor might be economically out of reach for the typical local club's swim team, some interesting thematic variations are worth noting that also exploit data connectivity.

The organizers of a small but progressive swim team in southern New Hampshire historically posted its individual members' results in real time to their Web site. As they became more knowledgeable with their use of the Web, they started to also post race schedules, including lane assignments and start times. (As many parents of swim team members will commiserate, a swim meet is typically 4 to 6 hours of nothing but waiting for your child to swim two 30-second events.)

They then discovered that many parents at the swim meet would call home to ask someone with Web access to learn of the actual result times or lane assignments. To remove that informational speed bump, the organizers decided to bring a wireless hub to each event that provides free WiFi-based Internet access to anyone at the event. Poolside.

Many parents now bring their laptops to the swim meets to monitor individual race results, and to surf the Web while waiting between important events. (In the Inescapable Data world, a pervasive communicator [i.e., cell phone or PDA device] would be the choice of connectivity mavens.) Nonetheless, the data is there, and with a few innocent key-clicks, parents can drop the results into an Excel spreadsheet and compare a favorite swimmer's results against others in the same age group, against local weather conditions, time of day, what the swimmer had for breakfast, water temperature—whatever. Why? Because they can—armed with their connectivity toys.

Running with Inescapable Data

In 2004, Adidas introduced a consumer-priced computer sneaker called "1." Think of it as the first high-tech sneaker. It sports an embedded force sensor, computing chip, and micromotors. So, in addition to it being the latest in geek fashion, think of it also as a member of a new apparel category—wearable technology.

The sensor, located in the sneaker's heel, takes up to 20,000 force readings per second. It communicates these readings to the embedded computer chip that, in turn, directs tiny motors distributed throughout the shoe to make small shape changes. Adidas claims that this is the first footwear product that can change (and personalize) its characteristics in real time. As noted, manufacturers in general are increasingly using technology to differentiate products and capture market interest. So, if it is a customized running fit you're after, 1 is the shoe for you.

As useful as a shape-changing sneaker is in providing a customized fit, there is another dimension that perhaps Adidas has not embraced yet. Although 1 is not an Inescapable Data collection device, it could be, much like the swimming or car sensors. If the sneaker were Bluetooth-enabled and could dump its data to a computer in some XML format, runners could gain new performance insights just like swimmers can by using the finger-attached force sensors. Using embedded GPS sensors, runners could also correlate the force sensor data with GPS data to map performance during a race to course conditions (uphill, downhill, flat) and save that data for historical trend analysis.

Adidas could also sell special software that allows runners to self-coach and pattern-match running styles against famous athletes, or simply others of the same age and weight. Avid runners are typically concerned about overall health effects of running—both good and bad. Although the cardio workout is good, the pounding done to the knees and other body parts is not so good. As runners ourselves, we would value occasional insight into style, force impact, and speed. Plus, as natural competitors, we are also interested in comparative data. (How does my running style compare to other middle-aged, slightly overweight, and slightly bald men?) We like scorecards, and we use them as personal motivators.

The Inescapable Data Racquet

Sports equipment manufacturer Head makes a line of tennis racquets using some very special materials and a computer chip. The "Intelligence Series," such as the i.X16, uses a technology Head calls ChipSystem. Intelligence Series racquets are strung with Intellifiber, a proprietary fiber that has piezoelectric properties. Much like the flame-starter on your gas grill, when a tennis ball hits the fibers and imparts mechanical energy, the fibers turn that energy into electrical power. A chip embedded in the racquet handle is then energized by that power, which in turn reverses the power back to the strings. The effect is a tightening of the strings within 1 millisecond of impact which not only imparts more power back to the ball, but as importantly, reduces 20 percent of the vibration (vibration is wasted and uncomfortable energy).

With a little more work, the truly intelligent racquet could also measure strike angle, velocity, and impact in much the same way that the sneaker-based force sensor system, and could do so as inexpensively. In tennis (or any sport that uses a racquet or club), it is notoriously difficult to tune one's swing to the proper angle, speed, and general motion. Taking another step forward, suppose you as the tennis buff were to correlate the data from your "smart" tennis racquet with the data emanating from your equally smart tennis shoes. New relationships could emerge that provide a better total picture of your game that could be used by you and your favorite pro. What—too busy for tennis lessons? For sure, there's a creative sports marketer out there somewhere who will leverage the data of thousands and make available a piece of software you can run on your WiFi-enabled laptop that gives you expert advice tailored to your playing style. Or, accessing such aggregated data, some faraway Net surfer might uncover an inverse relationship between declining energy levels exhibited during a match and the use of a smoother stroke that could then be correlated to higher win record, simply by running a few Excel macros.

Teams and Fans: Real-Time Participation

Team sports steeped in tradition and history (baseball, football, and soccer, for example) will have a difficult time crossing the connectivity divide, at least for some aspects of the game. Fear that inserting more technology will alter the original balance or nature of a game is the major impediment. Change will come slowly and incrementally.

Nevertheless, those incremental changes are already evident. Major league baseball stadiums are rolling out WiFi services now in an effort to enhance the fan experience with—what else—more data. Team stats, pitching stats, individual hitting stats correlated with stats on other players—merely tap your wireless PDA screen or full-function cell phone and a river of baseball data starts flowing your way. The 2004 All Star Game in Houston offered WiFi access throughout the stadium. San Francisco's SBC Giants Stadium and now many others are offering free WiFi service throughout the entire park.

In addition to stats in real time, fans are also treated to streaming video— dugout views of the players, instant replays, and much more. Of course, full Internet access is also there for the connected cognoscenti in the crowd—some of whom may actually be trying to disguise the fact that they are playing hooky from work by keeping current with e-mails and instant messages. Forget your laptop. Why risk having an exuberant fan spill his beer onto its keyboard? You will need at least a wireless-enabled PDA to play in the big leagues here. So, although you might be picturing the awkwardness of lugging your 11-inch laptop into the stadium—fagetaboudit! Get the right gear.

SMS and Audiences

The wildly successful TV show *American Idol* catapulted the use of SMS (short messaging via cell phone) and created a new dimension in audience participation. No longer was the use of handheld voting appliances popularized by shows such as *Who Wants to Be a Millionaire?* limited to an in-studio audience. Now, literally millions of viewers can participate in

continues

SMS and Audiences (*Continued*)

some aspect of a TV show by merely thumbing a few cell phone keys. 13.5 million SMS messages were delivered during the *American Idol* season in 2004. More interesting is the fact that 40 percent of the people sending those messages say they had never sent an SMS message before. Something about the show and the messaging capability was compelling enough to mobilize millions of new SMS users.

SMS is also in evidence at major sporting events. Oakland Athletics fans can use their cell phone to SMS a response to messages posted to the in-stadium megaboard.[1] The megaboard then displays the results. Although it might currently be used for idle-time entertainment, SMS can also be used for more serious game-related activities. Was the runner safe? Key 112 for "Yes," 113 for "No." Second-guessing the officials is as much of the fan experience as any other facet of a game. The power of being able to survey tens of thousands of spectators within seconds is mind-numbing for fans and could be very intimidating to officials.

Although the business of sports is entertaining and satisfying fans, with WiFi-enabled stadiums and devices only a bit more capable than traditional cell phones, a club manager or coach can receive valuable "fan sentiment summaries" in real time. Should the pitcher be pulled now? Which relief pitcher would fans rather see take over? The expectations to have our voices heard will climb as a result of the use of pervasive devices directly connected to computers and networks that can instantly process millions of packets seemingly at once and display the results to a massive audience.

The entire fan experience from ticket sales onward is getting more connected. "Like movie theaters, we now have online ticket sales for our fans," describes Will Gartner, head of sports information technology at Boston College. "We're working hard to allow our fans to have easy access to our games and to enhance their game-day experience. In fact, we're exploring using a new technology that allows fans to check in ticketlessly simply by having their cell phone with them. Because we're rolling out WiFi and other technologies for the press areas, it seems sensible that cell phones and PDAs will be one more way for our

---

[1] http://mobilemomentum.msn.com/article.aspx?aid=18.

fans to both get game time data and communicate about the game as it is happening, as opposed to waiting to they get back to their rooms or homes."

So, in forthcoming modern stadiums, fans may not even need their wallets. They enter the park authenticated via their PDA (or cell device). They can similarly use the device to charge their food and beer purchases. While waiting in the beer line, they can be reviewing replays from different camera angles. When seated they can "blog" with distant Webbers about the game and possibly cast an SMS vote for the game's MVP—all this by using their pervasive PDA device, bringing them closer and more *connected* to the game.

Player Tracking and Analysis

"It's still about the game," says Gene DeFilippo, athletic director of Boston College, "but technology is being used aggressively throughout training and analysis, and our athletes continue to look for any advantage technology can offer." Technology is effectively being used as a surveillance and understanding tool largely focused on the competition but also inwardly on a team's own players: post-game analysis via video capture, Internet-based rumblings of other teams, and detailed player tracking on the field to name just a few.

"We've had video play analysis in football for many years," continues DeFilippo, "but the new digital and communication technology offers us significant benefits." In years prior, coaches would watch VHS tapes of various games (both their own team and an upcoming opposing team). Tediously, they would scan for plays and maybe go so far as to boil down a set of plays to another tape for detailed analysis by a particular coach or set of team members. "Today, all coaches have laptops and can watch plays at home or on the airplane or here in the office. The software and tools operate more like a database now. They can rapidly call up all the first-down plays, or all the second and shorts, or second and longs, and really focus on whatever aspect they care to study. The players, too, can analyze plays in the comfort of their own room, over and over again. The data and technology is no longer only available in some backroom video-monitoring area, and it can be shared rapidly."

DeFilippo next describes how the larger community of schools is tighter now as a result of communication efficiency. "The technology has brought the sports world into a tighter group across colleges throughout the country. The Internet online groups exchange information so fast, if something happens in North

Carolina everyone knows about it momentarily," cites DeFilippo. "If some player has an outstanding game, good or bad, everyone knows about it immediately. In the past, it was hard for news to even reach the local papers a day later. The connectivity gives us more information and faster than ever before." Players are essentially tracked by their fans via the Internet in perhaps a less-formal but nevertheless detailed fashion. A good pass, a rough hit, or a notice of a fatigued left ankle, all become part of the global information to be exploited for the next match.

Sports statisticians have long since tabulated useful metrics such as innings pitched, balls thrown, yards run, player played minutes, pass attempts, and so forth. Often, these values are used during a game to guess at player fatigue level or readiness for a particular play. Cairos (a German company) is making small radio-frequency (RF) transmitters that are embedded in the shin guards of soccer players. They then outfit the field with the necessary receivers and computer uplinks. This produces volumes of time and geographic data that then gets boiled down into individual player details. For instance, exactly how many minutes was player X on the field? How many minutes was he in the goal zone? How much total distance has he run this game and at what average speed? How many ball kicks did he achieve and at what velocity? Such data leads to a better total understanding of a player's abilities and vulnerabilities and ultimately better game strategy.

Bean Pot

The Boston Bean Pot is a traditional hockey competition among four prominent large Boston-area colleges. The 2004 Boston Bean Pot used a similar tracking technology developed by Trakus. Trakus puts a small RF patch into every hockey player's helmet; the patch transmits accurate geographic and velocity information continuously. This data could be critical for game-time decisions about player rotation and player positioning and even more so for post-game analysis and training. Furthermore, by having individual player tracking, television media providers and in-stadium media providers could provide a whole new level in presentation to the audience. Three-dimensional time-ordered spatial information of games will allow for fantastic post-play analysis and simulated replays. These new forms of detailed per-player real-time information gathering devices are starting to show up across various sports.

Technology is used throughout training but not always as elaborate as a wired-up swimmer or hockey player. For example, some universities use student ID cards (or similar technology) to accurately track workout schedules and uses of various training equipment (primarily in the weight-training rooms). A coach can act a bit more like a doctor and prescribe a set of exercises or activities and understand better how the athlete responds. Some systems use video capture, and the coach can then show the athlete before and after progress of a particular exercise. Data and data sharing allows both the coach and the athlete to have better knowledge and insight. Has athlete X been training less as the months past? Does his amount of training on a particular apparatus compare to others of a higher talent level? Is his arm motion as smooth as the top athlete ever recorded by this school? Such information is now available, and the savvy players and coaches will exploit all tools at their disposal.

Where does the use of technology cross the line in sports? Most agree that any use of nondrug technology prior to a game (as in training) is acceptable. Whether it is deeper analysis of the opposing team via video or body-wired inertia analysis during training exercises or massive statistical analysis and cross-correlations of data, if its pre-game no one seems to question its legality. As game time gets closer, the area gets grayer. If a coach keeps track of a player in-game time via a clipboard, no one worries. If he uses a passive shin-guard tracking device simply to save the labor of the clipboard, might anyone worry? What if now (as a result of the shin-guard tracking) he has a far deeper picture into a given athlete's energy consumption, is he unfairly using technology? What if his computer system is able to real-time correlate a given player's energy level to the 48-hour caloric intake as reported by his meal card against historically similar situations? Although books could be written strictly on technology and sports, the Inescapable Data interest is in the cross-use of data and connectivity. If there is data available, someone will figure out values of relationships and such information could be exploited even in real time, game time.

In pro football, the coach today has a wireless transmitter to the quarterback and is allowed to call in plays while the team is in a huddle. How was that allowed? The observation was that coaches were calling plays anyway by using either hand signals or voice or coded voice to carry the message. The wireless headsets simply streamlined the process and perhaps allowed for faster huddles and a more exciting game pace. So, we're okay with wireless voice technology and quarterback headsets up until the huddle breaks it seems, as if play time is still off-limits for nonplayer communication. Yet, in baseball, as the runner rounds second base, he is clearly taking commands from the third-base coach, wirelessly (albeit, hand signals and screaming). The point is this: Coaching indeed happens during plays already. How soon before baseball runners have wireless headsets much like quarterbacks, under the same guise of streamlining an already existing communication path? How soon before the message "run to third" is emphasized by real-time automatic computer analysis of all the players' field positions and ball location (via shin-guard data or stadium video analysis)?

In a pre-Inescapable Data world, the sports technology scene was more black and white. Whatever use of technology occurred off the field or pre-game was a team's own business and fell into the general category of "training." By in large, there wasn't much electronic data aside from the standard metrics such as innings pitched, times at bat, etc. Now, things start to get a bit blurry merely with passive-monitoring tools at game time (such as detailed time played in a game) and simple real-time access to databases and computers that can do rapid correlations. Add in some direct use of newer technology such as wireless headsets and opponent player tracking and the door is wedged open to the deeper opportunities.

Participatory Games

There are a variety of new sports entering the scene made possible by GPS and Internet connectivity. "The first real GPS sport is, without a doubt, geocaching," explain Adrian Kingsley-Hughes, a renowned GPS expert and notable author on GPS. "Geocaching is a high-tech GPS treasure hunt where the participants load waypoints that they download from the Internet onto their GPS receivers and go out in search of the treasure." The "treasure" is often a tin or plastic box that contains a log book and small trinkets. Kinglsey-Hughes states that geocaching is the fastest-growing participatory sport in America and likely the world. The Clinton administration's removal of the deliberate accuracy error in GPS paved the way for many new GPS applications, including these participatory games. *Participatory games...allowing the players a deeper connection and experience.*

New sports that are born in the wireless technology era will be less subject to a sense of fairness when it comes to technology exploitation. Perhaps American football will never have full heads-up displays inside of every helmet showing all player locations and best-move suggestions, but brand new sports certainly could. There is a huge swell of people entering the ages of 20 to 30 who were just a couple of years ago our video-game fanatics. This generation was born when cell phones were invented and grew up with their ubiquity (unlike the rest of us over 30). This same generation understands the value and power of GPS, can read XML fluently, and uses handheld devices to communicate by text more than voice. The point is this: Their tastes for competitive sports could be different from ours and of generations past and will have a deeper expectation for the use of technology.

Related to the new generation, the old paper- and mail-based fantasy sports game is now a raging Internet industry complete withits own "Fantasy Sports Trade Association" (www.fsta.org). According to FSTA, there are now more than 15 million adults playing fantasy sports game and the number is growing dramatically. The growth is largely attributed to the Internet, which brings real-time statistics tabulation and automation to an otherwise laborious and slow game.

What Is "Fantasy Sports"?

Fantasy sports started many decades ago as a way for fans to get closer involvement in their favorite professional sport such as football or baseball. Through the mail (snail mail), virtual leagues were formed and each participant managed his or her own personally created team. Although their team names would be made up, the players on a given team were selected from the inventory of real players on the professional teams. The fantasy players act as general managers and draft players or trade players and eventually build up a custom team of their own (but comprised of real players).

Each week when the real world would play a game, statistics about the individual players would be tabulated (such as yards passed, yards run, sacks, interceptions, and so forth). For each "event," some numeric point value would be associated (perhaps a touchdown is worth 20 fantasy points, or each 9-yard run is worth 1 fantasy point). After all the real games had been completed, painstakingly the Fantasy organizers would tally all the points of the artificial team conglomerations and decide winners and losers. Today, Fantasy sports are all Internet based, which allows for all the scoring to be real time and automatic. Furthermore, the process of creating teams and leagues and drafting players is all far more convenient given the ubiquity of Web access.

Every major television network hosts Fantasy sports Web sites, from football to basketball to baseball and others (racing, golf...the list goes on). Many players participate in several leagues at the same time. Although there is no charge to join certain leagues, most charge a per-team fee, then pay out part of the proceeds to the winning team of a season.

Many leagues are self-run by average citizens who pay a television network site a fee for hosting the league and using the network's Internet tools. However, after the network "home" has been established, each league sets its own rules (regarding point scoring, trading, etc.), builds its own financial base, and establishes its own pay-out values...all done via the Internet and by your ordinary Average Joe. In a way, Fantasy sports is a cross between The Matrix and Dungeons and Dragons—there are clear elements of the real world (and real data) coupled with a hefty dose of imaginary play, blurring reality and fantasy.

The average Fantasy player spends more than three hours a week managing his or her team and examining statistics. This is aside from the time spent watching televised games or doing individual research on players. The popularity is so strong and so synergistic with televised sports that many sport shows now will have an onscreen "crawl" detailing various player stats for the current game that are likely the key "scoring" metrics in the Fantasy games. Fantasy league Web sites are a community unto themselves, complete with blogs and trash-talk chat rooms, bringing together the various team managers in an ad-hoc *society*. Some sites are now sophisticated enough to send SMS text messages to player's cell phones announcing trades, new score additions, or changes in the team standings, as if the importance of such activities is as high as any business-class event. The users strive to be connected to their teams at all times, especially during game times when scoring is happening at its fastest.

The teams in Fantasy sports do not really exist. They are made from data of real-world people. They are managed in a fashion that mimics real-world transactions. They are fiercely competitive, and there is typically physical-world money at stake. Teams can even be bought and sold just like their real-world counterparts. Fantasy sports fills a void in the sports person's world—to be closer to the game, team, and players and to actually *participate*. Pervasive sports online data sources and wireless "everywhere" networks have enabled a sport within a sport.

Stepping back, is this any different from being a mutual fund manager?

Let's switch now to online gaming. The traditional video-console gaming industry is no doubt enormous, around $7 billion yearly in U.S. sales,[2] but is slowing and even declining in dollar growth. The gaming market is evolving and widening and now has to contend with significant PC-based games and cell phone/PDA games, which are notably suitable for connecting to an online community.

The online gaming industry was a little slow in gaining significance. Broadband to the home is seen as the critical enabler and finally by the end of 2003 more than 81 million households (worldwide) had broadband connections.[3] Demographically, the market for video games has been overwhelmingly male dominated (and typically under 30), but broadband has enabled a reach to a better-mixed audience. Services such as Yahoo!, MSN, and Pogo make online gaming available to a broader demographic, and some games now even have a 50-50 male-to-female following. Because the majority of online gaming is through a PC (versus a game console), the majority of the online crowd is older than the console crowd. But even consoles, such as Xbox, offer an online capability, but have had difficulty getting traction (partly due to the younger audience, partly due to the challenge of getting the console attached to the home network).

Predictions for growth are staggering. It is estimated that by 2005, the worldwide market for online gaming should be more than $5 billion and nearly $10 billion by 2009 (at which time there is expected to be 228 million broadband users worldwide). As interestingly, the "mobile" online gaming market (cell, PDA) is expected to reach nearly $2 billion by 2009 as well.[4] The key to the growth is *connectivity*. Until recently, video games were a solitary entertainment form—more captivating and engaging than perhaps TV, but essentially an easy time-fill regardless of weather or time of day. Online gaming adds two new important dimensions: socialization and a more dynamic environment.

Early online games were essentially the same as their offline counterparts but enhanced by allowing other players (anywhere in the world) to be part of the scene and action. This not only allows the junior high kid a chance to play with

---

[2] http://www.npd.com/press/releases/press 040722.htm.

[3] http://www.forbes.com/prnewswire/feeds/prnewswire/2004/08/03/
prnewswire200408030702PR NEWS B WES LA LATU034.html.

[4] http://www.clickz.com/stats/big picture/applications/article.php/3403931.

his school friends without ever picking up a phone or messing up each other's houses, but also allows him to play with (or against) anyone else in the world regardless of time of day. This has led to the creation of what's known as massively multiplayer online role playing games, MMORPGS, where thousands of players are simultaneously in some grand adventure. Less of a peer-to-peer configuration and more of a central server one, service providers run the simulations in more powerful computers that can even keep players "in the game" when they are logged off. Similar to the old role-playing game Dungeons and Dragons, MMORPGS sessions can last many days and even weeks. Notably, the sophistication of a "mission" is far higher than a simple "shoot 'em up" console game and can draw on an aging gamer population.

As games move more "into the network," the power of the games increases in both terms of dynamic scenery and complexity of the software. No longer is there just a single machine's worth of horsepower involved. There are networks of higher-end servers and thousands of endpoints, all of which can add energy to the environment. Essentially, federated computing. The newest trend, that of enabling mobile/cellular devices to the mix, will bring even more penetration to the market and perhaps further change the gaming mode. Games may start to be more like Fantasy Football, wherein users are continually "checking in" (all day long) and tweaking their characters and teams and in general monitoring the operation...from anywhere and everywhere they go.

Gaming is changing. It is no longer strictly for 8- to 15-year-old boys. It is no longer something that adults and managers can ignore or categorize as a momentary diversion for a young age set. That age set has aged (with replacements coming in as well) and has now evolved to a far more connected and societal life ...entering our work force in great numbers. They are living a life daily that is remote, high-excitement, sensory rich, and collaborative. Drop them in an undifferentiated office cube with a pile of reports to read and they'll fail. The power and importance of gaming (and in particular online gaming) among the young is not so much in its own contribution to GNP but rather what implications it has for us trying to manage this future worker.

TV: Yielding to User-Designed Viewing

Paul LaCamera, general manager of WCVB in the Boston area, has some keen observations on the broadcast industry in general and in particular the news industry. "Consumers are demanding more immediacy from news, particularly among the younger viewers that seem to be designing their own personal delivery systems. The emerging generation is not looking for news at 6 P.M. and 11 P.M., but rather expects news to available at all times and from a wide variety of sources, which they choose and in a format they've created."

LaCamera uses the term *fractionalized* when discussing how the audience has changed over the years. Essentially, the total viewership is about the same but no longer can the industry count on having the audience all present at either 6 P.M. or 11 P.M. The standard broadcast hours have a much smaller audience than in years past, yet the size of the overall news-needing audience and their appetite for news has grown. Like we have seen in many other businesses we have studied so far, this in turn places a need to have tighter distribution to a more targeted customer. WCVB addresses this through a relationship with a local 24-hour cable news station, NECN (which they part-own). This provides another mechanism for distribution of their material and on a more continuously available format. WCVB, like other stations, also has a relationship with various cable companies and offers many of their stories as video-on-demand elements. TV station Web sites are yet another format for distribution of the stories and actual news video (enabled by pervasive in-home broadband).

"TV stations are still a good business. Far higher returns than a typical business. But we do have to work harder to deal with smaller audiences for any single distribution venue. The world has shifted to a more on-demand and customized mentality, even for news," describes LaCamera. "As of the late 1980s, 80% of the people that watched prime-time TV were watching one of the three main broadcast networks. Today, it's under 50%, with the other 50% watching cable. Cable, with its volume of channel selection, offers viewers a wide range of distractions."

Tivo and Tivo-like devices have added to the changing landscape. Tivo essentially enables users to watch any show any time they desire because it transparently records shows locally. (You could, for example, watch the 6 P.M. newscast at 6:10 P.M. if you like, and even "pause" it while on a phone call.) Cable companies are scurrying to offer Tivo-like services through their new digital set-top boxes. (Who needs yet another box at home? This is much the same way that some telephone companies have offered answering services to reduce the clutter of the old in-home answering machines.) With Tivo-like capabilities and the broadness of cable (e.g., news channels, sports channels, science channels, etc.), "connected" viewers are truly able to design their own viewing experience. For advertisers, this trend toward more narrowcasting can be a good thing.

For years, the broadcast industry has struggled with a changing demographic of the nightly viewer. As cable viewership increased and viewers have more avenues for news watching (including Web and more news hours during the day), the nightly audience faded. "Today, the average age of someone watching any of the national nightly news shows is *well* into the 50s," exclaims LaCamera. "By contrast, if you want to reach that almost-impossible young male audience, you'll want to have placement with NESN (sports network). Whether it is broadcast or cable or Internet, the trend is clear: Audiences are getting fractionalized into more narrow buckets, which is probably good for advertisers that desire better targeting and somewhat more challenging for those of us that need to fill more pipes and delivery mechanisms."

Although tight connectivity between computer, cable, and the Internet has been envisioned for quite some time, no solution to date has been well received. But there are some technologies blending as well as a different set of desires from the viewership. In the Boston area, 82 percent of the homes have cable TV, and quite likely a large percent of those are also receiving their Internet from that cable company. In the new world, while watching a live broadcast such as the news (or perhaps more specifically, The Top National Political stories, or The Top Local High School Sports stories, or The Top International Pet stories), viewers can press Pause on their clicker in order to answer the phone, adjust the stove, or assist with homework. Should a well-targeted advertisement appear (say, a campaign-contribution solicitation, or a new exercise device), "connected" viewers could press Play on their clicker to momentarily suspend the original program, view the advertisement, and then resume their live program.

The acceptance of Tivo-like technology (as well as a general love for interfacing to *only* a clicker while in the Lazy Boy) will enable narrowcasting to benefit both the viewers and the advertisers alike in the connected world. When you're designing your own daily TV viewing experiences, including even the live news shows, you know you've crossed the connectivity divide. Those who don't will only be able to watch that which is broadcast over the air waves, which will effectively be its own narrowcast to the single audience demographic that remains unconnected.

Video Business, Connected Style

The video rental industry has survived despite numerous historical predictions of its demise. The typical cause (cited years ago) was video on demand. Many decades long after promised, we might finally be in an age where the video rental industry has to finally succumb to both the Internet and cable companies (and other carriers).

Blockbuster has been reporting declining video rental sales quarter after quarter throughout 2004 and before. (Revenue has been somewhat balanced out throughout the industry by a dramatic increase in video "sales"—it is nearly as cheap to buy a movie as it is to rent once with a two-day late fee.) Rental customers are angered by late fees and the hassles related to returning videos. A number of alternatives have entered the scene. For one, video on demand is now real, and most cable subscribers can watch a wide selection of movies any time they want (including pausing and rewatching) and for a lower rental fee than a video store. Second, services such as Netflix offer mail-based rentals with no late fees and value priced. (They claim that typically the movies arrive the next day.... The post office has evidently become faster with all of us sending e-mails instead of post.) Last, online computer downloads are getting some steam from companies such as www.movielink.com or www.internetmovies.com. Tivo is even rumored to be in discussions with some DVD mail-rental firms to allow streaming and buffering of movies electronically.

Video-Quality Challenges

We all welcomed DVDs when they entered our lives, partly because of the smaller form factor but mostly because of the vastly improved picture quality (and no degradation from usage, aside from those nasty scratches). The quality of a DVD is good enough to hold up to home-theater projection (using theater-like computer projectors that can illuminate an image to six feet wide or more).

Sadly, the image quality of digital television is closer to VHS or worse. In an effort to cram thousands of streams onto a limited pipe, bit rate has to be compromised (and thus quality). The quality issue is different than with VHS, however. The problem is what is known as macro blocks. Video images are compressed in a "lossy" manner, meaning some data is

continues

Video-Quality Challenges *(Continued)*

lost. An image is divided into thousands of squares, and each square gets compressed. In an effort to better use the limited pipe, successive scenes are often sent as "deltas" from a base image. If the scene does not change much, the bandwidth can be used to sharpen the picture. This can be annoying to watch, and the macro blocks are often visible (as well as the subsequent sharpening that occurs). This is even the case with HD (high definition). Downloaded movies (from movielink for example) suffer from the same problem because they too have to deal with limited-capacity pipes today. Fortunately, time has shown us that data rates go up and prices come down in the communications industry. In the meantime, video quality is a barrier to wider acceptance of Internet-style downloads.

Let's not overlook the wireless industry (cellular). The wireless players are huge industry players and always looking for a way to increase their monthly fee. Might we see a day soon where the speed of wireless would be sufficient for video? In 2003, in South Korea, SK (the area's leading mobile operator) launched a video download service using its new 3G network. (3G is the third generation of mobile technology and many times faster than predecessors.) Customers were able to download movies to their cell phone or similar devices. The service was so well received it was overloaded in no time.[5] SK is more recently using some satellite technology with special satellite-enabled distribution mechanism.

The point is this: The video rental and nontheater movie business is dramatically changing and seems to be moving to a fully connected (and perhaps wireless) and real-time experience. Once again, we desire to be in control of our entertainment experience and want it on demand. And, we are starting to expect movies and videos to be available no matter where we are and no matter what device we might be in front of at the time—computer, TV, cell phone. Inescapable Data!

---

[5] http://www.economist.com/business/displayStory.cfm?story id=3150731.

Summary

For the sports participant, gaining a competitive edge always had a history of data attached, long before data could be acquired electronically. The new world is hurling sports-related data at us for both personal-skills growth and for a better participant experience. Advances in what used to be futuristic virtual display technology are now available to the average consumer. Data-emitting devices are appearing in our sports gear, which we will exploit for personal-skills growth. Similar devices are appearing on our sports heroes for our benefit (a richer audience experience) and for their benefit (better coaching). We are interfacing with our own personal sports and public sports using the tools we use in our daily and business lives: wireless communicators, the Internet, GPS, and, of course, our computers. Connectedness has created a new breed of participatory and online games that are retraining our expected level of interaction of entertainment with each other. Even our TV- and video-viewing desires are now moving toward viewer controlled, real time, and interactive. In the connected world, our sports and entertainment diversions are being driven more directly by us and tying us closer to the event.

CHAPTER TEN

Connecting to Retail

Merchandisers are in the dark ages when it comes to having any sort of basic data about the people making purchases in their stores. This type of data is essential for growth in the hotly competitive retail world.
—*Robert Watson, owner, Watson-Janssens Marketing Agency*

Introduction

When the needs of retail businesses and consumers are aligned, both can win. Retailers want our loyalty. They want us to buy from their stores more efficiently and in ways that are less costly to them. Deeper knowledge of what we buy and how we buy it will provide them with much needed insight.

Using Inescapable Data technologies, shrinkage can be more tightly controlled resulting in lower costs for consumers and higher value for stockholders. Digital video-surveillance cameras can watch us both as shoppers (to better understand our shopping patterns) and as store employees, tying video images to corporate goals. Volumes of new data on each of us as consumers can now be collected by Inescapable Data collection techniques—both at the checkout isle and while in the store or online. If it can be measured, retailers will measure it, and the data will be exploited. Inescapable Data collection devices will feed this new data to back-end systems, enabling retailers to achieve unprecedented efficiencies—focusing on products that will actually sell, streamlining the process aspects, and directly targeting marketing efforts to appropriate buyers.

To realize these efficiencies, retailers must first entice us into their newly retooled stores, and then keep us as loyal customers after the sale. To do so, they will have to offer greater levels of personalization, customization, and value. If we demand more personalization and efficiency, Inescapable Data technologies will enable that kind of shopping experience, and we will find savvy retail businesses that can fulfill our desires.

However, at the same time, we are already seeing evidence that many of us may become wary, if not downright fearful, of a concurrent loss of personal privacy. When we enter a store equipped with video-surveillance, GPS, and RFID technologies, our movements and our individual product selections can be tracked in real time. The in-store system will be watching. Will we as consumers thrive in this new shopping environment and use it to our advantage, or see it as an unwelcome intrusion into our personal lives and privacy that reminds us more of Orwell's Big Brother?

RFID and the Grand Retail Vision

Chapter 8, "Real-Time Manufacturing," explored how RFID tags are being used throughout the manufacturing, logistics, and warehousing processes (the "supply chain") to greatly reduce costs and increase efficiency. As the price and size of RFID tags come down, they will start to appear on actual consumer goods, translating into cost savings and efficiencies for retailers as well. But there's another dimension—the consumer dimension—where having products RFID-tagged can also add value if we as consumers wish to exploit the technology.

For retailers, the values include (but are not limited to) the following:

+ Decreased shrinkage at the retail level
+ Increased retail sales (fewer shelf stock outages)

For consumers, the values include the following:

+ Improved in-store shopping experience via RFID-enabled PDAs
+ Increased checkout speeds (nearly instantaneous)
+ Strengthened (or heightened) value in the home for locating and tracking products

Large retailers such as the Gap and Benneton have already done regionalized in-store field trials, embedding RFID tags into many lines of clothes and installing shelf-based RFID readers. An immediate return on investment can be realized simply by reducing the number of shelf out-of-stock situations (rapidly replacing items as soon as the shelf location for a given style and size is near empty). As importantly, RFID tags provide the retailer a tighter tracking mechanism against theft; many apparel retailers claim they loose between 10 percent and 25% of their inventory in the overall supply chain due to shrinkage.

The current cost of RFID tags varies, but falls generally in the range of 20 to 30 cents per tag (retailer cost). For this reason, they may only appear on the more high-valued retail items costing more than $10 for the next few years. As demand increases, the cost is expected to drop to 5 cents per tag, making them more cost-effective to deploy on many more less-costly items. Gillette alone ordered more than 500 million tags in 2004, and Benetton ordered 80 million.[1] Do not think tags are heading your way yet? Indeed, we will see RFID-tagged products in some of the largest retail outlets in the very near future. Wal-Mart has mandated RFID product tagging wherever practical by mid 2005.

The consumer shopping experience is expected to improve notably as a result of RFID-tagged merchandise. Checkouts can be nearly instantaneous because RFID readers can scan all tagged items in a shopping basket or cart in seconds without any items needing to physically removed and handled. Similarly, the process of returning products is expected to be superior because the authenticity of the product and purchase can be immediately verified.

Some stores are conceiving and experimenting with both customer-owned and store-owned PDAs equipped with built-in RFID readers that could be "wanded" near an item to determine its price, whether it is part of a special in-store promotion, and whether it is connected to past or present tie-ins with other in-store promotions. Borrowing a trick from the online retailers such as Amazon, they can advertise directly to you; perhaps that blouse you picked out has a special promotional value given who you are and what else you're buying or not buying at the moment. As a consumer, you will be given the option (for

---

[1] http://www.computerworld.com/managementtopics/ebusiness/story/0,10801,79286,00.html.

privacy concerns) to share more, less, or none at all of your shopping experience with your retailer, but the more you are willing to share, the more they will reward you with conveniences and price.

Chapter 5, "Pervading the Home," discussed the values of having products with RFID tags in your house. Using them in conjunction with an appliance equipped with an RFID reader, you can determine the contents of your refrigerator or washing machine from any Internet device that can access your home network. This will allow for better home inventory tracking, better meal planning, and better outfit planning. From within a retail store, your PDA or cell phone will be able to query your home to find out whether you are out of milk and the actual waist size of that last pair of jeans you bought and whether you really have the right color of shoes for that skirt.

Boston Marathon

The Boston Marathon has been using RFID tags on sneakers for many years.[2] As runners pass various station points en route to the finish line, their status and time is immediately updated on a Web site for anyone to view. This nearly eliminates cheating—a notorious problem that occurs when runners mysteriously appear on the route close to the finish and cross the line barely breaking a sweat. For the legitimate runners who are forced to start literally minutes behind the starting line because of the size of the pack, the RFID tag trips a sensor at the starting gate that records their actual start time. As a result, runners get far more accurate "personal" times for the race.

As the proliferation of RFID on retail products occurs, people and businesses will find creative ways to exploit the data in ways that were previously unanticipated. Tracking runners during a race certainly is one way. As for a more creative use, perhaps your waste management company will charge you a variable weekly fee based on refunding the number of recyclable containers it can detect in the garbage you take out to the curb. Perhaps airport and building security systems will automatically scan for dangerous or undesired articles

---

[2] http://www.ti.com/tiris/docs/solutions/sports.shtml.

entering their premises. Possibly, you will be able to find your golf ball easier in the rough. Or maybe your cell phone will be able to alert you if you open the incorrect prescription drug medication in the dark.

RFID tagging of consumer products is occurring now and will become more pervasive over a short number of years. Tracking these objects from their creation through to your last use can provide benefits to retailers and consenting consumers, both in store and at home and beyond. There are indeed some concerns about privacy and who will access and exploit this new data source. Will passers-by on the street be able to "wand" me with their cell phone as they pass and know the details of my attire? Then again, they are using their eyes today anyway, and furthermore could snap a cell-phone picture discretely. We, as consumers, may at first elect to have our tags "neutralized" upon purchase. Quite likely, however, over time, we will relax our worries much like we now think nothing of using a bank card in the supermarket, which clearly puts our name on that huge list of purchases.

Mining Retail E-Commerce

Retail has notably changed since the advent of the Web. No longer must we visit brick-and-mortar locations to purchase goods. Far from catalog shopping, e-commerce offers us many benefits, including faster comparison shopping, greater price efficiency, and 24/7 shopping (truly a "shop 'til ya drop" experience).

The U.S. retail industry is a $3.6 trillion industry. The industry currently spends 2.1 percent of its income per year on technology (up from 1.8 percent in 2001) according to IBM Global Services 2003 survey of 78 chief information officers. That is a 15 percent increase in technology spending, much of which is targeted at creating a more effective e-commerce-channel. Currently, e-commerce accounts for more than $60 billion per year, but that is a paltry 1.7 percent of the total retail expenditures. Experts expect this to grow to 12 percent, nearly $430 billion dollars, by 2010.[3] This represents significant growth in consumer use as well as a matching back-end infrastructure build-out.

---

[3] http://www.clickz.com/stats/markets/retailing/article.php/3401181.

E-commerce shifts the balance of power from the retailer to the consumer (although the retailer also experiences many gains). Web-based shopping gives consumers nearly an endless set of tools for

+ Price comparison of competing retailers
+ Competition between shipping methods and cost
+ Formal and informal product comparisons

In general, e-commerce gives us the time and the freedom to be better-informed shoppers. It is an environment where we vote with our dollars. E-commerce is good for retailers, too. The information they can glean from a Web-based shopping experience is all electronic, and gathering this data does not require video cameras, RFID tags in stores, etc. For example, when a shopper is referred to a Web site via a search engine, the site gets what is called a "referrer" header in the HTTP transaction. This enables the retailer to better track how its customers got to its site and where they are coming from.

After the shopper is on a Web site, the retailer can track not only how much time a shopper spends on any given Web page, but also how often the shopper puts things into and takes thing out of an electronic shopping cart, and even how often the shopper completely abandons a cart (easy to do on the Web, whereas it is more intimidating at a brick-and-mortar store). Conversion rates are still appropriately measured (that is, how often a basket of items turns into a real purchase), along with other metrics as well, yielding data that goes far beyond what can be gathered in-store—data that helps retailers better understand the effects of their marketing campaigns. Many sites solicit feedback and ask questions that help them get closer to the consumer, and consumers are more willing to provide information when it is just a matter of clicking a check box or selecting a pull-down rating level. Because there is no physical interaction, all the interaction is electronic, and thus quite naturally in a form to be scrutinized and analyzed and cross-correlated with other data streams.

Are retailers with a presence in shopping malls suffering as a result of the rise of e-commerce? Not now, at least according to parking and foot-traffic measurements. Shopping malls are becoming more and more a social and entertainment experience. Perhaps the new-found freedom of fewer in-office work hours and increased personal efficiencies made possible by cell based e-mail and messaging have given people both the time and the need for casual physical shopping experiences. Many consumers now spend time in malls "taking in" the new fashions and getting an understanding of prices and trends and simply just meandering about. A percentage of these consumers, who relish the convenience and shop-on-your-terms experience of e-commerce, will then choose to purchase online at a later time.

Over time, however, the Web's vast array of information and efficiencies may not eliminate storefronts, but perhaps will reduce their numbers. Shopping malls (and the stores themselves) might get physically much larger, but quite possibly fewer and further apart, which may make them even more of a "destination" (much like a theme park). Or, perhaps the larger retail stores of the future will survive with less square footage and personnel, given that the educated consumers has first learned most of what they need to know ahead of time. In either case, the physical shopping experience for many products appears to be here for a while—albeit augmented with the virtual one. The Web adds convenience and expediency, but is not a total replacement. (We have to do something with all the time Inescapable Data technology saves us, and strolling the aisles is among those sustaining distractions.)

Charting the Course of Customers

Retail stores have used video-surveillance (tape-based) technology for many years as both a theft-deterrence tool and as an employee-monitoring tool. We strongly believe that usage of digitized video surveillance will soar to unprecedented levels because of a coming proliferation of low-cost charge coupled display (CCD) cells (the vision part of a digital camera) equipped with wireless IP technology. Although we recognize the value of this Inescapable Data technology as a crime-fighting tool, we also believe it will be exploited by retailers for another as yet little-known use: customer tracking.

For decades, merchandisers have desired a tool to better analyze customer buying habits. RFID helps in this effort, but in the end all that is truly known is what items are actually purchased (and perhaps at what time of the day and perhaps with what other purchases). What a merchandiser still does not know includes the following:

- Was the person male or female? Young or old? African American, Caucasian, or Hispanic?
- Was the person alone or with children?

- How long did the person pause in front of a particular display?
- What paths through the store did the person take, and how many places did he or she stop and for what time periods?

"We are so convinced of the value of such data that we looked into manufacturing some sort of small handheld device that we'd give to people as they entered our store," explains Robert Watson, owner of Watson-Janssens Marketing Agency, and former owner of the Black Lion retail chain. "Now, obviously, no consumer is going to want to carry something that is essentially watching them, so we abandoned that approach. Nevertheless, merchandisers are in the dark ages when it comes to having any sort of basic data about the people making purchases in their stores. This type of data is essential for growth in the hotly competitive retail world."

Using multiple, low-cost digital video-surveillance cameras that can be deployed easily (i.e., without wires), a retailer can now achieve 100 percent floor coverage and make visual fingerprints of individual shoppers or "shopping groups" as they enter a store. For example, Cognex, a major supplier of intelligent image-processing systems, offers a system that can accurately identify the pertinent details of individuals as they pass through a doorway. Even from above and at fairly modest resolution, the system can identify predominant and secondary clothing colors, approximate body shape and height, and the number of people in a shopping group—enough to fingerprint shoppers and then *track* them as they pass from camera view to camera view.

At the checkout, a camera aimed at face level can also distinguish major race and sex. Cameras will be in stores in any event, primarily for theft or security reasons. Adding a few additional units for shopper tracking (made possible by low cost, wireless enablement, and computer processing advances) gives store owners a completely new source of customer data. Retail stores are hungry for as much information about their shoppers as they can possibly acquire. Jan Davis, CEO of ShopperTrak, says, "More and more leading retailers are adopting conversion rate[4] as one of their most powerful measures of success. They use the trend and level of conversion to assess how successful they are at driving customers to stores through advertising, meeting their customers' needs

---

[4] The number of potential shoppers divided by the number of transactions a store sees over a given period.

for service through adequate staffing, and offering their customers appropriate merchandise in attractive surroundings. A one-point change in conversion drives double-digit improvements in revenue."

Traffic data is an important measure for the sales potential of a store (conversion opportunity). For the most part, this data has been unavailable, and so retailers used far less useful data, such as sales figures, for many operational decisions. For example, staffing decisions would be mostly based on historical sales figures for given times of the day (or days of the week), data that does not correctly account for unserviced customers. The impact of out-of-stock situations, which occur frequently for a hotly sought-after sale or new-release item, cannot be understood by just a lack of sales; traffic analysis around the location could at least offer some insight into the missed opportunity. Fundamentally, having traffic data changes how stores are managed. Instead of supplying a particular retail outlet with X units of an item based on past sales, the quantity could be based on more knowledge about the number of shoppers for a certain category of product. Similarly, stores, particular in-mall stores, rely heavily on window displays to attract shoppers into the store; however, they currently have no metric regarding window observers compared to how many then enter the store. A given "promotion" of some item can now measure the amount of attention the item received in terms of shoppers observing. With simply low sales figures, it would be difficult to know whether the low sales resulted from a lack of promotion, poor in-store placement, or price. Digital video enables retailers to passively acquire a set of behavioral shopping details that would have been impractical to gather otherwise.

ShopperTrak's Orbit

A Chicago company, ShopperTrak, makes a product that is very close to fulfilling the full video vision. The Orbit is a small four-inch by four-inch device that includes a camera and some computer processing technology. The device is located in ceilings and other locations throughout the store or mall. The system's primary application is counting the number of customers as they enter and leave a store or mall. It unobtrusively tracks customer movements and converts that data into counts. The video images are not stored, and thus individual privacy is protected. It is an improvement upon many other "customer-counting" devices in that it can better

continues

ShopperTrak's Orbit *(Continued)*

distinguish shoppers even in highly dense traffic such as in grand open-
ings and in difficult entrances or areas of a store or mall. It counts people
as they enter, as they exit, or as they pass by the store. It can also count
people as they move throughout the store and measure intra-store traffic.

This data is then used by store, district, and corporate managers to understand traffic patterns, manage staffing levels, and measure the impact of
advertising and promotion as well as the attractiveness of the store layout
and merchandising. Traffic data can help better gauge how to staff the
store. (Using just historical sales data alone does not account for how
many people are left unserviced and unhappy.) If the owner has several
stores, he or she can better understand how different layouts and merchandising affect sales of particular products. This system is currently
used in many retail stores and malls already, with nearly 40,000 cameras
installed throughout the world, including in more than 100 Louis
Vuitton[5] locations in North America. Knowing the conversion rate, these
owners have a better understanding of the performance of stores. In retail,
owners are constantly trying to raise their conversion rate.

According to Jan Davis, CEO of ShopperTrak, sales of their device have
been brisk—growing at double-digit rates for more than 8 years with
more than 40,000 installed by the end of 2004. Tracking shoppers as they
shop is a reality.

There is an old urban legend about how one large retail company, through
extensive data mining (detailed mathematical relationship analysis of their sales
databases), discovered that there was a correlation between the sale of beer and
diapers in the early evening hours. It has been conjectured that this was due to
the fact that husbands were stopping by the corner store on their way home
from work (instead of the local bar) and buying diapers for the baby and beer
for themselves. Whether this particular urban legend is true, such analysis is at
the heart of data mining, the results of which can give retailers an edge over
their competitors. Remember that for the power and size of mass retailers such

[5] http://www.shoppertrak.com/news article53.html.

as Wal-Mart, even a small change in the merchandising of one item on one day can lead to millions of dollars in new revenue the next day. Retailers are now driven by numbers and live in an age of grand analysis.

Suppose the retail relationship of diapers to six packs, for example, is proven through statistical analysis. How does a store now exploit this fact through better merchandising? There are two opposing choices. One choice is to place the diapers conveniently near the beer (next to or opposite the cooler, we assume). The other is to separate the two as far as possible. The first approach supposes that the shopper is in a hurry and has no other purchase desires and, in fact, may choose that store because it offers a faster shopping experience, assuming others are as convenient to stop at on the way home. The second approach attempts to capture and capitalize on the impulsive nature of a shopper who enjoys seeing other merchandise between the two sought-after objects and might choose to spend more time (and money) in the store, en route from the diaper rack to the cooler. (This is the more like the classic supermarket separation of the milk isle from the bread isle.) However, neither strategy could be known to be better than the other without more data. To know exactly which strategy has the best chance of boosting sales, the store owner needs to know the duration of shopping visits and the paths taken through the store. Was the shopper deliberate and focused, or did the new snack display en route cause a path pause? How many beer and diapers customers were in fact male?

Armed with new sources of digital video data, the information is finally becoming available.

Watching Store Operations

Monitoring retail store employees using video-surveillance techniques is already a well-established practice. These black-and-white closed-circuit television (CCTV) systems are typically limited to recording what goes on in a few camera views. Only after an actual crime has been committed, or in cases where a rise in store shrinkage would those tapes ever be analyzed. Why? Watching an in-store videotape for hours on end would otherwise be a complete waste of time.

Today, using videotape, video searching is done by eyeballs scanning time codes and choosing camera locations (e.g., show me yesterday afternoon's tape of the cash register). The current operation mode of "let's just capture it and hope the camera presence alone is the deterrent" no longer suffices. Retail store owners are now demanding better service from their employees and zero loss due to shrinkage. From the point of view of the retailer, far more value can be gained using wireless, digitized video beyond simply being a theft deterrent.

Imagine a "Google for video" capability. For example, a store owner could query the system to find only video clips that have "moving people with hats on." Or "parents with children in tow." The system would then return only those clips for viewing in a matter of minutes. Sophisticated new software, using algorithms for image processing, will come from both commercial vendors and the open-source community to help simplify and automate much of the monitoring operations and to derive new automated metrics (e.g., how often Clerk Jane spends assisting shoppers in a given isle). To start, the data must be captured and stored. Much like having 10 years of x-ray data amassed, at any time in the future re-analysis can take place on this accumulated gold mine. Perhaps a new software technique for matching people on repeat visits will become available and reveal some additional tidbit of shopping behavior that the retailer can exploit.

Monitoring could also be done more effectively by service bureaus monitoring many remote stores from centralized locations, resulting in the birth of a new industry: retail video management as an outsourced business, much like payroll is outsourced. Today, many homes and businesses outsource their security to some remote monitoring firm. Monitoring firms can now tap new retail markets where theft and security issues are just as prevalent. This is somewhat akin to the remote monitoring of intensive-care units (ICUs) now being used by some hospitals—having an expert on staff at all times for all locations but cost-leveraged through volume.

Metro's Future Store: A Look at Where It All Comes Together

The Metro Group is the world's fourth-largest retail and trading group in the world, with more than 2,300 store locations in 28 countries (mainly in Europe) and approximately 240,000 employees. Like Wal-Mart, Metro has the ability to profoundly influence the entire retail landscape.

Metro's Future Store initiative (www.future-store.org) is a cooperative project supported by many computing vendors, including IBM, Intel, and

SAP. As part of the project, technologies and systems are invented, tested, debugged, and then showcased to the world of retailing.

Part of the vision of Future Store is to combine total product and inventory tracking with as much data as the individual consumer is willing to share with Metro, in the belief that the more Metro's system knows about you the shopper, the better—for both the shopper and for Metro.

We will walk through a Future Store supermarket from entrance to exit to understand what this means. Although some of this is hypothetical, all the technology elements are real and much of it is already in use in some Metro experimental stores in Europe.

As you enter the store, you grab a shopping carriage as you normally would. However, this is no ordinary shopping cart. In fact, the magic cart is a focal point for a number of technology vectors, including WiFi, GPS, and RFID—all of which are built in.

After you identify yourself using a personal identification card, you can build your shopping list and load it into a PDA-like device attached to the handle. The PDA includes a flat-panel display—far larger than the normal PDA screen but not overly obtrusive—that is attached near the handle so that you can interact with it as needed.

Because the cart is WiFi connected to both the store's internal computing system and the Internet, you can build your shopping list using data saved from your last shopping trips. For example, the system tracks what you commonly buy for weekly grocery items and will include them on the list automatically. You can then make additions and deletions. To maintain your loyalty, the shopping cart will offer you special discounts on items that it knows you have purchased in the past, or as rewards for being a frequent shopper.

If your refrigerator is RFID enabled, using the cart's WiFi connection to the Internet, you can also check in with your refrigerator to see what you need. If other parts of your living space are RFID enabled, you can check them, too. In addition, Metro plans to make a service available that enables you to send and store your own personal "product desire" messages to your account at the store. Perhaps earlier in the week, your daughter noticed that she was about to run out of toothpaste. Using her PDA, she just queues a message to buy more the next time you shop. When you are at the store, these can be aggregated with other shopping list sources. It is conceivable that the store's internal system could actually help you plan out menus as well, perhaps showing a week's calendar and assignments of various key items to the days (steak on Tuesday with broccoli, fresh fish tonight with asparagus, etc.).

Now armed with your shopping list, the magic cart operates somewhat like a mini-GPS system. The display gives you a top-down map of the store aisles while it pinpoints your current location. If you want, it will map out a route for you and highlight areas you need to specifically visit. As you pass the cart by certain shelves, targeted advertisements for nearby products such as toilet tissue—on sale this week only—light up the PDA screen. Specials on connected products—bacon with eggs, ham with cheese, corned beef with cabbage—are offered especially to you, the valued customer.

The store shelves are "smart shelves," meaning that they know exactly what products are on them and in what quantity. Before an item runs out on the shelf, the system has alerted the storage room and called for replenishing. The storage room is tightly tied system-wise to the supply chain and in-store inventory systems. As pallets are unloaded from a shipping truck, the contents of the entire pallet are instantly known (and accurately, without human inspection) and registered in the inventory system. When a shelf calls for a new carton of chicken soup, for example, as the carton is passed through the doors of the back room and onto the store floor, the inventory system is updated and marked as "in store." Once placed on the shelf, the smart shelf updates the inventory as "on shelf." The product can be completely tracked by RFID technology—from manufacturer, to store shelf, into a shopping cart, and finally to home.

By virtue of RFID-tagged products, the shopping cart knows exactly what is in it and can show you your local inventory neatly on the screen at all times—perhaps sorted by product type, or alphabetically if you want. As the shopping cart passes through a special gate at checkout, the RFID–tagged items are instantly known to the in-store system. There is no need for you to line up and pile these items on to a checkout conveyor belt, only to have them individually scanned and rehandled back into your shopping cart. For non-RFID-tagged items, camera-enabled weight scales allow for automatic recognition of your produce selection. Place the bananas on the scale and the system recognizes them, weighs them, and associates the cost to your cart. Advances in video capture and image analysis make this possible.

In the future, it might not even be necessary to pay interactively given that you have identified yourself to the store. (Perhaps your account will simply be debited.) As you exit the store, you might choose to have some product's RFID tags deactivated (if you are concerned about privacy implications, for instance).

In the Metro view, there will be a station where you can pass individual products under a scanner and have their RFID tag zero'd out.

Stop & Shop

Stop & Shop is a large, multibillion-dollar New England area grocery store chain (and more) with more than 345 stores and 57,000 employees. They have been discretely testing a new shopping cart system called the Shopping Buddy in a few stores south of Boston. In 2003, Stop & Shop started introducing the Shopping Buddy, a wireless cart-attached computer with an attractive color display. Shopping Buddy is based on a smattering of WiFi, infrared, ceiling sensors, and Bluetooth technology to assist in tracking and communicating with the carts.

When shoppers swipe their Stop & Shop discount cards through the display, Shopping Buddy calls up the shopper's most recent purchases and calls out the locations of these products. An in-store positioning system also allows Stop & Shop to display discounts on items that are in close proximity to Shopping Buddy. Shopping Buddy is also used for targeted advertising campaigns. For added convenience, shoppers can place deli orders while careening through the isles, and then pick up their deli merchandise as they pass by. The system even has a bar code scanning wand that enables customers to record their own selections for more easy review as they shop (because RFID-tagged products are not here yet).

Shopping Buddy "learns" as time goes on. It gets to know individual shopping preferences, and therefore can better offer discounts and accompanying purchases. One of Stop & Shop's ultimate goals is customer loyalty. Might such a system increase loyalty and cause shoppers to return to the stores that know them best? Many retailers are thinking this is one more tool to retain customers, especially those who relish convenience and expediency (and personalization).

Many parts of this Metro Future Store are real today and in use in the actual Metro stores in Europe (with similar capabilities within Stop & Shops in the United States). Regarding RFID, there are experimental stores with smart shelves that can track those products that are currently shipping with RFID tags. Once the list of retail products sporting RFID tags becomes pervasive, more shelves and more stores will exploit the technology. It will perhaps be a while before our carts can "talk" to our homes and learn what is out of stock, but the WiFi carts and personal shopping assistance technology is here today. RFID is at the heart of this concept of future stores, but so is WiFi and disjointed data streams and a general notion of "connect everything" to achieve higher values.

Buying Shoes—How Extreme Customization Is Possible

We found evidence of how Inescapable Data could change the way retailers do business in an experience as simple as buying a pair of shoes when we spoke to Charles Redepenning, president of Stride Rite International.

Since 1927, shoe retailers have relied on the Brannock Device to find the right-sized shoe for you. (Yes, that is what that shiny, flat contraption that measures your foot length and width, and that you only see in shoe stores, is called.) Like the utility of a nail clipper, it is hard to improve much on the simple elegance of the Brannock Device. For the most part, it does a fine job. As we all know from sometimes painful experience, however, it does not do a perfect job. In fact, the Brannock Device is essentially optimized to match you to a shoe manufacturing process that cares only about length and width, as opposed to the actual pair of shoes you want to buy and wear.

Redepenning is focused on what happens after a pair of shoes leaves the manufacturing facility:

> At Stride Rite, we take pride in the expert training we provide our salespeople. We are quite serious when we say that we want a child to leave the store with the best fitting shoe. Parents are increasingly concerned about problems brought on by poorly fitted shoes. We have tremendous loyalty among our buyers as a result of the personal attention to the shoe-fitting process.

He believes in leveraging data to deliver a better, more personalize fit; improve sales speed; and simplify the re-order process for busy parents. To do so, Redepenning envisions a Brannock Device replacement that is better able to capture more metrics about the foot. In addition to width and length, it could capture other important metrics such as arch size, instep height and length, foot-waist length, calf circumference, and body height. Low-cost technology and components exist today that could instantly "image" a foot placed into a shallow box-like device (infrared, digital image capture, ultrasound—a variety of technologies to completely map out the dimensions of the foot). Not all shoes are sensitive to all metrics—a low-profile sneaker has no interest in upper-calf circumference, for instance. Yet, there is great potential utility in saving this data.

Redepenning continues:

> *When a parent brings a child in for a fitting, each child could be processed through some device that would be even simpler than the Brannock Device in that there are no mechanical adjustments. It would be wirelessly connected to the POS [point-of-sale] system and ultimately to [our] corporate systems. Look at all the useful data we could get: all the normal foot metrics, all the extended foot metrics such as foot-waist and arch height and calf circumference, but also the subject's weight; and we could ask and note age and sex...All shoe brands and styles are made slightly differently, which is why one size eight fits differently than another size eight in a different brand. Without even talking about changing the back-end manufacturing process, we can simply find the better-fitting shoe faster and bring out only those that we know will be acceptable to the customer.*
>
> *This data could then be fed back into our manufacturing suppliers. We could design new shoes based on these metrics. We could quite possibly decide that length and width are not the only manufacturing variables for some shoes, and we would definitely see a relationships with the other metrics that we wouldn't know otherwise, such as the discontinuous relationship of the arch height to foot width. This could revolutionize our operations as we would see geographic trends in sizes and shapes that we never would have seen before and inject that back into our manufacturing through to marketing.*

The actual retail-purchase experience could be better for parents, too. Upon the initial visit to the shoe store, a parent could be in and out faster than ever and with the perfect-fitting shoe. Now that the retailer has an accurate record of foot and body metrics, a parent could confidently re-order shoes from a shoe retailer's Web site (with the site perhaps presenting accurate pictures of the child wearing a chosen shoe, viewed from a variety of angles). Over time, data gathered from a large population sample would allow the shoe retailer to predict the perfect-fitting shoe even as the child grows older.

Scaling of 1

Retail "personalization" is an increasing trend, especially in e-commerce, but also among the high-volume, brick-and-mortar retailers of more personal items such as clothing. A physical store cannot stock every conceivable shape, color, and size of a particular item such as slacks or shirts. However, we all truly appreciate a good-fitting pair of pants and a well-tailored shirt, and sometimes brand loyalty is made stronger if a consumer is able to find the right color shade with special stylistic features he or she is looking for.

The bigger retailers with both real and online storefronts offer extreme customizations via the Web. Polo, Nike, and Lands End are among those sites that are attempting to offer consumers custom-tailored clothes, orderable from the comfort of the kitchen while in pajamas. On the Ralph Lauren Polo site, a buyer can choose the color of a jersey, details about the size, and the color of the embroidered logo. Lands End is far more extreme, and a series of Web pages ask questions not only about shirt size and in-seam length, but also shoe size, shoulder broadness, and thickness of forearms. All of this data, they claim, is compared against five million other measurements and will result in the most proper "mathematical model of your body." Inescapable Data at work!

IBM has termed this new phenomenon the *well curve*—an upside-down bell curve. At one extreme are products, such as hammers. We do not very much care about differentiating or customizing them. Instead, we want the most efficient way to purchase them (in terms of price mostly, but also convenience of purchase). On the other end, anything that expresses ourselves personally, such as clothing or cars or nearly anything expensive, we want a lot of control over. Dell conveniently builds PCs "to order" (at no additional cost). Car makers will custom make you a car (color, finish, options, and interior) at no extra cost. The trend now extends to fashion items. Experts are calling this new *craze mass customization*. This trend simply would not be possible without extreme interconnectivity of business systems and a reduction of direct labor to the custom order.

Stride Rite could also allow its customers to use their measurement data to buy shoes from noncompeting retailers (for example, soccer cleats or ski boots).

The database could be made available to public health groups that want to use the data to show trends in increased childhood obesity and the related effects on foot shape and posture as the child's body develops under the increasing weight. Stride Rite could also make its data available to pediatricians as part of an effort to monitor a child's overall health. (Pediatricians have argued for years that proper foot care is as essential as proper dental care.)

If use of the new foot-measuring device grows, Stride Rite could allow competitors to use it and jointly share the data it collects. Why? As adoption of the technology increases, the cost of these devices to retailers falls. Using the data generated by the device, more manufacturers who supply shoes to Stride Rite could become more efficient, again reducing cost while producing better-fitting shoes. It is even possible that a mass-market version of the device embedded in the common bathroom scale will become available, wirelessly transmitting its data to your home health database, available to your doctor as well as your favorite shoe retailer.

Summary

The retail industry is going through some monumental changes made possible by the accumulation of vast amounts of new data and some new sources of streaming data such as RFID and video. New devices will emerge that allow for better fit and function of a wide range of items. A prevalent theme in the retail world to come will be personalization and customization, made possible by massive data collection and correlation. Wireless backbones will exist throughout stores and our homes and will provide the necessary conduit for joining those data sources together. RFID tags on products will provide both the retailer and the customer new levels of inventory tracking. Video will surely be one of the thickest streams of data and will be used in new ways to analyze our behaviors to a level never before possible. Video, merchandise tags, and other data sources will ultimately save significant costs in shrinkage and result in cheaper, more efficient purchases for all of us. The blending of these new pervasive sources enables new levels of information, and that information in turn gives retailers efficiency, knowledge, and new loyalty enablers for their customers.

CHAPTER ELEVEN

Computer Storage Impacted by Inescapable Data

We'd have to hollow out Mars to hold all the new data if it weren't for the massive increases in storage densities and reduced cost.

—*Jack McDonnell, the "Mc" in McData and former CEO of the prominent storage networking company*

Introduction

The essence of Inescapable Data is the aggregation of potentially massive amounts of data in ways that yield new sources of information. To accomplish the aggregation, one of the goals is to keep data moving—because data in motion has an opportunity to be accessed by more applications, resulting in greater value. Data has to rest sometime, however, and classically, it rests on storage devices. What is happening in the data storage world has a direct bearing on the functioning of an Inescapable Data world. Improvements and changes to the way data is stored and made available are coming—ones that will facilitate the use and management of the huge amounts of data that Inescapable Data devices will generate.

There is a general trend toward storing all data indefinitely that causes the volumes of stored data to proliferate. Some of this pack-rat behavior is motivated by regulatory agencies (SEC, FDA, etc.) bearing down on business in that they now require the saving of data for seven years (and more in some cases). E-mail messages are now being saved for indefinite periods of time by many organizations because they are considered public documents by law.

Whereas many companies now save terabytes of data, Inescapable Data devices will drive many organizations to the point of saving volumes measured in petabytes. RFID, digital video and image capture, PDAs, and cell phones all will generate massive amounts of data. The heft of digital video data alone needs to be appreciated, because it might be the last (and perhaps crippling) frontier for massive storage growth. The major challenges include the following:

- Developing the ability to sift through all of this data, often in real time, in a way that extracts information of value
- Protecting massive data volumes from loss or corruption
- Securing data that is often "in flight" over wired and wireless connections from theft or destruction by malicious forces

Data Classification

Mark Bregman, CTO of Veritas, observes that Inescapable Data devices are causing a rethinking of data classification. "We're going to need to categorize data in a new way. In the past, we tended to think of data as 'valuable' or 'not valuable.' With pervasive devices, transient data needs to be managed accordingly and managed in real time, but for shorter life cycles. Quite possibly, this leads to new types of data management software (for transient data) in this seemingly green field," explains Bregman.

It is simpler in the traditional data management world. There are only two types of data: files (considered "unstructured data") and records in a database (considered "structured data"). Inescapable Data devices, such as RFID readers and digital cameras, generate massive volumes of transient data—data that has value for only a short period of time. Much of this transient data (or some distillation) will need to be stored for a period of time. The question is, for how long?

Companies that use, store, and manage data are now on the horns of a dilemma. To save or not to save—that is the question. For example, in a food-processing setting, it will be useful to have a record of a particular pallet crossing a particular loading dock at a certain time, perhaps because later the pallet is identified as one that inadvertently contains food contaminants. However, does the processing plant need to save every RFID blip for that pallet? Or would something more condensed suffice?

Storing digital video poses similar challenges. Would an automobile manufacturer need to save every image taken for a month of the robotic chassis welder? Or would it be more meaningful to store only the images of rejected chassis for exception analysis? On the other hand, if a year later when a particular vehicle is involved in a fatal accident and the investigators suspect a poor chassis weld made the car unstable at high speed, would the manufacturer be able to use the video images of a properly welded chassis to defend itself?

Inescapable Data and its vision for extracting greater value bring with it an added requirement to classify data properly. Data that has become less valuable over time for one business might be very valuable to another—perhaps another member of a particular value chain. With proper data classification over time and collaborative data-sharing agreements, significant value could be realized.

The data storage industry is entering an era when more classifications of data may be required than the traditional (and simple) file and database. These new classifications will carry with them their own unique data protection, availability, and management requirements. As Bergman points out, "The enabler for Inescapable Data and computing is not the endpoint devices creating the data but rather the new critical infrastructure supporting the flow and retention of that data."

Store Everything?

Are we are heading toward a world in which we might want to store absolutely everything for an indefinite period of time? As discussed in Chapter 6, "Connecting Medicine," digitized x-rays and other medical images are already being stored indefinitely. Why? There is tremendous research value in mining that data and correlating it with other forms of data. The value of this data will only be exploited if it is saved. The really difficult question of "for how long?" is only exacerbated by the fact that, in research endeavors, researchers cannot really know whether data that seems to have zero value now might be of tremendous value to another researcher in the future. Two decades worth of digitized x-ray images could prove invaluable to a cancer researcher studying the progress of a particular type of tumor, particularly when that data can be correlated with genomic data, diagnosis histories, and treatment regimens.

Your son's sixth-grade essay, created 10 years ago, on the demise of the U.S. cotton industry may seem valueless to you now. But, at some point in the future, some researcher's tool could analyze his essay against essays from various socio-economic backgrounds from that period and compare it to each year since. There could be an obscure correlation to the sales of video games or to certain uses of language evidenced in the captured history of those essays. At age 35, his career counselor could use his entire electronic history to understand and ex-pose useful patterns, true skills, and hidden aspirations. If the cost to retain this document is insignificant, why not keep it indefinitely? (Are you not right now just a little bit curious what it would be like to be able to revisit your own sixth-grade essays?)

As an investor in a particular company, wouldn't you like to have access to ab-solutely all electronic records for that company, no matter how many years have passed? The federal government requires companies to retain physical records for a set number of years (and more so now than ever before), but the time limi-tation is primarily rooted in the practicality of doing so and the attendant costs. Before the advent of digital storage, if businesses had to keep every record for-ever "we'd have to hollow out Mars just store everything!" exclaims John Mc-Donald (the "Mc" in McData and former CEO of that company). Storing physical paper documents requires warehouses and staffing and heating and cooling for what might be minor benefit to the government. So government rules for retention duration are based on a recognition that the likely utility of an aged document has to be balanced with an affordable cost for physically keeping it available.

Digital storage now replaces much physical storage. With that physical stor-age cost burden lifted, does that mean that companies will be required to store everything digitally forever? Although it is now conceivable that one could store nearly everything forever, it still becomes difficult, if not impossible, as a practi-cal matter. True, disk storage densities nearly double every year or so, meaning that one can store nearly twice as much data on roughly the same-sized disk with each new generation. At the same time, the cost of each new generation of disk remains roughly the same, meaning that one could take all the data stored on the previous disk, deposit it on the new disk (that costs the same as the old one), and still have room for lots more—space you may feel you get for free. As you will understand, however, there is always a price for storing data—and the longer we save it, the greater the cost. A storage media that lasts longer than paper has yet to be invented. Therefore, to preserve digital data, you have to keep moving the data bits from old media to new every 5 to 10 years for magnetic and 15 to 20 years for optical. Otherwise, it is lost. The cost for those successive migrations adds up over time. In fact, if you store files of family pictures for long periods of time, for example, it is still cheaper (and probably safer at this point if you want to pass them on to successive generations) just to have them printed and put them in a picture album.

MRAM

Magnetoresistive random access memory (MRAM) is a new type of data storage medium that may change the data storage world. Typical computer memory, dynamic random access memory (DRAM), stores data by using electricity. Electricity must be continuously fed to the RAM to keep it charged correctly, and this, of course, is why your laptop battery does not last 100 hours. MRAM uses magnetic charges instead and, as a result, needs virtually no power. Thus, like data on your hard drive, it will persist even when the power is turned off.

The U.S. Defense Advanced Research Projects Agency (DARPA) has been funding initiatives in MRAM since 1995.[1] A group of three companies (IBM, Motorola, and Honeywell) led the effort initially, and other companies have more recently joined in the fun.

Just another new storage media? Maybe not. How would you like to continuously record everything that happens to you throughout your life (in high fidelity detail no less) just by wearing a small digital recording device? Personal life recorders (PLRs), popularized by Don Norman in his 1992 book, *Turn Signals Are the Facial Expression of Automobiles*, could use MRAM storage to make the PLR possible given its density, low power, and cost advantages. Although manufacturers fabricating MRAM prototype devices are working out bugs, the expectation is that within 5 to 7 years, MRAMs will hold 400 times more data than today's tiniest hard drives within the same physical space and using far less power. Estimates of the projected revenue for this new type of storage device exceed $4 billion annually.

---

[1] http://whatis.techtarget.com/definition/0,289893,sid9gci539346,00.html.

We have almost come to expect that certain types of personal data will be stored and accessible for long periods of time. We might expect every banking deposit or withdrawal to be online and available to us going back to account creation. Certainly, we would like to have childhood orthodontic records when faced with oral surgery later in life. If you have a child getting braces now, it could be quite useful for you to compare your records to your child's, given the genetic relationship. In the future, we may find it distressing if we cannot make such comparisons. Accurate family history of anything medical is now extremely important. Even if your childhood orthodontist is no longer practicing, he probably had no reason or physical space to keep your records created 40 years ago, yet there *is* utility in those records to *you*.

Perhaps you would you find it useful to have electronic records of your grammar school grades and course work as your own children make their way through the school system. Perhaps you have forgotten that you, too, had troubles with abstract concepts up through the fifth grade, but then some change occurred and you turned out perfectly well. Does this compare to what a child of yours is going through? Your own history contains valuable data—both to you and to others. Increasingly, our personal digital histories are being recorded by companies and organizations with which we come into contact. Who owns that data? Would you like to own your data? Such personal records now exist and could be collected in a more organized manner.

The Inescapable Data world researchers of all kinds thrive on massive volumes of accumulated data. Through collection and analysis of this data, extremely useful knowledge and information will result. It might be patterns of espionage, or indicators of fraud, or confirmation of assets, or medical or personal social histories.

We have always used data to help us project forward or discover the past. The difference in the Inescapable Data world is that we will use staggering amounts of historical data and correlate it with various streams (sometimes unexpected or oven odd streams) to learn of hidden values. As Jack McDonnell puts it, "The ultimate goal is not reacting, but anticipating." The first step may be to store nearly everything nearly indefinitely.

The Data Preservation Challenge

Yes, we can store massive amounts of data for increasingly longer periods of time, and we may never run out of storage space, even if we save absolutely everything forever. Storing data bits that accumulate into data mountains over time is easy to do. Tape and new forms of optical media will store petabytes for centuries—as long as you do not want to retrieve it. It is when you want to get data back so that you can actually use it that things get increasingly difficult and expensive; As mentioned earlier, the storage industry has yet to devise a storage media that lasts longer than one or two decades at the most. Long-term data preservation requires periodically refreshing at least the storage media, and usually the underlying hardware as well. In normal practice, data centers replace disk arrays every 3 to 5 years and tape drives every 5 to 7 years. Fermi Lab migrates 3 terabytes of data per day from old tape cartridges to new just so that they can be assured of being able to retrieve the data if and when they need it.

Data preservation is becoming a hot topic among many information technology administrators within companies, universities, and government agencies such as the Library of Congress. Although our world has been digital for many decades, only recently has this problem of long-term data storage *and retrieval* become more acute, driven by two conflicting forces:

+ A broader need, imposed by regulatory agencies for more organizations to keep records online and available for longer time periods, and the need for historical preservation
+ Changes in computer "formats," both physical and data formats, that tend to more and more rapidly obsolete the very processes we need to retrieve and interpret that data

Suppose that you live in an old house in a historic New England town and you discover in your attic a cache of historic artifacts. In a sheaf of thin, yellowish-brown pages, you find letters, proclamations, debt notices, and arrest warrants, some of which date back to the early eighteenth century. They are handwritten in a script and syntax that gives you pause. But they are intelligible. As you leave your attic to announce your discovery, you accidentally knock over a box that contains a collection of old floppy disks that dates back to your first PC that you trashed long ago. You suddenly realize that to extract anything intelligible from them, you would have to carry them down to a computer museum. Even so, there is no guarantee that the museum will have the right version of Word-Perfect that you used to create many of the documents stored on those floppy disks or run the right version of DOS, all on a machine with a 5.25-inch floppy disk drive that no one makes any more. In fact, even if you were somehow able to find the right combination of hardware and software, the floppy disks themselves may have degraded to the point where their data is no longer readable.

If we want to store data for very long periods of time (hundreds of years in the cases of historians), we are now exposed to two significant problems that the storage industry is still years away from solving:

- Media degradation and the increasingly rapid obsolescence of "readers"
- Lack of a universal digital format for encoding

The first problem is about physical media: disks, diskettes, and tapes. These all have a physical lifespan that ranges from three to seven years. After that, they degrade (tape dries out and gets brittle if not stored properly, for example) and lose data. CDs buy more time, perhaps a few decades if properly protected, but keeping the hardware that reads these CDs functioning for the same time period is a significant challenge.

The problem of media format obsolescence was more apparent a few years ago and more confined to removable media (tape, for example). This will be less of an issue going forward because the storage industry is trending toward adopting a smaller number of standard formats that can be adhered to for longer periods of time, and toward depending more heavily on online storage for even long-term storage needs and for quick retrieval. For some applications, it is better to have the data online and stored in more than one location than to have a single copy stored offline in some removable form that is subject to physical decay and data loss. The cost per gigabyte of Serial ATA disk (SATA), for example, now allows this luxury. However, there is no free lunch. The higher density the disk media, the more the media is susceptible to data loss over time, meaning the data almost literally "evaporates" from the disk after a period of about five years. Therefore, if you want to keep data online and on disk for more than five years, you must migrate it from one online media format to a newer one. Then, there is the cost of electricity required to keep these mountains of data online and "spinning" continuously. For some, however, this seems a sensible tradeoff.

The real problem in data preservation lies within the actual encoding format. The problem is known as *semantic continuity*. Suppose that you have somehow managed to keep your 1988 Turbo Tax file online and available. (Go to the head of the long-term data storage class!) Do you have any mechanism for actually making use of it? Perhaps you can print out the return on hardware you have managed to preserve for all these years and store it away for safekeeping. The odds that your current Turbo Tax version can use this data electronically (meaning it would have to support a nearly 20-year-old format) are slim to none.

Getting Back Your Bits—Can You Make Sense of Them?

The Harvard University Library has two archival storage facilities, one analog (papers, books, photos, microfiche, etc.) and one digital, known as the Online Computer Library Center (OCLC). Here's how OCLC charges users for its services:

> OCLC's current prices are for "bit-preservation" services only. In other words, OCLC will preserve the data bits for as long as the OCLC remains in business— presumably forever—but it is then up to you to turn those bits back into information when you want to retrieve them 50 years from now.

> Bit-preservation services include data management and backup, ongoing virus checks, periodic media refreshment, disaster recovery, and support of administrative tools for owners to update metadata and generate reports. Prices have not yet been set for "full preservation," wherein OCLC would be obligated to provide standard bit-preservation services, plus the capability to render intellectual content accurately, regardless of technology changes over time.

"Full preservation," that is the really hard part. You can have your bits back anytime you want. If you want them back many years hence in the same format and with the same information content as before, however, well, perhaps you should generate a hard copy and walk it over to the analog preservation side of Harvard's archival storage library just in case.

Semantic continuity is really at the heart of the data preservation problem. When seen in this light, it is not really a problem storage vendors can solve. Solutions must come from the applications vendors (Microsoft and Oracle, for example) or from other sources within the scientific and engineering communities. It is an extremely important problem, perhaps not so much for the individual PC user as for commercial industries, research institutions, and governments. Legal documents, reports, digital pictures, presentations, and the list goes on—all need to be preserved. If we want decades of data available for Inescapable Data utility, we need to have mechanisms to ensure that we can extract information from saved data well into the future. Many organizations are starting to grapple with this challenge, but as of yet, there are no clear solutions.

State Government and Preservation

Document preservation is an acute problem for state governments. "We believe that we have the sacred responsibility to preserve history for future generations. That creates unique challenges in the digital world," says Peter Quinn, CIO of the State of Massachusetts. "Nobody has yet been able to figure out how to preserve this much information in the same way that history has used paper to preserve information. This is one of the top two or three issues in all of government that we have to deal with."

For decades, data was stored on a style of tape that changed slowly over time. The formats for accessing that data changed very little over time as well. Quinn points out that the computer language Cobol has withstood the test of time and lasted many decades. In contrast, in the past 10 years, he has seen dozens of hopeful replacement technologies come and go. Organizations with a high dependency on Cobol (or any platform for that matter) are in a quandary about where to go next. Too many promises for the next dominant programming language or platform have come and gone, leaving remnants of programs along the way that need continual maintenance.

To make matters worse, Massachusetts state government workers are aging, and Quinn believes this represents a significant threat to data preservation. Quinn states that a significant number of his IT staff members are between the ages of 50 and 65, add that number to those in their 40s and the majority of Quinn's work force is over 40 years old. "We're going to loose 30% of our workforce in the next 5 years due to retirement and maybe another 20% due to other attrition reasons. That's 50%, and they're taking with them the skills that built our tools that run the government," exclaims Quinn.

Other industries are experiencing the same problem, but it is more pronounced at the state and federal government level because turnover is typically lower and governmental agencies can therefore maintain legacy architectures for longer periods. As governments hire new computer engineering talent, they find that these new workers are more familiar with creating and maintaining Linux and Windows than with Cobol. Therefore, the crumbling IT infrastructure problem self-perpetuates and worsens as time goes on. An important requirement for data preservation is preservation of people skills to maintain and carry forward the "information" locked within the data.

To keep certain electronic documents safe from the ravages of time and planned obsolescence, some companies are choosing to convert Microsoft Word and Excel documents into image formats (TIFF, GIF, PDF) that are standard and well known. Although they too will age as current formats fall out of prevalent use, migration tools will not only copy the data to the newer-faster-cheaper-denser storage media, but also "convert" the image format to whatever is the prevailing standard. This approach has some merit, but has some important drawbacks as well. Namely, images of a Word document are orders of magnitude larger in terms of the storage capacity required than the original document stored in its original Word format. Second, although the text and embedded graphics are preserved, formatting attributes and file metadata are lost. For example, if you convert a spreadsheet to a picture, you lose the cell formulas and associations that reside behind each spreadsheet cell. If a spreadsheet is archived so as to preserve the underlying math, image or PDF conversion will not help. Another approach is to use XML, which is wonderful for allowing attributes and other metadata to be expressed in a more universal format. XML enables you to store much of the nonvisual information that many documents contain (such as relationships within a document such as spreadsheet cell formulas). However, XML might not fully describe the "look" of a document in the exact same way that a picture (or perfect re-rendering) can; sometimes, the purpose of retrieving an archived document is to prove (perhaps in court) that the information was laid out in a nonmisleading way (consumer label cases, for example). Therefore, not having a image-based rendering of the document could be troublesome for some industries and applications. Storing both an XML version and an image version of a document has been suggested as a workaround—however, it is one that consumes mega amounts of storage.

Another approach is to use a more versatile display format, such as Adobe PDF, with some added extensions. If both the format and the rendering logic are similarly well specified, it is conceivable that storing more of the raw contents of a document would be possible. Even so, you would also need to store much ancillary data with the file to be 100 percent sure that the "picture" and all of its associated data can be reconstituted. For example, the actual text fonts would have to be stored *in* the document (as opposed to merely referenced). Similarly, all color and layout information would have to be specified in some device-independent manner. Likely, there will be other blocks of information that would need to be stored as well to enable perfect reproduction. Finally, it will be of paramount importance to store the document and all of its associations as a 100 percent self-contained object so that it can be migrated and copied without external dependencies. For small documents, these requirements could exact a disproportionately high premium for storage capacity, making the approach impractical for many applications. However, it may well be a practical approach for aircraft manufacturers, for example, that must maintain engineering documents—normally large files—for as long as a plane is still flying.

There is some hope for limiting the runaway accumulation of stored digital documents. Intelligent storage devices can tease-out redundancies that occur *across* many files (as opposed to "compressing" within a file). If a given storage device is holding thousands or even millions of files, in its "spare time"—i.e., when not responding to normal read/write operations—it can be examining its contents for redundant data. For example, if you routinely use PowerPoint to create your corporate presentations and typically use the same base template, a healthy percentage of the storage space required by each of those presentations is allocated to data that is identical for every presentation that uses the same template. Similarly, if our new document-saving approach has to embed such things as fonts (over and over again, for each document), such a cross-file examination could lead to impressive compression. This significant amount of purely redundant date can be teased-out of each document and applied back to the document when it is retrieved.

In time and as Inescapable Data devices force companies to store and manage petabytes as opposed to terabytes of data, storage devices will become available that use embedded intelligence to "mine-out" repetitive patterns and redundancies. Fat files will be transparently replaced by smaller ones that embody the unique contents *only* plus pointers to the "shared" or redundant information common to many files. The user of the file will be unaware of the magic going on behind the scenes. This process is not unlike what a RAID (acronym for Redundant Array of Independent Disks) storage system does today in that that takes a file and breaks it up into thousands of data "pieces" that are "sprayed" or "striped" (in the disk storage vernacular) across a number of physical disks in a RAID group. Intelligence in the RAID system reconstructs the file when it is recalled. Should one of the physical disks fail, the RAID system reconstructs the missing data by virtue of parity data stored on the other disk members of the RAID group, all done transparently to the application user. Intelligent storage devices are in use today. More intelligence is coming.

Walking Information Through Time: The Universal Virtual Computer

Imagine that you are a twenty-fourth-century archeologist. Digging among the ruins of what was once the house of an eminent twenty-first-century scientist and professor in residence at the university you now call home, you find a sealed metal box that contains an odd looking piece of plastic. When you bring it back to your university home base, a fellow researcher identifies it as a holographic storage "disk"—a once popular but now extinct form of computer storage. Wow, you think. Maybe the old professor preserved his research notes and other important documents, and deposited them in some sort of digital time capsule. What a find!

Luckily, the university computer museum has a device that can still extract data from the disk. However, you still have a problem. How do you decode the data bits and turn them into something you can understand? For that, you turn to another friend in the university's computer lab who has a universal virtual computer (UVC). This digital version of the ancient Rosetta Stone discovers that the old professor anticipated that future generations would be able to create such a machine, and saved his documents in an appropriate format. Voilà. The digital time capsule has been truly unlocked.

continues

Walking Information Through Time: The Universal Virtual Computer   *(Continued)*
Here's how the UVC works: It is built from coded instructions (a program) contained in a paper document of about 15 written pages. (Paper is still a perfectly acceptable analog storage medium in the twenty-fourth century, as it was in the sixteenth century.) The program simulates the most basic components common to all computers to create a processing environment that is essentially the same, no matter when or who made the computer. All it has to do is something all computers do—run a program. So, as long as you know "the code," you can build a UVC that will retrieve digitized information that was stored in a format that can be understood by the UVC.

The UVC is in fact the brainchild of an IBM researcher named Raymond Lorie. He and a UVC project team have already created a prototype UVC that can decode text and image formats such as JPEG and Adobe PDF. The goal is to propagate the UVC as a feature of a modern culture that now understands the present fragility of alls thing digital and wants to preserve its information stores for the benefit of future generations.

Breakthrough Compression

It may be impractical to store "thick files" until some sort of storage break-through occurs in the storage space. Compression software—software that compresses files down to one-third or even one-fourth of their original size storage-wise—can achieve wonderfully high compression ratios. However, achieving these higher compression ratios typically engenders some form of data loss—however slight. "Lossless" schemes typically only achieve 2:1 or slightly better compression ratios.

For legal, financial, and archival document preservation, one may not be able to tolerate any data loss and must be able to reconstitute 100 percent correctly a document or record. (Just 1 data bit missing from a bank record could mean the difference between being solvent or in debt, for example. On the other hand, a digital video file could lose a data bit without anyone ever noticing the missing pixel.)

The data compression world is presently divided into two distinct camps. One tolerates "lossy" techniques for digital imaging applications (videos and pictures) as a tradeoff for saving huge amounts of storage capacity. The other "lossless" camp wants high storage savings ratios coupled with a guarantee of data consistency when a compressed document is retrieved. What is needed is something in the middle: a technique that achieves 100 × storage capacity savings (even if it eats a lot of CPU cycles to get there) while at the same time perfectly re-assembles the data upon recall.

Wavelets are a newer form of compression, lossy however, that looks at a much broader sampling of data "chunks" and analyzes them more deeply in an effort to find and extract greater amounts of redundancy—the magic of data compression. Any compression method simply applied to a single file will probably not yield significant storage capacity savings, but as the scope of input data is expanded, the value of high-ratio data compression dramatically increases.

The promise of using wavelet-based compression is, that given plenty of processing horsepower, there may be no limit to the amount of redundancy that can be squeezed out of a stream of data. Imagine the sequence of characters ABCDEFGHIJ. Such a sequence is hard, if not impossible, to compress. If, on the other hand, it were ABCCCCCHIJ, the redundant Cs could be replaced by a count digit followed by a single C. Most compression algorithms look for such obvious opportunities. A less obvious solution (requiring more CPU time to detect) would be to realize that the string of letters may contain "ramps" where successive letters are one higher (or lower) than the previous letter. The compression scheme could then, for example, encode the starting value (A) and a ramp rate up or down of (1). A further less-obvious solution would be to realize that the majority of that pattern exists in other documents and, therefore, it might not be necessary to re-store all of it, once again at the cost of many more CPU cycles.

Sometimes, data can be "folded," like bed linens (or even more creatively rearranged), and when folded more redundancy appears. The point is this: Myopically looking at small streams of data misses the larger redundancies that can be found by looking through huge chunks of data for commonalities among a great many files—a broader type of folding—or whose differences can be "described" (like the ramp example). To get to this elimination of greater amounts of redundancy that can be extracted when data is stored, and added back when its retrieved, storage devices need to have more "extra time" on their hands (to be able to find and catalog all their data), more clues about the contents of the files they contain (for more efficient searches), more advanced compression algorithms, and, most importantly, terabytes of data to sift through in order to find redundant patterns. But once there, 100 × improvements in density might just be the beginning.

Video and Media Driving Storage Growth

We believe that TiVo-like technology and devices will become more prevalent because they will address an important need that is now just emerging. These devices hold video and audio files that come across from TV broadcasters but do so in a way that is mostly transparent to the viewer. In the future, your new DVD player or new cable "set-top" box will sport perhaps a few terabytes of disk space, capacity that will be invisible to you. Your preferred cable company will then be able to stream hundreds of movies down into your cable box each night, making use of idle bandwidth during the "wee hours" and allowing you a much faster pay-per-view experience should you eventually elect to watch some of them. In fact, your cable box full of stored videos may allow you to transfer movies to a handheld video player at super high speed (a few seconds of transfer) so that you can take them along for a long car ride. This is far less practical if the video/audio stream has to originate from cable TV headquarters and fight its way along the cable pipes among all the real-time viewing and Internet traffic streams. Storing content locally for use at some future point in time, *caching*, will become a general trend within the cable broadcast.

PVRs and DVRs

Personal video recorders (PRVs or DVRs), popularized by TiVo, are finally taking off. These devices, which enable users to record broadcast and other TV signals to disk, were first introduced to the market in 1999. They were somewhat slow to take off, and sales were low through 2001, only reaching 1.2 million units by 2002.[2] During 2003, sales tripled to 4.6 million units, and 2004 will see sales around 11 million units. According to Price Waterhouse Coopers, by 2008, 20 percent of households will have

---

[2] http://pvrhw.goldfish.org/tiki-read article.php?articleId=39.

DVRs, up from 3 percent at the end of 2003.[3] Comcast, Time Warner, and Cox are all now promoting their versions of a DVR. In addition, PCs and laptops can be turned into video recorders quite easily. Microsoft Windows Media Center Edition enables the hard drive to essentially provide PVR services. Similarly, the familiar consumer electronic companies (Sony, Toshiba, and others) are now configuring DVD recorders with hard disks in order to offer similar capabilities. To be clear: We and others see an enormous number of home-based devices soaking up massive amounts of disk space to save movies and other forms of broadcast content.

Local data caching allows the users of data to experience dramatically increased performance when retrieving stored content. Under a content-caching scenario, the material (be it a movie or song or a picture of your dog) is "stored" in multiple locations throughout a network, possibly in addition to your own home entertainment system. A new movie (for example, one of the *Lord of the Rings* sequence) is initially released for video and cable viewers only. A large cable provider starts with a single electronic copy of part three of the trilogy that has been transmitted to them by the movie distributor. The cable company then places the movie on its main content server in a location that is central to their coverage area. The cable provider then broadcasts the movie out to each regional cable office, which stores it and rebroadcasts it out to each cable head end (the in-town distribution point). The cable head end may then rebroadcast it to neighborhood waypoints, and then in turn down to your local set-top box, perhaps without you ever asking for it or knowing about it beforehand. Why? The closer (geographically) to its final destination the content is stored, the less performance impact there will be on the cable provider's network when it comes time for you to actually watch the movie.

It is conceivable, therefore, as cable providers move forward with digital content, that the *Lord of the Rings* movie will be stored on 80 million different disk drives across the United States. If a typical DVD-quality movie is 4 gigabytes large, one movie alone could consume as much as 300 million billion bytes.

[3] http://www.usatoday.com/money/industries/technology/2004-07-28-tivo-cov x.htm.

(The storage industry has not yet invented a term like terabyte or petabyte to describe this much data.) In a bit of an odd twist, as rapid and massive as all this storage growth around us will be, we will be increasingly *unaware* of it.

Today, we know perfectly well that our home computers and laptops contain disk drives. Disk drives store our files and pictures and audio and video media. We select which files to store, and we occasionally manage them (move material around, delete some, add some, etc.). We have to interact with them when they run out of space or performance begins to suffer, or, heaven forbid, they crash and we have to replace them and the data they once contained. By contrast, TiVo-like devices shield us from all of that. We do not see a C: drive. Instead, we are presented a view that is far more application-tailored. We believe the box is holding movies, but we are indifferent as to whether they are on some spinning disk or coming in from some wired or wireless signal, or some of both.

In the Inescapable Data world, repository-type data will be stored in a caching fashion all along a series of access points, and we will be unaware of the actual location or type of media holding the data; we will be thinking only in terms of the business or consumer object (e.g. the movie), and the infrastructure will shield us from the underlying complexity. We are moving toward a world where the network seems to hold our data rather than specific devices (or specific locations), driven by the super-thick movie and video files that value the significant performance gain.

From Blocks to Files to Objects

Today, when data bits are stored electronically within a computerized storage device, the data bits are collected into "blocks" (typically 512 bytes). When an operating system issues a command to transfer data to or from a disk, it typically reads or writes the data in a series of blocks. Each block carries with it a block number that identifies it. Higher software functions contained within a file system (on the host or attached computer) logically string many blocks together (that are likely scattered across a disk) into a unit typically known as a file. However, today's disk drives only have knowledge of the lower-level blocks and their associated unique identifiers. They have no knowledge of files—a knowledge reserved for file systems that run somewhere else, usually in the application host processor.

Many guiding lights within the storage industry now believe that the more knowledge a storage device has about the data contained within it, the more optimally it can operate. Today, a disk drive has no knowledge that block 482 is related to block 1,988 and that both blocks contain data used by a critical application (a banking application that manages your checking account, for example). It therefore cannot know whether those blocks need a greater level of data protection than a block that has some temporary data in it that will simply be discarded in a short period of time. The software that understands that blocks are sequenced to form files, and that some files contain data that is more critical to the ongoing function of a business (for example), is higher up the processing chain, and is likely residing on the host computer. This was acceptable when disk drives were typically "inside" of a computer.

Today's medium- to large-scale corporate data centers use networked storage architectures—storage devices, such as disk arrays, that are physically outside of host application processors and are networked with other processors so that their resources and data can be shared. Various business requirements drove IT administrators in this direction during the late 1990s, primarily because large disk "arrays" were relatively expensive to own and manage when they were held captive by single application servers (because of sophisticated RAID technology and electrical power and cooling requirements). Networking them among other application servers allowed their costs to be amortized across several connected computers. The storage area network (SAN) industry was born.

SANs allow many computers to share storage resources via a high-performance fiber-optic fabric (Fibre Channel). Storage elements can be more easily added to and removed from the fabric as needed, and administrators in charge of the host systems benefit by leveraging the infrastructure costs across many systems. However, in spite of this advance in resource sharing and storage efficiency, the standard block access methods did not change. The servers still use "block" concepts when talking to storage arrays over a SAN even though the storage arrays can now be hundreds of feet or even miles away.

Think back to Chapter 8, "Real-Time Manufacturing," in which you learned that massive increases in business efficiency and values come when barriers are torn down and interface points become more abstract. (For example, do not ask what the inventory level of thumb tacks is; instead, ask whether the ability to complete bulletin board packages is in jeopardy due to supply-chain fulfillment issues.) Most vendors of storage-related products are still not delivering solutions that enable the administrators of storage "data centers" to radically optimize their operations. Not having learned how to "see" (per the Muda concept), these vendors focus myopically on those 10 percent improvement targets. They deliver faster SANs, better SAN switches, and more SAN software to manage and configure and monitor. All Muda. What storage administrators really want is better application program value from storage.

Although SANs were (and are) useful for amortizing the cost of storage physical operations, because they did not fundamentally change the "unit of access," they did not introduce any major process benefit. If SAN elements (storage, switches, etc.) knew of the higher-level business object in transit, the files, more optimization and management automation could take place. If you are a traffic officer in a busy intersection downtown, you can myopically manage the flow of vehicles (disk blocks); if you are the city mayor, however, you can synchronize sporting events with bus schedules and office hours against public-transport availability. Keeping data access at the block level does not allow the infrastructure to capture enough of the value chain and falls short in providing higher optimizations. It also introduces more rigidity, and the SAN manufacturers only response is to focus on the pipes and blocks and attempt to squeeze value by increasing speeds or connections instead of working up to higher values.

Some storage vendors currently offer local area network (LAN)-based file access to network-attached storage (NAS) devices. NAS devices typically do not expose blocks to the host application, but rather expose a file-level interface. These vendors have observed (correctly to users of NAS devices) that ultimately the business object of interest is a file. Using NAS, storage administrators can more easily manage access to files that have common requirements for quality of service, performance, and protection. For them, NAS is clearly the right direction. The NAS device can behind the scenes operate on "blocks that comprise a file" as a set (perhaps to replicate, to index, alter the location for performance, etc.). Some NAS manufacturers have been extremely successful with a model that is still resisted by others because of performance concerns. Why? The typical interface technology for NAS devices is TCP/IP on Ethernet—a somewhat slower and higher-overhead protocol than the Fibre Channel protocol used for raw block access. However, the real reason in their minds is that NAS essentially requires a storage transaction to be processed twice—once to pass through the "computer" in the NAS itself and once more when the actual data moves through the host computer for the application. Corporate data-center storage administrators who grew up in the mainframe world spent decades through the 1970s, 1980s, and 1990s looking at removing all possible I/O bottlenecks—storage being uppermost on the list. They instinctively reject any access method that is not the fastest one possible. However, for many, NAS performance is good enough, and the cost of NAS can be one-half to one-third the cost of SAN.

Hybrid Approaches

Some interesting hybrid solutions exist to outboard data storage. SANergy is one such product that allows computers to view storage as if it is NAS, but the actual payload contents of files is moved directly as blocks via a faster alternative path like that of a fibre-channel SAN. Other products imitating this approach are IBM's SAN file system and ADIC's StorNext file system. But the performance improvements gained by these solutions are only stop-gap measures, and the modest deployment of such techniques by data-center managers suggests that the need for faster "network file systems" is less acute than currently perceived by storage administrators; that is, speed is not the real issue. Network-attached storage changed the data management paradigm in a way that many administrators were not yet willing to embrace; for years, their hosts accessed raw blocks, and changing to a file mentality was as difficult as it was for some to switch from being phone-centric to e-mail-centric.

Business processes and operations on data need to be abstracted better, and then they can be optimized in the storage infrastructure. The reason that NAS and SAN are only incremental improvements in the ways needed to manage large accumulations of data, such as the ones generated by Inescapable Data devices, can be seen when one examines the problem storage administrators are faced with when responding to new regulations governing data-retention periods. The rules for retention (HIPPA, Sarbanes-Oxley, SEC 17-a4, etc.) can be somewhat more complicated than just "retain for seven years." It might be this: Retain for seven years once the account is closed, or after broker X leaves, or retain indefinitely while the audit is underway. Different types of material carry different retention periods and rules. (An e-mail might be required to be retained for one period, and a proposal might have a different requirement.) To manage data more effectively, data-center storage managers need to assign more management criteria to individual files—additional information about files (metadata) beyond name and date and owner that are now needed to properly protect and manage files.

Inescapable Data generates big data—data in the petabyte range. To manage and process it in such a way that yields meaningful information in real or near-real time, a new level of abstraction has to be introduced—higher than file level. This new abstraction layer could take the form of a "super file" or some sort of macro file that is built out of XML components (but clearly something beyond the current approach that keeps a parallel database for the extra metadata that is very limited in its scope to begin with). We think that a fundamental problem worth solving is essentially one of scalability. Data blocks are too small to be stored and accessed individually, so they are aggregated into files and file systems for the sake of processing efficiency as more and more data block accumulate. Similarly, files have become too small of a denominator as well. A super-file concept will allow many components in storage fabrics and storage arrays to self-optimize and manage the data better. Essentially, this drives data management intelligence deeper into the storage domain and away from the application host environment. In the Inescapable Data world, optimizations occur not just by connectivity alone but by virtue of information that allows for intelligent optimizations.

Although the super-file concept is not yet evidenced in today's market offerings, something called Object Store is close and getting some market traction. The Storage Network Industry Association (SNIA) has a technical working group focused on object-based storage, `http://www.snia.org/app/org/workgroup/osd/description.php`. The base concept rejects the notion of accessing physical storage "block by block" whose meaning is only understood by a host file system. Instead, Object Store uses an object number to reference a file (object), and then uses commands to read/write pieces of that object. This process is roughly similar to the way a network computer accesses a network file system; the difference is that processing of the new Object Store protocol is performed directly on the disks (or storage arrays) themselves, hopefully yielding a quantum leap in the performance and scalability of storage systems in service to the demands of big data. The goal of Object Store is to truly replace "block numbers" with "object ID object data."

A number of commercial activities are taking place aimed at popularizing OSDs (object-based storage devices). Many companies are now participating in establishing a standard version of this model so that, once implemented, all vendors conform to basically the same way of doing OSD. At the forefront are IBM, EMC, Veritas, Seagate, and HP, among others. In addition, there is an open-source file system, Lustre, developed for the National Laboratories (Livermore, Los Alamos, Sandia) by Cluster File Systems Inc., and marketed by HP as the StorageWorks scalable file system. Lustre uses an implementation of an object store called ObjectStore Target (OST). By driving an object-oriented access method directly into storage devices, hosts systems can more readily "share" access to data at storage-wire speeds (without funneling data through an intermediary controlling file server as is the case with NAS) and the storage element can more intelligent lay out files and optimize access. Although not as powerful as a true super file, this is evidence of the storage industry at least embracing the notion that more powerful forms of metadata and metadata processing will be needed to make high-value use of the masses of Inescapable Data that will beckon those wanting to extract that value.

Data Protection

There have been some subtle changes in the way we as users think of safeguarding our data. It was not that many years ago when those of us with home-based PCs likely backed up our PC disks periodically to a cartridge tape device or floppy disk. Some of us learned through painful experience that hard drive crashes could result in the loss of programs, documents, spreadsheets, photos, charts of family trees, closely guarded family recipes...you name it. They were gone forever if backup copies were not on hand when the replacement PC arrived. Even if we did not learn the value of this basic computing procedure the hard way, we almost certainly knew of someone who had.

A couple of interesting things transpired over the past few years. For one, the average user of a personal computer is no longer a techno geek; the majority of users are now "average citizens"—homemakers, students, independent consultants, retirees—just about anyone and everyone. At the same time, the capacity of a single PC disk drive grew from about 100MB to 100GB (an increase of 1,000×). For many reasons, we still do not properly back up the data we depend on daily. In no specific order, they are as follows:

- *We think we cannot.* The disk drives have become too big. A quarter or half a terabyte cannot be backed up in any reasonable time. We could use CDs or DVDs, but we would be feeding the machine for days and wind up with a stack of DVDs several feet high. (However, online backup services are now available that will store as much data as we want to give them—for a price, of course.)

- *We do not know that we should.* Many computer users still do not understand where and how PC data is stored. Information appears at a mouse click. Storage? What's storage?

- *Trust.* Many of the newer breed of users just assume that either the machine will not break (or be stolen) or that someone else is responsible (the manufacturer maybe?) for data protection. Perhaps they are conditioned by their other life experiences. When one goes to the bank and hands the teller $10 to deposit (okay, no one actually goes to the bank anymore, but hang in there with us anyway), one has the 100 percent expectation that any branch or ATM connected to that bank will give you your $10 back when you want it. A bank that says, "We had a computer glitch and lost the record of your deposit" would arouse great ire. One simply does not expect to hear such a statement any more.

- *We do not know what to back up or do not have the time to sort out the replaceable data from that which is irreplaceable.* We think that much of the data could be redownloaded (if it originated during a Web surfing expedition), but we also know that some of the data is very unique to us—the tax return from two years ago, school reports, and customizations of various software applications that we've grown to depend on, for example. It is just too difficult to find those unique items among the massive tangle of other data and back up just those items.

For the previous decade or two, the computer world has been divided into two different major user camps: business users and home users. Business users truly owned the most important data and had the most to lose if it was irretrievably lost or corrupted. However, as a business user, the job of data protection fell (and still falls) on the shoulders of IT administrators. On the other hand, and up until recently, home users did not store that much data electronically that was considered critical for one reason or another, so the exposure to loss for the home user has traditionally been limited.

This situation has now turned upside down for both camps. Today, most business professionals use laptops as their primary computer. Laptops are typically disconnected from corporate networks during the classic backup time (overnight). So, we now have business people with massive amounts of potentially critical corporate data that is susceptible to abuse and damage, yet is seldom connected to any corporate backbone. Furthermore, business people are more likely to self-create unique data than in the past; the traveling business person is creating his or her own PowerPoint presentations, proposals, and Word documents, whereas a few years ago these were created by marketing departments or administrators and thus protected by the centralized IT department. Not so any more. It is estimated by a number of industry analysts that 60 percent of a corporation's digital assets are now living on the "edge" in PCs and laptops and not protected *at all*.

Similarly, individuals now have critical data stored on their own home computers. There are more at-home independent consultants and more teachers creating material at home in the evenings for the next day. On home PCs, more mothers are organizing book groups and soccer schedules, and more kids are writing sixth-grade essays. The loss of data for the home PC user can now be just as devastating as it is for the business professional (resonating with the Inescapable Data theme that businesses and individuals increasingly share common issues).

The Inescapable Data philosophy brings some solutions. In the Inescapable Data world, data is stored multiple times and in multiple locations, transparently. Consider how most modern applications, such as Microsoft Word, operate regarding mistakes. You can "undo" whatever it is you last did, and most programs enable you nearly unlimited "undo" (unwinding very far back through a series of edits of a document). We now depend on this undo capability, and it allows us to be more freewheeling when making changes to documents. We need the same level of comfort for the actual disk files themselves. We should be able to "go back" through old versions of files (or any data for that matter) and do so while at 30,000 feet in an airplane.

Versioning—The "Undo" Key

Twenty years ago, Digital Equipment Corporation's file system featured built-in versioning. Every time a file was created, a copy of that file was also made in the background and stored. Each time it was updated, the updated file was added to all of the prior versions. Why? If a file was accidentally corrupted, an administrator could roll back to a previous uncorrupted version of the file and start over.

However, the problem in "undoing" one's mistakes in this way becomes apparent when one realizes that, at the time, the average mini-computer's disk capacity was 50MB. The disk could quickly run out of space. Although the file system was busily storing past versions of every file, even those silly transient "binary" ones created by the computer itself, the amount of "litter" that accumulated on the disk got in the way of processing the useful data. The file system was not smart enough to know what to retain and for how long.

Some new "undo" approaches are smarter and offer a less-cluttered approach. IBM has a software package, VitalFile, that runs transparently on your laptop (or UNIX server) and knows the difference between user-created important files and chaff. User files that get updated have the older version tucked away in a discrete repository and can be restored immediately when needed. Chaff is auto-managed; versions of files are stored only for a certain amount of time, and as they age, older ones are deleted automatically. Other companies offer products that will "journal" changes to files out to a disk in the SAN fabric and allow an administrator to roll backward through past transactions to re-create the contents of a file at a certain point in time (although this is more useful for what is called "structured data" [i.e., databases] rather than user files). Over time, individual users will come to expect an "undo" function to fix or restore files that have been lost, destroyed, or have become unreadable from their home-based systems because they are receiving continuous protection (i.e., "undo") from nearly every other computerized tool they use.

Sun's view, in the words of Mark Canepa, senior vice president of storage and networking is this: "The fact that you have to perform backup is a bug." Sun suggests backup is less of a separate application and more of a feature of the components that actually store the data, such as the file system itself. "You simply cannot tolerate *ever* loosing data anymore," continues Canepa, whose new file system, ZFS, improves on the old "backup" paradigm. IBM's new file system, SAN FS (and its natural physical components, such as fabric replication services), also take the attitude that protection should be more transparent to both the IT storage administrator and the application user. Veritas also offers products that lean toward more continuous protection as well. For IBM, Sun, Veritas, and yes, even Microsoft, the direction is clear: Data protection will be assumed and transparent going forward because it will be provided as a standard storage infrastructure function.

Opportune Protection

Picture yourself (the typical laptop user) in this new world of transparent data protection. While flying over Chicago, you modify a PowerPoint pitch you gave yesterday to General Motors—the new pitch you intend to use in an upcoming appointment at Ford tomorrow. After making a few cuts and pastes of some spicier artwork, you click the Save button. Unfortunately, you "saved" it as the old General Motors presentation, essentially overwriting it with the Ford pitch. Oops.

In the Inescapable Data world, recovery is but a keystroke away. You are able to swiftly "recover" any instance of any file you have recently changed, even without being connected to the company network or calling for the assistance of a help desk or administrator. (This alone is a monumental step forward.) When you reach your WiFi-connected hotel room, you log on to the hotel's network. Via the Internet, your system automatically migrates some set of the changed files onto a remote system somewhere in the Internet *cloud*. Later, if your computer is misbehaving or misplaced, you have the comfort of knowing that your important materials are housed elsewhere in the grand network for protection against such mishaps.

At the heart of every computerized thing we do is data that is likely stored away in files on a computer. Proper protection of these files is of paramount importance, and for data to remain pervasive it has to first be assured of persistence—more so now than ever before because we are more integrated with data in the Inescapable Data world. The entire paradigm of data protection in the

world of computers is changing and moving toward real-time continuous dupli-
cation of all data, which is pushed somewhere into "the network." In the colorful
future, when data is changed, it will be sent into the network. The network will
manage its redundancy and retrievability. Today, "backup" is still a discrete operation, even using some of the software we have mentioned. The next chapter
covers some newer technologies and philosophies for overall network data management that will have a welcome home in the Inescapable Data world.

Groupware as Backup

There is a hidden value contained within groupware software. Using
groupware to create, maintain, and exchange files essentially results in redundant copies of data being stored in multiple locations. The Groove
software, mentioned earlier in this book, is a peer-to-peer product. There
is no "server" to buy and configure, meaning that setup time is not an issue.
There is no central data repository either that needs to be backed up. Instead, all the peer members within a groupware group end up having identical copies of files—created automatically behind the scenes and over a
very secure encrypted connection. As groupware members come online
and go offline, the Groove software automatically synchronizes shared
files with new updates. Offline group members files are resynchronized
with the most recent versions when they come back online. For group
members, a loss of a hard drive or a stolen laptop is less of a worry because
all other members have redundant copies of shared files. It is likely that
future Groove versions will support versioning, further protecting users
by providing "time-based" copies of files, which is essentially what backup
copies are.

Storage Utility

During the late 1990s, the storage industry caught the same Internet fever that
plagued the rest of the computer industry. The concept was deceptively simply:
Instead of storing data the old-fashioned way on disks safely housed in the corporate computer room, companies were told that they could store all their data
in offsite storage "utilities" and pay only for the actual capacity they used on a
monthly basis rather than buying all that storage hardware and software. The

data would come to them, from the storage utility, over all of those fat Internet pipes the telcos were investing in as they built-out the Internet. It was just like paying for electricity. The electric utility sold electrons. The storage utility sold data bits. Both were delivered over wires. The model was so compelling that even Enron got into the business.

Then came the Internet meltdown. Most storage utilities died a quick and horrible death, because, in the end, most wound up being housed within—and selling their services to—the very same facilities as other Internet services providers such as Exodus. As compelling as their model seemed during those "frothy" Internet days, the storage utilities failed to address one crucial issue: Storage is as much about data *protection* as it is about data *availability*. In addition to looking and acting like electric utilities (plug in, get data), the storage utilities also had to look and act like banks. The storage utilities could not convince enough big customers that their critical corporate data was not only safe from harm, but that they could actually get their data back if the utilities went under. David L. Black, CTO of EMC, puts it this way: "When outsourcing anything, you need to outsource *enough* of the total process; pulling out too little breaks things and leaves processes uncomfortable."

Bregman resonates with the balance of availability and protection. "Classical utilities, like power or water, are 'fungible'—completely interchangeable—but your data and mine are not." Bregman goes on to explain that the ill-fated storage utility model is actually alive and well, but *within* companies as opposed to an outsourced service. There are significant economies and efficiencies being realized today through the consolidation of storage devices, physical centralization, and the creation of common management structures. This is good, but incremental progress, such as what you read about in Chapter 8. Focusing on achieving 10 percent improvements often misses the 80 percent gain opportunities. Real gain comes from leveraging the entire storage value chain through tighter relationships.

Might this echo what Black is driving at? If enough of the interbusiness processes, along with the data, are carved out and separated from others, perhaps the right economy is realized and without unacceptable risks. If you are a manufacturer tying your fabrication operation closer each year with your plastics and glue providers (and using joint IT tools for messaging, schedule coordination, inventory balancing, and so forth), it might be sensible to have much of those data-driven processes housed elsewhere.

Bregman points out, however, that there are significant challenges, particularly in larger organizations. "For large scale brick-and-mortar companies, outsourcing of computer utilities is somewhat disruptive because all of a sudden they have excess capacity, people and/or real estate and machinery, which creates resistive inertia," explains Bregman. In contrast, smaller companies, particularly start-ups, will more readily embrace an outsourced model. In fact, smaller companies may, as a result, have an improved competitive edge by being able to get to this new efficiency more easily and grow (and shrink) more rapidly. "In an Inescapable Data world, I don't actually care where the data is as long as I can get it back," cites Bregman. Inescapable Data and its networking are once again changing the grounds of competition.

Summary

Storing data is key to Inescapable Data (until some magic occurs that allows data to be always in flight yet locatable). As such, it becomes increasingly important to protect data against loss or destruction, because this data will be our keys to analysis, correlation, and general utility in our lives. The current paradigm for protecting data (which could arguably be stated as a no paradigm) is insufficient for the new world of rapidly changing data. The industry will likely embrace the notion of continuous real-time and redundant protection. In a related way, we may find our machines and ourselves storing nearly all data nearly forever because key values come from historical analysis. Video streams from surveillance sources and general consumer movies (and caching) will drive dramatic increases in disk utilization and become our premiere data creator. Finally, we are discovering that the fundamental units of storage, blocks and files, are not adequate to truly enable the efficiencies expected in an Inescapable Data world where businesses desire to focus only on value-add operational tasks. The future will offer us concepts larger than files that will allow for intelligent protection, caching, and outsourcing to finally realize Inescapable Data goals for computer data operations.

CHAPTER TWELVE

Super Computers, Visualization, and Networks

We are a company that focuses on big data, some of the largest data sets in the world. Petabyte-size models kept in globally addressable RAM with thousands of processors operating. Discoveries made by such massive computation, data analysis, visualization, and the challenges of building these machines will propel computing to the next level. The current super-computing model needs rethinking.

—Dr. Eng Lim Goh, CTO of Silicon Graphics, Inc.

Introduction

The world of computing will forever go through changes and advancements. Some specific areas are worth exploring in the context of Inescapable Data: super-computer advances, visualization advances, networking changes, and perhaps new types of processing chips and new types of micro machines. Here, we explore these topic areas with a specific eye toward how these changes will hasten the realization of Inescapable Data values.

Super Computers

Silicon Graphics (SGI), Cray, IBM, and Sun all make super-computer class systems. Other players have come and gone, and in spite of their importance to the scientific community the market for super computers has not grown substantially over the past few years. But, the machines themselves have truly grown in power and capabilities, and the value of their contribution to society is rarely acknowledged.

The federated or grid computing models that we examined in Chapter 6, "Connecting Medicine," now threaten to take applications away from the current super-computing platforms because a great many problems are now solvable by these alternative architectures. Problems that can be cleanly broken up into smaller pieces, distributed outward to many small computing elements, and re-assembled later are now migrating over to the alternative models.

Even so, some of the hardest problems in the world can only be solved by super computers. In addition, studying the application, architecture, and deployment of super-computer solutions is useful in the context of Inescapable Data because over time, many large systems architectural approaches move downstream and add tremendous value to the general population of smaller computing platforms. Super computers are also critical to unlocking the value contained in the biggest data sets known in the fastest amount of time (albeit at significant cost), thus solving some of the most perplexing problems in areas such as meteorology, seismology, and medical research—all endeavors that will benefit from the future implementation of Inescapable Data gathering devices on Earth. Changes in present-day super-computing architectures are forthcoming that hold hope of step-function increases in capability without the requisite increases in physical size and cost.

Dr. Goh elaborates:

> Two years ago, we sat down and decided to go with a clean sheet of paper when designing our mew platform for production in 2007. One thing we observed, as HPC (high-performance computing) systems evolved, their peak performances were running away from sustainable application performances; that is, applications could only realize a small fraction of the claimed performance of the system. That "gap" has been growing and growing over the years.

The present gap between an application and the inability of the machine to use its massive compute resources efficiently occurs because it is presently difficult to optimize applications to today's multiprocessor super-computing architectures. Imagine being a waitress or waiter and needing to set 10 different tables for the dinner rush. You can set one table at a time or stage and carry all the knives on one loop through the tables, and then the forks, and so on. The former way is analogous to how most programmers tend to create software applications, because it is simpler to debug and understand. The latter way is similar to the way super-computer chips would rather see things organized. So, chips perform at their best when they are running handcrafted algorithms that are tailored to the needs of those CPUs. An application that has not been laboriously "trained" cannot extract maximum machine efficiency.

How big is the efficiency gap? Worst case, a user might only realize 10 percent or less of the super computer's rated performance for some applications. Given the multimillions of dollars these systems can cost, purchasers find this inefficiency hard to swallow, leaving many potentially solvable problems unsolved because the cost of a solution is simply too great. Another way to view the costliness of this gap is to consider the power consumed by the largest super computers in the world. It is in the order of a megawatt. If we are only getting 10 percent useful work out of them, this translates to effectively wasting 900,000 watts of power (and more, if we also consider the air-conditioning power required to remove this wasted heat).

Nevertheless super-computer customers continue to buy increasingly more powerful systems in an effort to throw more and more hardware at a problem to get to a suitable performance solution. Cost aside, this poses other significant problems. For example, cooling these massive systems is problematic. Manufacturers have gone back to air-cooling processors (fans) versus the more cumbersome liquid cooling methods. A 10,000-processor system generates a gigantic amount of heat that has to be cooled rapidly. The temperature on the surface of the near-microscopic working part of a computer chip reaches the same temperature as a nuclear reactor core. Consequently, air flow under the floors of these new computers has been known to approach 60 miles per hour. Needless to say, having *fewer* processors that do more useful work has to be one new direction manufacturers take.

As discussed in Chapter 4, "From Warfare to Government, Connectivity Is Vitality," super-computer–sized problems are mathematically intensive. Historically, nearly all of these problems have been "floating-point" intensive as well. Dr. Goh and his team set out to do some research to see to what extent this is still true today of the problems being solved by SGI's current customer base. As noted, any application suitable to a federated computing model has appropriately moved onward. The remaining applications in fact do have a different but common set of characteristics.

One of the hallmarks of a super-computer application is the requirement for the machine to support relatively enormous random access memory (RAM) usage, measured on a scale that most computers would measure disk space. A super computer could have a terabyte of RAM and have thousands of processors accessing that RAM simultaneously. RAM access patterns for super-computer applications differ from those of conventional applications.

Consequently, the design of super-computer RAM differs fundamentally from that of more conventional computers. Think of super-computer RAM as a series of cells organized in a similar fashion to that of a chessboard. As such, moving data into and out of memory cells is exceedingly expensive by conventional computing standards. Super computers are specially designed to make such operations better (but still challenging), and much of the performance increase comes from clever software that knows how to remap and move blocks of data in the most conducive manner.

Embedded Density

Case in point, Mercury Computer Systems (the company introduced in Chapter 4) is one of a number of companies that are known for "handcrafted" data movement and signal processing routines—software that is written in basic machine instruction code and uses nearly all the horsepower of computing machinery it embodies. Mercury's computing systems are essentially mini super computers embedded into equipment designed to withstand the rigors of harsh (and physically small) military-application environments.

Handcrafting is nearly a lost art in the computer world. The general-purpose computer industry is driven to mass producing hardware that runs applications written in higher-level programming languages and tools that can produce more "utility" with less development and debugging cost. (However, it does so at the expense of wasted CPU cycles.) Military applications have extreme constraints on heat and physical size, and so the effort has to focus largely on the development of algorithms that get the most efficiency out of embedded, special-purpose computers. On the other hand, commercial computer manufacturers can be more lax on processing efficiency as well as size and heat generation. Super-computer applications not only use enormous amounts of memory, they spend a fair amount of time simply moving data around—a thoroughly non-mathematical operation. Dr. Goh's research of his customers showed the actual dependency on floating-point operations, although still critical, was not the 95+ percent everyone assumed, plus dependency varied greatly from one application to the next. Some applications would require very few floating-point operations, but needed the super-computer memory architecture and other speed benefits. Others were closer to traditional dependency, but none as high as 90 percent. Memory rotations aside, today's typical high-end application now requires a sizeable amount of integer processing that needs to take place along with the floating-point operations and other work. The answer, Dr. Goh believes, is tightly integrated hybrid processing architectures.

Mercury Computer Systems has held the same belief for some time, necessitated by the military computing customers they largely serve. Nearly all Mercury systems are sold with a variety of processors (scalar and vector) tightly knitted together into a monolithic memory model with super-fast internal element interconnections. Mercury's systems are typically optimized for placement in very small spaces and harsh environments, and thus play in somewhat of specialty-market segment. SGI and other classic super-computer manufacturers are now heading the same direction.

Many challenges will remain, however. The need for different types of processors (floating-point plus scalar) within the same architecture adds a great deal of application complexity that the machine internal operating system software must shield. The open-source community will likely be the source of standard Linux-based application programming interfaces (APIs) that allow higher-level application engineers to write applications based on a "core" set of mathematical and data-movement services that nearly perfectly exploit the power of the hardware.

If super-computer makers continued along the path of squeezing only 10% performance improvements out of our highest-end computing solutions, we would never solve today's toughest computational problems. Instead, they have to step back, see the processing "Muda" and completely redesign. By so doing, they will hopefully be able to leap frog various problem spaces and advance data analysis and consumption at a rate that would take a decade or more by conventional measure. SGI, Mercury, and other forward-looking companies are designing new systems that have an appropriate variety of computing elements. If done correctly, the efficiency gap that forces applications to utilize as little as 10 percent of a machine's power could be improved to 50 percent or higher—a monumental leap that should yield significant advances in the number and types problems that super computers can solve. The new approaches and technologies developed will ultimately move downstream and wind up possibly in computers the size of today's workstations and maybe even laptops. (Note that today's laptops pack as much computing power as a small IBM mainframe of 20 years ago.) Imagine doing home weather prediction and personal protein-folding analysis as you watch Sunday-afternoon football. Such step-function advances will be critical to enabling localized processing of the massive amounts of data that will be available to us as citizens of the Inescapable Data world.

Visualization and 3D Graphics

We have already alluded to how fundamental limits are reached with regard to information absorption. That is, we need our new information sources more finely digested and presented in ways that we can understand and understand more rapidly. Passive data-display devices, such as the Orb, are useful. Heads-up eyewear and immersion devices are useful. Advances in 3D graphics and displays can bring an even deeper presentation of information.

The fundamental building block of computerized graphics is a small triangle, partly because a minimum of three points in space is required to describe a surface. Put enough triangles together and you can finely approximate any image. Creating a realistic scene or image in full motion can require hundreds of millions of triangles. "Ten years ago, the computerized models of a car would have 10,000 triangles and be rendered in real time at 20 to 30 frames per second and at a million pixels per frame," describes Dr. Goh. Each triangle (a mathematical model) is rendered into dots or "pixels" on the computer screen. The pixels fill in the shape of the object. "So, 10,000 triangles go into the system and 1 million pixels come out per frame. By contrast, today, we have data sets of hundreds of millions or even a billion triangles, but commonly 3 to 10 million pixels out. We've gone from a data *magnification* to a data *reduction* problem. The latter is therefore the focus of much of our visualization research."

A billion triangles per frame at 30 frames a second (for full-motion graphics) makes for a lot of processing in just 1 second. Such rendering capability is currently the province of super-computer-scale machines. Of those billion triangles, only a fraction of them will be visible from whatever the current view-point is that the computer presents to the viewer. The system first calculates which will be the visible ones. Then, it has to angle and rotate each remaining triangle to account for the current viewpoint. Shading, coloring, shadows, texture, and illumination all need to be calculated as well—all calculations are mathematically intensive. The result is a realistic rendering of a certain object at a given view angle under specific lighting and interference conditions (shadows, obstructions, etc.) for one-thirtieth of a second.

Why the dramatic increase in the number of triangles needing to be processed? Users of computer graphics software are now demanding a much more realistic rendering of an image. In years past, high-end computer-aided design (CAD) systems could model only one aspect of a car, for example, at a time, such as the exterior only or the tail section only. Today, automobile engineers want to model and view the entire car, including all the engine components, all the body panels, and the entire interior—a 100 percent complete model. Why? Because only then can engineers truly tell that absolutely everything fits together perfectly, has the right spaces around it, and is aesthetically acceptable overall. Given such a complete model, engineers can run extremely compute-intensive (and accurate) thermal simulations, weight-distribution calculations, air-foil simulations, air-flow simulations (around the engine and computer components), and place human models within the interior. The explosion of data needed for more complete modeling in turn begets another explosion of simulation data, and the requisite computing horsepower needed has to grow proportionally to keep pace.

Extremely complex simulations of automobiles, proteins, weather patterns, and earthquakes will in all likelihood get the processing power needed resulting from the new generation of super computers now on the horizon. However, Dr. Goh believes that the technology that goes along with these new computing forms will "trickle down" to smaller and more pervasive computing devices. Soon, PDA device displays will be available with XGA or better quality resolution—a turn of events Dr. Goh believes that will be highly disruptive. Currently, PDA displays are "good enough" for displaying text such as e-mail and very limited Web-style graphics. Greatly enhanced PDA displays that can render a Web page, for example, in finite detail, will make owning a PDA-like device far more compelling to those who have so far resisted the lure of anywhere-anytime connectivity. Furthermore, it will enable scientific and engineering applications to include PDAs as data gathering and presentation devices.

OLEDs

The physical form factor for PDA displays may change as a result of a new type of display technology. Imagine a flat-panel computer display with the flexibility of a sheet of plastic. Within three to four years, displays based on the use of organic, light-emitting diode materials (called OLEDs) will begin to replace the standard CRT and LCD screens in common use today. We say *replace* because OLEDs promise to be cheaper to make; consume far less power; and project a brighter, clearer image. As an added bonus, they will go almost anywhere.

Because they can use glass, plastic, and metal foil as substrates, OLEDs (and a derivative technology called PLEDs) will appear on wristbands, cylindrical columns in buildings, articles of clothing, and in all the places we now use electronic displays. They can be as big as billboards, as walls, and street signs, or as small as the face of your watch. They could even be embedded in virtual skin. But, their real benefit will be seen immediately by PDA and laptop users. Imagine a computer screen that rolls up and drops into your purse or pocket. Using OLEDs, PDA displays could actually display lots of readable, intelligible information (such as an entire Web page) exactly as you now see it on your laptop, and with better resolution. In fact, OLEDs could allow multifunction PDAs and laptops to converge into a single personal, portable, universal information unit.

The Holy Grail for some visual modeling applications is holographic displays. A holographic image is one that appears in three-dimensional space, as if suspended in air. Right now, the demand for such display technology is low, partly because the image quality is still poor. Systems still cannot process enough triangles in one-thirtieth of a second to give realistic depth perception. Today, a pixel (the picture cell) contains only enough information to display color and brightness. A "hogel" (the holographic cell equivalent of the triangle) needs to have more information (namely "phase" among other details). Looking at a holographic image is much like looking at a real physical scene through a windowpane. To render such detail in real time requires tremendous compute power, which today is only barely available even from super computers. With the help of Moore's law (a doubling of compute power every 18 months), scalability, innovative new hybrid computer architectures, and remote display technologies, the processing power will eventually percolate downward to workstations and PDAs. There are, however, still some challenges.

Another remaining challenge is determining what the actual display technology will be for holographics. Currently, images can be generated using three different colored lasers: red, green, and blue. It turns out that red lasers are inexpensive compared to green and blue. This is partly because of their mass-market use in every CD drive and related technology, and partly because of the fact that red-light wavelength, being longer that green and blue, makes red lasers easier to mass produce. Green and blue lasers are more expensive to produce given the shorter wavelength of the light they radiate, and so they are seldom used in commercial applications (and thus no economies of scale). A commercial application for green and blue lasers is now on the horizon: holographic storage.

Blue-laser data storage disks will be appearing in early 2005. Today, red-laser DVD-type devices can hold up to 4 gigabytes of data. Blue-laser disks have been shown to hold up to 50 gigabytes (equivalent to 4.5 hours of recorded HDTV) partly by virtue of shorter wavelength of blue light. In a few years, true 3D-storage holographic disks using blue lasers will be available, yielding a terabyte of storage per penny-costing disk of plastic. Some computer storage companies are driving this technology forward in earnest. As discussed in previous chapters, our desire to "store everything indefinitely" coupled with massive data sources, such as movies and videos, will soak up as much capacity as the storage industry can muster up—but only at the right price.

The amazing twist to all this is that the storage industry could essentially be building 3D holographic projection systems (granted, at a different granularity and designed, instead, to hold digital information for computer consumption). Nevertheless, Dr. Goh believes that it will be the massive deployment and success of such technology in the general computer storage sector that will *enable* holographic scene-projection devices to be built. As Dr. Goh states:

> We're essentially just waiting; the prices will come down and the component availability will go up—we'll wait until the prices are low enough and pieces are available, then knit them together and repurpose these storage components for display systems. Realistic holographic displays are no longer skeptical future fantasies. They will indeed be practical and will someday be ubiquitous.

No doubt, holographic displays could forever change the way in which we visualize information. If possible, 3D holographic images will prove to have value far beyond displaying simple scenes. The world will find ways to display "information" in useful 3D forms. Imagine "walking" through your medical records—turn your head left to see your genome and walk around your gene segments; turn right and wade through a 3D scan of your liver.

Thinking more abstractly and less pictorially, holographic displays will be a boon for the engineers of computer *programs* and *data connectivity* devices. Imagine being able to see the relationships of one database tied to another in some sort of artistic rendition. Imagine seeing computer subroutines floating and interacting with data. Computer programmers have seen nearly zero innovations in tools that help the programmer visualize relationships. Most attempts at pictorial programming models have used 2D displays based on "boxes" and lines to show relationships—a far cry from 3D holographic representations that could even show time as a component.

While building a program, the mind of the computer engineer swells with bizarre artificial models of relationships because no other models exist. No two programmers build the same fantasy model—one reason for the difficulty in maintaining software applications after they are built. In contrast, an engineer building a car or airplane is ultimately building something physical and therefore naturally uses tools to help him visualize the potential end result. Those same tools help others working on the same project—safety engineers, manufacturing engineers, artists, etc. Holographic display breakthroughs will come from an ability to visualize *information* that actually has no natural physical rendition, such as parts of a computer program itself, databases, and their relationships to other data sets, where color, texture, depth, age, interaction, and other attributes can be represented in 3D space. Watch for such innovations in "information" display, and then watch massive advances take place for a wide variety of data-centric applications that today have no opportunity for visualization.

XML and New CPUs?

We have discussed how XML is becoming a dominant description and interface "language." The first step in processing XML statements is to compile XML into native computer bits (machine language?)—a process that is CPU intensive (as well as memory and storage intensive). Interestingly, XML processing tends to be stream oriented, more so than other data sources. That is, there is a massive stream of XML syntax pouring into our CPUs, which are presently ill-equipped to turn that stream into another stream of computer bits. Might this need to convert XML streams into data streams that conventional CPUs can interpret lead to a new generation of XML-processing CPUs?

We are already seeing some evidence of this. One company, DataPower, makes a transparent XML pre-processing device that sits in the LAN between servers and watches for XML transactions. Their specialty device can decompose XML at wire speed (that is, it introduces no slowness or additional latency into the data stream) and provides a number of value-add features such as assurance that the syntax is correct (which is an expensive operation, processing-wise), encryption and decryption of the data stream for security, and other tasks. Without such a device, many enterprise applications would need the processing power of several to a dozen servers to match the same performance level and hence the value of a specialty network-based appliance to convert XML streams "on-the-fly."

Today, XML is primarily used on the "boundaries" of a computing network, the points at which a given computer system interfaces to another computer system. XML streams must be converted to another programming language so that they can be interpreted by today's conventional processors. It is likely that, over time, we will see more and more data streams remain in XML format throughout processing the processing steps (i.e., within a processor, between systems, and even stored on disk). This will be done to relieve the processing-overhead impact as XML streams are translated and untranslated multiple times.

A number of companies are chasing the XML chip opportunity, and a number of different approaches will emerge. Initially, these will all appear as niche market opportunities as opposed to the next Intel-class mainstream processor contender. It may be a while (if ever) for the market opportunity to develop to the point that an AMD, Intel, or an IBM/Motorola will build an XML main processor. In today's world, workstations and laptops are our personal bulk data processing devices. In the Inescapable Data world of tomorrow, PDAs and full-function cell phones or gaming handhelds will be the processing devices of choice out on the "edge." If wireless telecommunications take on more of an XML flavor, we can easily imagine that the DSPs (digital signal processors used in all cell phones) of today will be altered to be natural XML-streaming processors.

XML processing has the potential to upset the apple cart regarding the future of mainline networking devices and today's prevalent CPU architectures. Today, the typical LANs or SANs (storage networks) pass data back and forth between servers and storage devices. They are passive networks in that their switching and routing components have extremely little knowledge of the data passing through them. As such, they offer few capabilities for optimizing relationships between data streams and managing of those data streams. If the data elements of "packets" were encapsulated in XML packages, a far higher utility could arise from LAN and SAN components. XML could be used to describe the data inside each packet, thereby making the associations between data packets and servers, databases, and other data sources, for example, more obvious to switches and routers. Therefore, it seems sensible to assume that the encapsulation of data in XML packages is forthcoming, if we can simultaneously drive the performance of XML processors to the point where there is no discernable loss in network performance versus what users now experience. As suggested, it may not be the computer industry itself that drives XML encapsulation; it may be more driven by the communications industry, and then re-absorbed back into mainstream computing.

Intelligent Networking

"The question is not about the data, but about applying context to the data," states Cheng Wu, founder and chairman of Acopia Networks (and formerly founder of ArrowPoint Communications). The world of data networking is going through some powerful changes that might re-label the data networking industry as information networking. The old days of moving bits without knowledge of what they are or their purpose for existence seems to be coming to a close. Wu's new venture is squarely focused on more intelligently managing data motion and data location. (*Storage* might be too old of a word now, because storing implies keeping something in one place for a long period of time.)

Wu believes that there is a fundamental gap between applications that are seen more as services to the users of applications, and the computing infrastructure that supports them, and that this gap has to close for new efficiencies to be realized. Wu believes that the computing industry has been constrained by what is now a rigid architecture model that dictates how data is stored and moved. As a result, the industry can only achieve a yearly 10 percent improvement of some aspect (faster networking switches, faster server CPUs, faster disks, etc.) of the computing infrastructure. In his view, step-function improvements will come from a completely new attitude about what the "data network" really is.

"The core intelligence of the data moves away from computers and into the network. Endpoint intelligence goes into the network. Today, however, the network is assumed to only be a transport. We need to first change our own view of what a network can do for us and then match that with proper machinery," states Wu.

In Chapter 11, "Computer Storage Impacted by Inescapable Data," we looked at how the concept of a super file would allow storage systems to be far smarter than today regarding how they manage, secure, and protect data. The same notion applies to networking. The more information we can glom around data—information that describes data, otherwise known as "metadata" (data about data, if you will)—the better the chance that a data package will move efficiently and purposely throughout the network. Data today flies through a great many infrastructure components, first within a computer system itself, then throughout the network, and finally landing on a storage device. If each of those components has some understanding of what is inside the data package traversing the computing infrastructure, from source to destination, and the intended use of the data, the entire infrastructure would function far more efficiently.

Every network switch, every storage element, every router, and every computer along the way, each could pick apart a higher-order message contained in metadata and add value to the infrastructure that ultimately supports computing services as seen by application users by finding a faster route, caching the information for later faster access, better protecting the information by duplicating it, pregathering related information that might be useful soon, etc. Today, a typical storage request looks like this: "Fetch block 10,221 from disk 78." A typical LAN transaction looks like this: "Here's 768 bytes of something that needs to land on port 21 on host 551." Such messages make it difficult for the vast amount of gear between the endpoints to do anything more useful with it than send it along on its merry way. The newer view would be requests that perhaps look like, "Fetch employee record 556," or "Here is a picture of my hairy dog taken last Tuesday outside of Boston on a rainy day just before noon, and it's pretty important to me for my archives, but not as important as my work proposals, and I'm likely to access it a bunch of times this month but then almost never again. Now, go store it somewhere."

This new goal is not magic, and we have seen similar examples in history that at first seemed like science "hope." For example, consider how memory management inside of your computer works. When computers were first invented, a program was held in the computer's memory, and the program's data in one flat contiguous space. The machine language program itself specified exactly what memory locations were used to store instructions and data, and those instructions had to be hard coded into the program as well. At that time, computer memory was extremely expensive by today's standards. There was a real limitation on how much memory a manufacturer could build in to a system and still make it affordable by even the largest of corporate buyers. As programs got larger and more sophisticated, the need for more memory soon outstripped a manufacturer's ability to affordably attach it to the system. A need arose to make some other form of memory or storage appear to the system's processor as real memory. The concept of "virtual memory" was born.

Virtual memory allows a processor to still believe that a program and its data are loaded into a particular place in real memory. However, behind the scenes, the computing system machinery transparently moves data back and forth from real memory to some other storage location such as a disk, in essence fooling the processor into thinking it actually has more real memory than actually exists. Processing has progressed to the point that today the processor inside your laptop program has no knowledge about where programs and data physically live. At any given time, the bits could live in RAM, in some intermediate memory cache, on disk, or even out on the Internet somewhere. An intervening layer of technology presents a virtual view of data and the pathway to it, and hides the underlying complexity; program and data bits are shuffled around at will behind the scenes.

This is essentially the view that Wu has for the future of the general networking and data access world. Today, it may sound like future-ware to say, "Throw your Excel spreadsheet into the network, never specifying a destination for it, and never knowing where it actually physically lives at any instant." The network may fling it around, it may make copies of it, it may decompose it a bit and index parts of it, and it may move it far away from you without asking for your permission first. No matter. Don't worry. Let the network figure all that out. The network will respond to you instantly and get it back to you as soon as you need it. The approach is similar to the virtual memory concept at work inside your computer—you have no idea exactly where in the network your Excel spreadsheet is living, how much of it is actually in your laptop's memory or disk, and how often it cycles around to various other locations within the network. The value of this approach to Inescapable Data is enormous because it allows the network to handle the large volumes of data that will be generated by Inescapable Data devices automatically and with far greater speed.

Intelligent networking is currently in its infancy. We're seeing evidence in a new class of network switch that can decompose some amount of data on-the-fly and perform some optimizations as a result. XML-encapsulated (i.e., self-describing) data bundles allow devices such as the DataPower XML processor to add value to networks. If more and more data goes the encapsulation route, we stand a better chance of seeing significant information management benefits.

Internet Enterprise

Larry Geisel is the former CIO of Netscape, currently CEO of NexaWeb, and a well-known Internet networking guru. Geisel vision is of a world that is anxious for deeper business-to-business connections via the Internet, but is hindered by some basic architectural problems:

> Businesses greatly want to deploy more Internet-based services, but the Web metaphor is limited. Network connections are unreliable, slow, and HTML is just barely adequate for individual users, and too often inadequate for enterprise applications to be deployed in an Inescapable Data way.

Geisel's view is that serious enterprise applications cannot move to a pure Web-based model because, at the moment, Web-based applications cannot provide the requisite always-connected and rich application experience. Changes need to be made to the overall model that describes how Web-based applications work. Web-based applications need to move away from a page-download-and-connect mentality to one that gives users a "live" and fully interactive experience, in spite of the fact that the reality of pervasive endpoints is that they do not have 100 percent reliable connections to the Internet.

To make matters more difficult, as Web-based applications move toward the inclusion of more pervasive endpoints that are connected wirelessly, they must also contend, at least initially, with slower connection speeds The development of customer relationship management (CRM) applications, for example, that could really leverage wireless Inescapable Data devices for great added value, are currently being held back by such challenges. NexaWeb is one such company using newer Internet models that use current bandwidth availability in more efficient ways yet without compromising application richness, evidence that Web-based technologies are starting to appear that solve some of the inherent limitations to a more pervasive business deployment of endpoint devices.

Applications built around this new Internet computing model are being dubbed "rich internet applications" (RIA). They key critical components of RIA include the following:

- *Rich Web experience.* We take for granted such things as the ability to "drag-and-drop" when using normal workstation applications are notably missing from the current Web-based ones. These features are added back in.

- *Live data.* To be used pervasively, business application endpoints need to have "screens" and panels that show live data (live inventory, collaboration messages, etc.). In the existing world of Internet/HTML applications, such views are typically impossible.

- *Zero-install clients.* Users are relieved of the need to install applications and application upgrades on their computing devices. This need becomes more acute as the number of endpoint devices soars.

Today, a few companies offer RIA development environments for businesses to build rich pervasive Internet applications. Likely, we will see an escalation in the deployment of these business tools and, with that, perhaps some changes to underlying business models as businesses users discover new ways to deploy RIA.

"When data gets truly portable via XML and applications get truly portable via Web services, you will see opportunities to create expanded enterprises that are far more loosely coupled than they have ever been before," says Geisel. We may see a new type of company emerge: the momentary enterprise. For a relatively short period of time, an opportunistic business model is activated, loosely coupling existing businesses that, heretofore, were not associated with each other. The momentary enterprise takes advantage of an opportunity that may only exist for months. When it has been fully exploited, the momentary enterprise is reconfigured—Lego-like—to pursue another opportunity. A "pop-up" business model is born, changing the competitive balance, and leveraging Inescapable Data.

Motes

Motes are networked computing's answer to The Borg. Motes are miniature, thumb-sized computers attached to radio transceivers, powered by batteries or solar cells. Motes can even be as small as pinheads. *Smart dust* is a moniker applied to a pile of a few hundred pinhead-sized motes.

Motes are autonomous, always on, and sometimes invisible computing and networking devices. Hundreds, perhaps thousands of these little devices can be sprinkled about some geographical area or even the surface of a wall (think "smart paint"). They are extremely simple devices that know how to do just a few things well: listen for each other and pass along information that is sensed among all motes in a network, for example. They form a virtual ad-hoc network that can "self-organize" into little computer "societies."

Motes are real. You can buy them today. They are currently too expensive and bulky for most of their envisioned applications but are nonetheless demonstrable. Time will drive down size and cost. They represent a long-sought-after mode of computing wherein devices with minimal processing power are networked together to produce major intelligence. They are every bit a part of the Inescapable Data revolution in that they can be deployed pervasively, communicate wirelessly, and gather and forward data that is digested into information in real time.

Motes can be fitted with a range of sensors that can detect light, sound, vibration, airborne chemicals, radiation—just about anything that is detectable electronically. They can be mounted on trees, machines, warehouse racks, telephone poles, even miniature planes and robotic devices. They develop an "awareness" of each other using radio transceivers to talk to each other, relaying their data messages back though a wireless mesh-like network, from mote to mote, to centralized data aggregators connected to the Internet. Motes can also be interfaced to other Inescapable Data technologies such as RFID.

Mote Details

Motes were created by the University of California at Berkley and Intel several years ago. There are more than 100 groups around the world today using motes for various exploratory and research topics.[1] DARPA somewhat gave life to the idea, which was originally known as smart dust. The original idea was to sprinkle thousands of these devices around battlefields to monitor troop movements.

Motes can be as small as a small stack of quarters. (The battery still dominates the size.) Although they are not yet at an inconsequential price, the goal is to have sub-$25 motes within a few years. Advances are occurring along compressing more CPU power into a smaller size (including the radio and RAM parts). Motes today are typically as powerful as the old 8088-based IBM PC, vintage 1982—a pretty hefty amount of power in such a small package. A number of firms are building motes and mote-like devices. Crossbow (www.xbow.com) is one such company.

Computers typically run operating systems, and motes are no exception. They run TinyOS and store data in a distributed database called TinyDB, both are products of the "open-source" movement. TinyDB can be queried from outside the mesh network via the Internet when it comes time to harvest their bounty of collected data. Or they can communicate data in real time, sensing and identifying the source of a toxic chemical spill in a factory, for example.

So far, motes have been used by scientists to collect data from large spaces over time without the necessity of having to constantly be on site (such as climate data in pristine forests or bird-nesting behaviors on uninhabited islands). However, potential commercial and military applications abound. For example, motes that sense movement and are attached to mobile anti-tank mines could triangulate among themselves the location of a moving tank on a battlefield and reposition themselves accordingly.

Motes indeed leverage the combined use of relay communication (and mesh communication) as well as data collection, to a scale unthinkable before their invention. Whether it is actually "motes" that become pervasive or something else like semi-intelligent RFID tags, we will most assuredly see mass-deployable

---

[1] http://www.eetimes.com/at/news/OEG20030128S0028.

devices that wirelessly communicate with each other and a centralized processing system while gathering data.

Summary

As followers of the Inescapable Data vision, we are particularly interested in
certain changes to computing and networking technologies. The processing capabilities of super computers are noteworthy because many of the far-reaching
values derived from data-stream correlations will require tremendous amounts
of computing horsepower, attainable at commodity prices. Similarly, advancement in the visualization of information and data is needed to transform a 2D
world into one where the 3D holographic presentation of information yields
new ways to "see" abstract concepts.

As networked computing models progress, we are seeing deep value in
richly described data—data that remains essentially in one highly inter-
pretable form throughout its travels. Such data can be routed efficiently, automatically managed, and intelligently cross-connected to other data sources—all
in the network if need be and without specific host involvement. The emergence of pervasive endpoint devices are tempting businesses to do away with
more and more of their legacy, non-Internet-based applications. Finally, a new
class of devices—motes—will finally get us to self-organized and Inescapable
Data collection networks producing volumes of data crying out for totally new
associations and analysis.

CHAPTER THIRTEEN

Inescapable Data in Perspective

Our hope is that the readers of this book will internalize what Inescapable Data means and be on the lookout for emerging examples both as a means to improving one's quality of life or business, and possibly as a way to protect oneself from those who would harness the reach of Inescapable Data in intrusive or undesirable ways. The power of Inescapable Data will be ours to exploit. We may be on the cusp of a new world wherein we are able to leverage each other's presence, data, and capabilities and enable a magnified and rapid set of benefits. With the coming emergence of full-function, handheld wireless devices, the power will literally be in our hands.

What Is Inescapable Data?

Computing technology surrounds us. More is coming. However, computing technology is not necessarily Inescapable Data technology. In the world of Inescapable Data, most of the following attributes must be at play:

+ Data rich
+ Wireless
+ Real time

- Leverage historical data
- Combine data streams for new values
- Asynchronous but immediate
- Self-describing and trivially interfaced with other streams
- Crossing traditionally business control boundaries

Often, we will find the following technologies at play:

- Wireless data networks
- Cellular networks
- RFID
- GPS
- Video
- XML

Are cell phones themselves Inescapable Data elements? No, cell phones are just better phones in that they are untethered, far more so than your cordless home phone. But if it can take and transmit a picture, it takes a step closer. If it can do that and send and receive asynchronous messages (text), it gets closer again. If it does all this and integrates with your calendar and scans embedded product tags for details or is used to pay for purchases, it definitely is.

Is your furnace an Inescapable Data element? Just having a programmable thermostat would not be enough. However, if the thermostat communicates with your home network, it gets closer. If the furnace has an embedded processor and can store historical data such as operating statistics, it gets closer still. If that data is self-describing and announced to your home computing network via a Web interface, it arrives. If you can build value-add programs and Web views to monitor, control, and automate your furnace, it attains full citizenship.

Merely being electronic and having a computer with a networking interface is not enough to be an Inescapable Data element. We are looking for the magic that comes when a historical approach to solving a problem is catapulted to a new level in utility by mixing multiple data streams, exploiting real-time information, distilling tons of data into meaningful information, and in general using technology in creative and "mixed" ways.

So, whereas a toaster with advanced settings does not exemplify Inescapable Data, one that is wirelessly interconnected to your heating, ventilation, and air-conditioning (HVAC) system via your home network and can thus adjust itself by exploiting collected humidity data does (perhaps to cook longer in higher humidity to provide a more consistent "toast" experience). Whereas a business system that reduces time through internal record simplification does not exemplify Inescapable Data, one that ties directly to suppliers' systems and avoids management worry over inventory levels by instead automatically reordering components does. Whereas a doctor's office that uses a high-tech gadget to instantly measure glucose level is not Inescapable Data, one that wirelessly updates your personal health record with the information and is then used properly by a pharmacy for prescription refill is.

It is a crossing of boundaries seamlessly, sharing information wirelessly, with other information sources, and without any delays or gaps (Muda). That's Inescapable Data. The art of combining these technologies will produce the significant twenty-first-century advances. Businesses and manufacturers are seeing this, too, and steadily creating products and connections along this theme.

Venture and Investment

Where is the venture and investment world heading? Post the Internet bubble, venture capitalists (VCs) are still a bit cautious. We sat down with several of the largest VC firms and tried to get a sense of where their emotions are with regard to investing in computing technology. (Investing, especially in the technology space, can be quite emotional.)

David Skok, partner at Matrix Ventures, says, "We're coming off of the worst down market ever seen in this industry. No one ever saw anything this bad. Sure, it has a cleansing effect, and we're still cleansing the financial aspect. There are still too many money firms chasing too few good deals."

Rick Burnes, partner at Charles River Ventures, puts into perspective part of the runup experienced in the late 1990s:

> The industry went through a very rapid period of expansion in the last half of the 90s—much more so than ever before. Why? Productivity numbers on computing became imperative. It became strategically imperative to have really good systems or you could not compete. That was the main driver of capital equipment in that timeframe. Wal-Mart is a very good example. The concept of Wal-Mart could not have existed in 1980—the equipment was too expensive. Wal-Mart was enabled by technology and it is very important that that be understood. Then the market became saturated—too much investment, which led to the decline in the first part of this decade.

The investment community is regrouping and regenerating steam and courage. "The areas that interest us now are RFID, wireless, open-source software, and the digital home," states Skok. "We see the enormous values brought forth by new advancements in these categories. Information and speed are at the heart of a changing method for doing business and the open-source initiatives are changing the balance of the incumbents," continues Skok.

Burnes observes that the communications and computer industries are going through an important change of customer:

> We now have a very large technology industry that is moving downstream in cost—moving down from productivity equipment in business now to the consumer and entertainment area. Some of the most sophisticated semiconductors are going into consumer gear. Our industry typically evaluates investment opportunities based on ROI, and now in the consumer market, we have to somehow evaluate Sponge Bob.

Of course, there is the common theme of compressing time. "In the 1970s, we didn't even have breakfast meetings," starts Burnes, "and today if we haven't exchanged a dozen business correspondences before we leave for the office, we feel we're under serving our employer."

So there appears to be some optimism for opportunities related to communications and tying data sources more tightly together. Throughout this book, we have highlighted the importance of cell phones (with advanced features) and cellular service (in addition to other wireless communication forms). It would seem sensible that the "communications" market would be picking up steam. The hesitation is partly due to a hangover of the late 1990s when telecom opportunities, the biggest growth hopes, led to unrealistic market runups. Have fundamental aspects of the economy changed enough to allow for a more sane resumption of communication investment?

An earlier chapter of this book discussed a number of changes that could spell the beginnings of fresh opportunity, including the following:

- Reduction of the number of in-office workers driven by an ability to create virtual office environments via combined voice and new data connectivity such as virtual officeware and beyond
- The adoption and growth of instant messaging and text messaging, driving home the value of asynchronous yet immediate correspondence

+ The willingness of businesses to remove intercompany barriers and tie in outside systems more closely, driven by desires for 80 percent to 90 percent improvements in time-to market efficiencies

+ Massive data volumes emanating from devices such as RFID tags and digital video cameras driving needs for improvement in wireless speeds and penetration from back-end warehouses through retail shelves and even on factory floors

+ Mass-market demand for real-time information while watching TV, while playing electronic games, and while at sporting events, all of which now demands a two-way interactive communication mechanism

+ Need for higher-coupled military intelligence built on real-time wireless extremely data-rich streams

Because so many "intelligent" devices can or will be wirelessly interconnected (refrigerators, automobiles, bathroom scales), there will emerge a new demand to give them the ability to exchange meaningful information in addition to raw data.

So, yes, a number of significant changes and advances have taken place over the past handful of years that likely will rejuvenate many "communications" areas.

Technological advances have occurred all throughout our lives. What's new, and where the opportunities now lie, is the ability for data sources to be intertwined more rapidly, plus a massive increase in the number of data sources themselves (medical data, video data, location/GPS data, identity data [RFID], and so forth). The intertwining, enabled by wireless-everywhere and standards (and self-describing data), brings new levels of efficiency, safety, and flexibility.

The opportunities are so vast they are almost intractable. What makes the new future attainable is that standards more than ever are helping interoperability, and creators of data streams are utilizing self-describing styles. These two events are allowing huge numbers of Average Joes to sit down and self-create solutions and values. Whereas the past required teams of programmers, some problems of the future will be solved by Web-savvy people using standard software tools. Whereas the past required special hardware engineers to design components, many of the device-to-device interconnections of the future will fall out as naturally as today plugging your blender into the wall outlet (although the future communication is primarily without wires). As a world community, we have learned how to do this new style of software creation called the open source and we suspect that legions of ordinary people will be creating sharable and high-quality nearly free software. Why? Because the devices are begging for some attention, and the manufacturers would rather leverage resources outside of their payroll.

Should I Worry About Too Much Data and Connectivity?

In a word: yeah. There are definitely things going on that should concern you from at least a privacy point of view, not to mention a general "always-tethered, wirelessly, life." Putting that thought aside for a moment, a significant worry is being able to jump on board this train and survive among your peers, your managers, and your children. Certainly through other times in history we have seen major industrial and computer revolutions create a massive paradigm shift in our lives. This one may be different. This one may come on faster and stronger and more quickly separate the connected from the unconnected.

The automobile was a notable invention. Not everyone could have one. Those who did had more freedom and flexibility; however, there were not many paved roads and not many gas stations, so the new freedom was bridled. The automobile revolution (if you could call it that) actually took decades, and steadily (but slowly) adoption rose and infrastructure matched the needs. The computer revolution was not too much different. It did not happen overnight either. Computers were around in business back offices running operations all through the late 1960s and through the 1970s. During the 1980s, they started to enter our homes, and through the 1990s they became pervasive on every business desk and home alike. Someone born in the 1960s was 30 years old by the time computers truly became pervasive. Hardly overnight.

The Internet adoption *appeared* faster (and it was faster, to some extent). Most people do not realize that the Internet was quite heavily in use in the government, military, and public spaces throughout the 1980s and 1990s. So, to many of us, it seemed like the Internet started taking hold in the mid 1990s and by the turn of the century was a completely pervasive tool. In either case, it was well under 30 or even 20 years, but not as fast as 3 or 5 years.

Regarding adoption rates, what should we expect from this impending move to wireless-everything and data-everywhere watching-everything? Rapid. Like pet-rock rapid, except that it will not go away after adoption peaks. Because of the reasons laid out many times in this book, this forthcoming revolution has advantages of a well-oiled machine and five billion hungry lions that will enable it to come in faster and more pervasively than prior revolutions. Although we have talked about the low cost of the new technology and the high business value as well as ease of exploitation, there is one more element that will significantly drive penetration rates: our youth generation.

Prior revolutions had to mostly entice the wealthy large corporations or wealthy consumers first and then slowly move more mainstream. (You may recall the 1980s when microwave ovens and VHS players were mostly for the upper middle class; today, hardly anyone goes without a cell phone or broadband regardless of class or age.) This revolution is different. Our kids can afford the same technology that our businesses can, and they relish the opportunity to exploit and overuse and perhaps misuse it...because it is cool and fun and because they can. We see it today. Kids are the number one cell phone text-messaging user. They probably rack up the most cell minutes as well (among the nonbusiness reimbursed group). They are playing massive multiplayer online role playing games in stunning numbers (when most of us still can't even spell MMORPG). They are using (if not defining) groupware tools to a level of comfort that is dizzying to the nonconnected among us.

The point is this: Other revolutions took time—decades typically—so you had plenty of time to get prepared to go mainstream. Technology changes, in general, have a natural habit of coming on faster and more furious as time goes by. But this time it is a bit different because many of the drivers of Inescapable Data are available to our children and completely embraceable by them. They are not only growing up in Internet times but are walking around deeply understanding XML, wireless connectivity, and can coordinate more trigger squeezes on a complex Nintendo controller while most of us struggle thumbing text messages with a cell phone. The business productivity tools and life-efficiency tools of the coming future are more synergistic with our kids than with us. Growing up, what did our home and personal lives share with our parent wage earner? A stapler, perhaps a phone, and it would be a stretch to say a typewriter.

So, your first worry should be how fast can you understand and embrace the onslaught of data devices and connectivity technology compared to eager younger wage earners.

Your next set of worries may include the following:

+ *Insurance.* You should worry about an inability to be insured without forgoing a level of privacy never considered before. Has your homeowner's insurance company already called you if you own a backyard trampoline and threatened cancellation? This is actually happening now. Imagine if they knew every time you bought Ginsu knives, or carbohydrate-laden bread, or a windsurfer. They need to manage their risk, and the more they know about what you do, the more profitable they can be.

How about medical insurance? Your genome might fairly accurately predict the cost of your longer-term health care. Won't the medical insurers try to charge a premium if you are predisposed to certain illnesses? After all, it will certainly cost them more to take care of you and they can demonstrate actuals to their point (and thus justify to regulators a difference in rates). Why should Healthy Sally pay more for insurance if she's perfectly normal and has certifiable evidence to that fact, simply to balance those who aren't? Might the insurers forcefully restrict elements of your lifestyle such as particular food consumption and insist on being tied into your food purchases for verification?

You could choose an insurer that might not have such invasive requirements—or could you, if the price is 1,000 times higher? Do you not already choose the "higher-deductible" option on your automotive insurance because you know you are a good driver? Won't you similarly be tempted to select the better insurance value because you are in fact a nonsmoker who does indeed go to the gym twice a week and seldom eat sausage so why not let them know that you are who you claim to be...? Is this goodness or worry?

• *Identity theft.* You should worry about identify theft on such a grand and comprehensive scale that it might be impossible to prove you are you. The new world will most assuredly use more and more biometric information, such as retinal scans and thumbprints, to help us identify ourselves. The trouble is, such information seems to imply a presumption of fact, that when the unique information itself is stolen or altered, it may be impossible to disprove. Could you not seeing the following conversation:

Gates to Fund Manager: "I'd like to withdraw a few billion dollars."

Fund Manager: "I'm sorry, Mr. Gates, but you're not truly the real Mr. Gates."

Gates: "Sir, look into my eyes, rescan my retina, rescan my thumbs, ask me my mother's maiden name."

Fund Manager: "We've done that. We know you're someone else. We have comprehensive tamper-proof records. Why, we triple encode our records with 2,000-bit encryption even the government is afraid to use and our data is replicated to 14.5 different global servers, including the space station and the new Mars colony. The real Gates's all-electronic records show that his thumbprints and retinal scans, done yearly, have not changed a single bit for the past 30 years."

The point is this: Although most of the advances in secure transactions and identity will benefit us, when broken, it will be broken real bad.

- *Marketeers.* Marketing professionals will be able to reach you to an uncomfortable level. You allowed this at first because of the promise of better prices and more personalized service and products. You sold your soul, and now you must be part of their machine or they'll cut you off. They will have more ability to reach you directly (as will your spouse or children). You will dream of the days when your biggest annoyance was merely a telemarketer calling during dinner. Now, you need to take their surveys (wirelessly, of course, but quite immediate because they need the information right away), you need to respond to their instant messages as you enter their stores, and you need to allow yourself to be monitored and watched. If you don't, you will not have affordable access (if any access at all) to their goods. They want you to be a partner in their corporation; because, after all, you truly are the riches of their life. Would you not similarly exploit ways to be closer to your customers?

- *Work life.* You should worry that this extreme blending of personal and business life ultimately means that you work continuously. Sure, it started off that you could be at your child's bus stop more often and seldom miss a soccer game, but it turned out that you never actually "watched" the swim meet, no longer waved as the school musical started, and hardly ever swam while on vacation...because you were too engrossed in that new full-immersion (yet see-through) helmet with touchless keying per your mere thoughts. Although that helmet might be a decade away or more, we can already see the beginning of devices that capture our *constant* attention no matter where we are. Using your PDA in the bathroom today is not outrageous anymore. Synagogue or church is not off limits. Certainly, restaurants and bars too often have patrons engaged with their wireless device (but we'll note, at least less distractingly as we move away from voice communication). We have squeezed more time out of our busy lives, but have we blurred our lives beyond being *life*?

- *Unreal sports.* We might worry that sports of the future become completely virtual if not artificial. We are inching there now. Even while physically at a game, we now find ourselves distracted by the pull of whatever handheld device is near us. We find that our biggest interest in professional sports is not how a given city's team is doing but rather how their player's contribution effects our virtual team's situation. Might we choose to stop going to games? Might we care only about our own personalized sports situation? Might it not even matter if the players themselves are real, much like it doesn't matter in Dungeons and Dragons? Perhaps the online virtual games will simply take over our "sports needs."

- *People.* We might worry that people we care about might start to know more about us than we desire them to. As we pass people in the hallways at work or in the mall or on the street, they might be able to "absorb" data about our clothes, where we shop, how much we paid, and maybe even our food preferences. When they enter our house and simply walk near our medicine cabinet, they may know more about our medical life than we would like. Our "virtual" cube neighbors in the workplace may now know every project we ever worked on and exactly how well we performed. Our next employer may as well. Our friends at a dinner party might giggle as they see into our previous night's adventures at the Halloween party by virtue of our global calendar absorbing cell photographs automatically into our public view.

But in perspective...yes, there are worries, and the issues raised above (and a great deal more) need to be seriously considered. But simply because these (very real) issues are possible, we must not attempt to run and hide. The introduction of the automobile was not without horrible consequences, even to this day ... cars crash and people get very hurt. Should we not use cars because of that? Can you imagine a world without cars? Can you imagine a world without computers? Or a world without cell phones for that matter? Our children will not be able to imagine a world without the massive conveniences that the new wireless and connected world brings us. Our employers will not imagine going back to less-productive times. Our deep interest in medical knowledge and military prowess will not imagine going back to the days of guesswork and exposure. So, the grandness of "data everywhere" (wirelessly) will come upon us, and it is our responsibility to be careful and cognizant of both the downsides and the upsides.

What Should I Be Doing to Exploit the New World?

As a regular citizen, you should consider the following:

- *E-mail PDA.* If you do not already have a digital "data" wireless device, get one. Being able to access e-mail (and Web pages, scant as they may be right now) is a critical tool in staying connected. Ignore the worry of being "too connected." You can control how often and when you glance to see whether you have new e-mail or text messages. You will likely discover that being able to lightly keep up with e-mail wherever you are is a stress *reliever*. No longer will you be running to your home computer the moment you come in the door. As people learn that you receive e-mail wherever you are, they will call you less often, which will save you time. You will have phone numbers and soccer field directions and correspondences at your fingertips no matter where you are. You will be able to stay closer in touch with your children, who will naturally choose to communicate this way.

- *Work@home.* If you have not done so already, speak with your employer about working some hours at home. Perhaps you can avoid rush-hour traffic entirely by working 10 to 2. Or work Mondays and Fridays at home like some major companies are doing today. Remind your manager of increased "work" time due to less travel and that you're willing to take customer calls at odd hours. If necessary, ask your employer to pay for your cell phone and/or home office phone and subscribe to a cell e-mail service along with a newer device to better handle text messaging. If you choose to work offsite more, you must back fill with requisite technology to smooth out the overall operation.

- *Get your kids a text/cell device.* Get your kids and spouse all on the same wireless plan, which hopefully offers free cell-to-cell calls. The cost for an additional line from most carriers is incredibly low, and most offer free cell-to-cell air time on the same plan. Staying closely connected to your kids and spouse is of paramount importance in the new world. Problems can arise faster than ever before, and the consequences can be higher than in the past. Do you really want to be less connected to your family members? Consider getting one of the new text-only devices for your kids, which is not only cheaper but more in sync with efficient information exchange in a less-interruptive fashion.

- *Get your doctors to send SMS and e-mail reminders.* Ask your doctors whether they have considered using electronic reminders. At a minimum, they should be able to send e-mail notification of appointments. (If you have an e-mail-capable PDA, that is all you will need.) It is in their interest (as well as yours), but they may be far enough behind the connected curve to not know that such capabilities are easily provided by their Internet provider.

- *Get your doctors to move to electronic records and get access.* Ask your doctors whether they are using electronic records now. If they are not, you should be insistent that they move toward an electronic record-keeping system soon. If they are, ask whether you can have access to your and your family member's records. If you do get access, be sure to archive and save any records you have access to.

- *Consider home video-surveillance devices.* Wireless IP cameras are quite inexpensive and likely you have at least one stationary computer in your house. Hooking up a wireless surveillance system is not very difficult. It does not have to be a "spy"-type camera hiding behind a bookshelf. It can be a simple device trained on a back entryway or a staircase to the bedroom. If there was ever a break-in or theft, the value of such data could be enormous. Furthermore, it is not a bad idea to be able to glance at your PDA while at a restaurant and be able to see that your house is not burning.

As an employer, you should consider the following:

- *Instant messaging.* If you are not insisting that all your employees run an instant messaging application at all times, you are missing out on one of the biggest productivity tools created in the past two decades. Beyond productivity, IM brings back a sense of community to your workers, and they will more happily "log on" in the evenings and off hours because, unlike e-mail, they can see who else is on and have an interactive correspondence. They will be more productive on conference calls, and, in general, command and control will have fewer barriers and more expediency throughout your organization (as we saw even in military operations).

- *Groupware.* Similarly, if your company is not exploiting the newer groupware technologies, it is missing out on a huge productivity boost. Many companies run applications such as Lotus Notes or use Web servers to share materials. Although that is fine, it is a far cry from the more modern tools that allow highly secure and rapid setup that spans customers and partners easily. Groove is one such application that we used to create this book. Imagine producing a 100,000-word book in full collaboration with a partner and never actually meeting in person (to discuss the book, that is). This entire book was done through virtual office collaboration software as well as a constant stream of e-mails and IMs and text messages. As an employer, any projects you have going with partner companies or customers should consider using groupware tools for document exchange and efficient information and project sharing.

+ *Work@home.* Work@home is good for companies and employers alike. Put aside the annual savings of no (or limited) office space; in the new world, flexibility will be the key attractor to successful businesses. The big challenge, as an employer, is successfully navigating these flexible waters. As an employer, do not be afraid to worry about how to successfully manage this new work force. There are agencies and consultants that can help manage the control anxiety and provide tips on successful remote management tactics. It is not without concern. Flexibility could be abused by the remote work force, and astute managers will stay very close to their remote employees...virtually, of course.

As a factory owner, you should consider the following:

+ *Open up.* First and foremost, relax, and open up your business systems. Allow your value chain to tie deeply into your systems and require a corresponding relationship yourself. Use tools that provide the right level of encryption and security, but be very open-minded to a new self-serve and automated-fulfillment mentality. Barriers and checkpoints will only slow your business down. We have grown through decades of business barriers that we do not even recognize because to us they are normal boundaries, much like lanes on a highway. Now, imagine no lanes. Are you ready to manage this new flexibility? Beware, your competitors might be.

+ *Turn upside down.* Manufacturing business in the developed nations will return, but only to those that are able to forget about 10 percent improvements. Business managers who are able to see the 100 percent or 500 percent improvement methods will allow major manufacturing businesses to return to the developed nations. Why? Because the primary reason for offshoring is labor costs, and when we eliminate or reduce the majority of labor costs (through automation and advanced tools), we can once again manufacture locally. The big win in local manufacturing: meeting the new breed of customer expectations for customization and rapid delivery (which simply cannot be adequately achieved if manufactured 12,000 miles away). Turn your operations upside down. Do not think inventory, think wireless, RFID, humanless business tie-ins, GPS on transport equipment and containers, and continuous contact to all principals of the value chain. Pioneer, and ye shall reap the rewards.

+ *Video.* Consider exploiting the power of video-controlled production. Wireless intelligent video-processing systems have come a long way and can reduce labor costs while improving speed and, most importantly, quality. Furthermore, there is significant historical value in accumulated images, somewhat similar to Massachusetts General accumulating decades' worth of radiological data. You may able to mine your own manufacturing-image data. At a minimum, you should be able to achieve automation and real-time control, hopefully to the extent that you can increase the amount of manufacturing done in the developed nations (to allow for faster time-to-customer and more customizations). Wireless video can also be used simply to allow for better two-way visual links between people on a manufacturing line and the storeroom or management offices. In the past, setting up CCTV links was expensive and cumbersome; today, it is trivial and trivial to rearrange. Bring the manufacturing people and operation closer together via video.

+ *RFID.* To what extent are you currently using RFID? What are your plans going forward? Not having a plan and being in manufacturing is like ignoring the automobile and staying with a horse-drawn carriage. Tracking in-process and finished goods from end to end and throughout the value chain is of paramount importance going forward. Wireless sensing technology such as RFID allows for more efficient tracking (than bar code wanding). Even if your products will not carry RFID tags for a few years, you can begin by tagging your mobile equipment such as forklifts, pallets, large containers, and so forth. Improve your business systems to absorb this new data and associate it to products in process and transit. The data will not only cut down on shrinkage, it will be an open window to efficiency improvements teased out of the accumulated data.

+ *Wireless.* Wireless technology is not just about allowing computers and laptops to be able to communicate with your corporate infrastructure. A great many other wireless devices can be inexpensively tied into your production facility. We saw how GM was using "easily movable" wireless buttons on assembly lines to simply notify forklift trucks of the need for more materials. The new world is all about rapid reconfiguration and providing signals, and communications without wires can greatly improve reconfiguration time. Step back and see your whole manufacturing operation as a highly flexible invisibly connected set of people and machines.

As a retail owner, you should consider the following:

+ *RFID.* RFID tags are forthcoming on products as well as crates and packages. Are you currently gearing up for this change? RFID will notably help cut down on shrinkage, which is a clear concern to every retailer. As importantly, however, it will increase sales by better shelf-inventory management. Start thinking of other creative uses of RFID-tagged goods beyond the obvious of instant-checkout and shrinkage-related uses. There will be an enormous amount of data spewing out of these tags ready to be mined by the curious retailer—shopping patterns (which products are selected before others), time in the basket or cart, frequency of withdrawals from the cart, to name just a few.

+ *Video tracking.* As you learned in Chapter 10, "Connecting to Retail," we are at the very beginning phases of passively monitoring our shoppers through the use of video-surveillance systems. Video cameras, now wireless, are affordable and can be deployed in large numbers to perfectly cover a retail location. New software will emerge that helps not just count but also track customers, which will provide invaluable data for the retailer.

+ *Customization.* Going forward, the convenience and 24-hour nature of the Web will continue to threaten many physical retail establishments. Extreme service, including detailed customizations of products, will help retain customers (both for physical and virtual stores). We are seeing a customer base that wants some control and differentiation over the products they buy and at the same time are not looking to pay a premium or experience a delay. Successful retailers (and manufacturers) will exploit real-time technologies and business integration to better produce custom products. Similarly, physical stores will have to grow in services and entertainment to draw people away from the Web and into their store.

As a doctor, you should consider the following:

- *Electronic records.* If you have not already moved to electronic patient records, do so quickly. Work with consortiums and medical groups to drive standards and commonality. Strive to provide XML-based exports of records and allow patients access to the records themselves. The values in so doing are both higher efficiency/convenience but also far better patient care as a result of more accurate patient histories and better doctor-to-doctor patient hand-offs.

- *Calendaring.* Missed appointments are not just aggravating but incredibly expensive, for both doctors and the patients alike. In the new world, we are squeezed to an unprecedented degree for near-perfect utilization of time. We simply cannot afford schedule and calendar boo boos (for either party). The good news is that our patients are more "connected" than ever before (because of wireless cellular devices mostly), and thus, we should be able to have rapid bidirectional schedule communication conversations (hopefully nonvoice). Similarly, patients have a need to self-schedule and reschedule, but need the doctors to provide convenient access to their calendars. As an industry, doctors should come together and drive standards so that patients do not have to relearn each doctor's own tools and technology for something as basic as making an appointment.

- *Amass data.* Amassing patient data will allow yourself and various researchers to gather insight from a growing body of medical information. These new insights will lead to better diagnosis, more expediency, and higher confidence in prescribed treatments. As a civilization, the more accumulated data on our medical conditions and treatments, the better our chances for higher survival and quality of life. It begins with accumulating data in readily reusable form and then the application of analytical tools to that data.

We could go on and on throughout every vertical segment we examined in the course of this book. Many of the themes repeat over and over again: Exploit wireless, exploit RFID, exploit GPS, use XML everywhere possible, amass data, cross data streams for higher insight, provide customers/patrons with higher participation, and so forth. Many suggestions are obvious, but the bigger values will come from a further step back and reexamining your overall operation (or life situation) with a fresh perspective about how these new exciting technologies can be combined for some impressive benefits.

Predictions

What book about technology and futures would be complete without a section on predictions? Predictions are fun. They do not have to be right; just plausible and sensible given the discussions throughout the book. Here are some various predictions.

Communications

- *Global calendars.* E-mail is pervasive partly because the foundation technology, SMTP (Simple Mail Transport Protocol) is pervasive, and every e-mail package in the universe knows how to speak that language. We will soon see a similar widespread (likely de facto) standard for calendar coordinating, and it will span from business executives to kindergartners. A universal set of protocols will emerge that allow various calendars to blend down (or render) to views that are suitable for any schedulable event. No longer will we fumble at the dentist office for a pocket daytimer; rather, the dentist will have access to your calendar and correctly know what times truly are amenable to you. Should you rearrange events, even at the last minute, updates throughout your life will automatically be made aware. We will be connected at a grand level and yet not sacrifice privacy (we hope).

- *Personal communication.* The move toward always-available communication is occurring swiftly. Unlike the slow (but steady) adoption of cell phones through the 1990s (from business users to eventually everyone), the move toward always-reachable communication will be more rapid. The value of nonverbal, immediate, yet asynchronous communication such as text and objects (pictures, songs, directions, purchase orders, etc.) is now understood by business professionals as well as the general population. The importance of being able to reach our children or business associates and in a nonintrusive yet quick way will drive this change even further. The values realized will be higher safety, personal efficiency, and business productivity.

By 2007, every cell-type device sold will be biased toward data communications (text and objects) because you will less frequently "call" someone compared to text messaging them. Case in point: AT&T's new cell phone that is text-only.

- *Singular device.* Our cell phones will truly become our wallets and "jack knives." By 2007, they will perform all of the following: MP3 device (both downloaded and streaming style), e-mail and text messaging, GPS to both provide our location info and guide us to destinations, RFID reading capable to allow for in-store/on-location product details, replacement for both video and cameras, oh, and of course, still voice-capable. We further expect them to be an authentication device soon after, for both in-store purchases as well as security for access to buildings, homes, and vehicles.

Entertainment

- *Sports.* Sports events have always held an important position for both entertainment and diversion from life-pressing problems. Entertainment, such as movies and plays and dinner, will blur with sports. All entertainment will be more interactive and under our control, whether we are at the local high school production of *Annie* or at the final game of the World Series. Our PDA-type devices will be integral to our sports experience, and we will look for deeper ways to be part of the action.

- *Dining out.* We may order our dinners at a restaurant via a tablet-based interface (or more drinks), but we will still cherish the interaction with the waiter (on our own terms). We may interact with the restaurant chef's kitchen prior to the evening and tune our selection. In general, our desire to dine out will increase (given all that new work flexibility) coupled with our ever-busy personal lives allowing for less cooking time (and the accompanying aggravation). Essentially, we will outsource our meals to those who can provide the correct quality and health at efficient prices.

Money

- *Cashless society.* The acceptance of bank cards and other plastic or wireless devices may finally spell the end to cash transactions. Retail stores will begin to charge a premium if paying by cash, much like airlines now charge for purchasing a ticket through an agent or on the phone versus via the Web. Cash in retail has an annoying theft risk, introduces float losses, and very often means consumers are more frugal with their purchases. Consumers will become more and more comfortable with using noncash methods because their trust in Internet and other purchase styles (gas station pumps and so on) has matured. Retailers will relish the level of detailed transactions they will have for all purchases. Low-cost cards will emerge, somewhat like phone cards, that allow parents to provide money to a child's card stretching the reach of this new trend. (Most public school lunch systems no longer use cash in favor of use a form of debit card for a variety of reasons—notably, ensuring all children can eat by preventing theft from bullying.)

+ *Single-key society.* We will move toward a society that wants a single physical device as means of payment and "activation" at purchase or use locations. Whether it is a single credit/debit card or a cell phone/PDA, a single device allows consumers to simplify their lives. The device quite likely will also be used for activating a car, unlocking car and home doors, and entry into office buildings (for those that even go to the office), and very likely will require the user to enter a code. Quite possibly also require some biometric such as fingerprint or eye scan. Thus, it is 1) something you posses (the device), 2) something you know (the code), and 3) something that identifies you—the holy trinity of security.

+ *Single bill, no bill.* We are rapidly moving to a society that loves electronic banking and is automating as many billing transactions as we can. Instead of automating bill payment, it will be observed that it is far simpler to have all suppliers of our consumer goods have an on-file billing target (credit or bank card—many do this today). If you had everything billed to your MasterCard, and your MasterCard was supplied by one of the three remaining world banks, which was your bank, new efficiencies are realized. You may never have to pay a bill again (so to speak).

Home and Life

+ *Home automation.* Our major home appliances will all be wireless-enabled by 2008. The cost of WiFi or similar technology will become insignificant compared to a $500 or $1,500 appliance. Consumers will initially value the remote-control capabilities (controlling HVAC systems or ovens from soccer fields or while at work) and later appreciate RFID capabilities once products proliferate with such tags. Manufacturers will derive far higher "usage" data that will in turn allow them to better match features to customers (e.g., how many times is the "gentle" cycle run? How often is the device used in the winter or after 6 P.M.? etc.). Given increasingly robust levels of networking, some appliances may even start appearing with rudimentary robotic/mechanical interfaces. For example, an innovative washer-dryer combination could be mechanically linked to avoid the need for human transfer. The washer itself could be fed by the laundry chute that separates whites from colors (either by RFID tag or visual/camera sensed) by a simple deflector. Refrigerators with cooking apparatus built-in (or vice versa) will similarly be more useful.

• *Location crazy.* We are heading toward fully understanding where everyone is at all times geographically, and desiring to know immediately how to get wherever we want to go. No longer will we require an in-car navigation system. It will be part of our everywhere-network (PDA, cell). It will not only tell us were to go based on just addresses, but also how to get to a particular office cube in a large building or a particular store in the super mall. It will not be a specialty add-on of cell phones or cars or buses; it will be built in to everything we care about. Our prized positions such as expensive hospital equipment or designer jeans will be somehow announcing themselves to something that can transmit location information. We will become location crazy.

• *Work@home.* Of the 80 million "information workers" in the United States, 50 percent will be working from home by 2010 and have no assigned office "cube" anywhere. This will continue to be driven equally by the new generation of workers who value improved home quality of life higher than any earlier generation and by employers seeking to gain more work hours out of the work force while saving on fixed costs. The effectiveness of remote work will be greatly enhanced by the changes in "personal communication" (being more reachable) as well as in new generations of groupware/virtual officeware. The changes will bring back the important attributes of happenstance, community, impromptu sharing, and yet maintain accepted social-hierarchy protocols.

Work and Business

+ *Momentary enterprise.* We will see sizable businesses (based on yearly revenue) come and go at alarming speeds. No longer will a business be measured by its staying power. Instead, businesses will be instantly created to capitalize on whatever important trend or desire is happening in the wider community. Energy will not be required for establishing the brick-and-mortar or all the billing and accounting systems or the transport or supply systems. Such commodities will be expertly and automatically leveraged by super-deep, business-to-business automation, and new enterprises will start up focusing all of their energy on their differentiating value. They will be willing to be short-lived (measure in months or a short number of years) and allowed to exit as rapidly and with nearly no cost. Investors and consumers win.

+ *Matrix workers.* As more and more people allow their skills to be better published and exploited, a new form of professional, the modern consultant, will emerge. He or she may work for a large company that routinely has suitable assignments lined up, or he/she may be part of a larger fabric of remote workers. Many of us will be matrixed among many employers, even some competing ones.

+ *Office space.* Nearly 50 percent of today's office workers will work entirely at home and likely have improved home lives in spite of working more total hours. The office space will not go unused. Our need for socialization still exists, and office space will be converted into specialized retail locations, city short-term dwellings for lonely suburbanites, and, of course, more restaurants (one of the last vestiges that the virtual world can not eliminate).

+ *Manufacturing.* Improvements throughout manufacturing will be so significant that by 2010, it will no longer be more efficient to manufacture high-volume products offshore. Manufacturing will swing back in the direction of home country because the value of having real-time customized manufacturing closer to the buyer will be affordable. Labor costs will be more than offset by significant advances in video-controlled production and inspection plus additional automation and interbusiness efficiencies. Notoriously long cycle times such as in the apparel business will be reduced from 9 months down to days, largely as a result of avoiding transocean voyages and all the accompanying Muda. Consumers will want to customize their appliances, durable goods, and fashion items, and yet not incur any delay in receiving those goods.

Miscellaneous

- *Data protection.* We will lose the word backup from our vocabulary, for business and personal computer needs. We will not worry about protecting our important data. The "network" and our service providers will ensure that our data is available from multiple sources and in multiple instances (in case we need to go back in time). The network will be our storage and storage will be something that only the network providers worry about (much like how you no longer save your paper bank statements any longer).

- *Miniature everything.* We will see computing power and data storage dash to levels never thought useful. Data will be collected by every conceivable device that has the lifeblood of just a trickle of energy. The data will be stored and digested and rebroadcast to a variety of nearby devices in case they can make use of it. This insane level of density and miniaturization will allow intelligence and "power" to invade most everything we touch. (Computerized tennis racquets will be pale in comparison.)

- *RFID.* RFID will steadily creep into our lives, but probably not with a single-year explosion. It will take time, but by 2010, most every consumer item from cereal to clothes to electronics will come with RFID tags built in. Today, we have to pick up something and look for a printed panel for a manufacture and model number, whereas in 2010, we will "wand" the device with our cell phone to learn of its details. Home automation and personal shopping experiences will greatly improve, as we will experience reduced shrinkage and better customer behavior/understanding on the part of retailers.

- *Medical records.* By 2010, we will have our own DNA sequenced and carry the electronic code with us (or referenced to some electronic repository). Furthermore, researchers will have Internet access to millions of other's DNA codes and medical histories, depersonalized, allowing them to discover important correlations. In 2010, all of our medical records ranging from the dentist to our heart specialist will be stored in a single common repository managed by our HMO, but we will retain control over who has access to individual components.

Summary

We have taken a broad look through a variety of technologies and industries. We started by looking at what might be the new key ingredients in the future computing world:

+ *Data*. Data-everywhere devices (which, like a fuel in a rocket) leads to far higher *potential*.

+ *Communications*. Changes to more "asynchronous-yet-immediate" technologies such as instant messaging nets higher *efficiency*.

+ *Networking*. Radical new strategies for networking "everything," even the tiniest of devices, will lead to higher *utility* in our lives.

+ *Infochange*. Data will race toward openness and self-describing styles allowing for far higher exchange and *automation*.

Data is the heart of it all, hence the title *Inescapable Data*. This is a little misleading because a hallmark of the new world is "information" rather than raw data, information enabled by new approaches to representing data and compute architectures powerful enough to process verbose definitions even if in a wristwatch. Networking has always been important, but wireless networking means that massive infrastructures can change and migrate faster than ever in our past. Connectivity, as it is now called, is more than networking: It is about gainful information sharing in a timely fashion. Finally, we have grown to understand that although we want everything fast, we want it asynchronous, including our own personal correspondences, because there are significant efficiencies to be gained.

We have tried to point out that our business and personal lives have blurred on many fronts. Perhaps the most important is that the two share common goals: efficiency, flexibility, and security. To get to the new levels of efficiency, we now know to look beyond our own business boundaries plus be relentless in our desire to mix streams of information. Regarding the new dimension of flexibility, we know that we will better retain employees and customers if we can be amazingly supple and accommodating. Finally, from terrorism to bullying to personal theft, security is dear to our hearts and we will look for common technology to relieve us in both business and domestic life.

The new world is not merely about technology. Technology has been here for decades...generations...centuries. Technology will continue to advance to bring linear advances in the single utilities they focus. The Inescapable Data vision is bigger: technologies intertwining for exponential benefits along the themes of efficiency, flexibility, and security. Look not for individual advances, but rather step-functions made possible by marrying information sources together, mostly in real time, and mostly wirelessly.

Therein lies the Inescapable Data vision.

Index